THE
EVERYTHING®
GUIDE TO CODEPENDENCY

I have been a licensed clinical psychologist for twenty-five years. During my career, clients have trusted me with their most intimate thoughts and feelings. Couples have invited me into their relationships, hoping I could help them find the best in each other.

When I was asked to write this book, I felt both challenged and excited by the idea. Over the years, identifying and working with codependency has been a challenging part of my therapy with individuals and couples.

I often recommend quality self-help books for my clients, but in the case of codependency, I had trouble finding one single book that illuminates the issue in all its forms. I was still referring clients to *Codependent No More*, written more than twenty-five years ago by Melody Beattie. As I handed the book to a client, I'd say something like, "This is about alcoholism, but I think it will help with your codependency issues."

Now I will recommend *The Everything® Guide to Codependency*, knowing I can hand it to a patient or a couple and simply say, "Read this; it will help you with your therapy."

Jennifer J. Sowle, PhD
Licensed Psychologist

Welcome to the EVERYTHING® Series!

These handy, accessible books give you all you need to tackle a difficult project, gain a new hobby, comprehend a fascinating topic, prepare for an exam, or even brush up on something you learned back in school but have since forgotten.

You can choose to read an Everything® book from cover to cover or just pick out the information you want from our four useful boxes: e-questions, e-facts, e-alerts, and e-ssentials.

We give you everything you need to know on the subject, but throw in a lot of fun stuff along the way, too.

We now have more than 400 Everything® books in print, spanning such wide-ranging categories as weddings, pregnancy, cooking, music instruction, foreign language, crafts, pets, New Age, and so much more. When you're done reading them all, you can finally say you know Everything®!

QUESTION

Answers to
common questions

FACT

Important snippets
of information

ALERT

Urgent
warnings

ESSENTIAL

Quick
handy tips

PUBLISHER Karen Cooper

MANAGING EDITOR, EVERYTHING® SERIES Lisa Laing

COPY CHIEF Casey Ebert

ASSISTANT PRODUCTION EDITOR Alex Guarco

ACQUISITIONS EDITOR Lisa Laing

SENIOR DEVELOPMENT EDITOR Brett Palana-Shanahan

EVERYTHING® SERIES COVER DESIGNER Erin Alexander

Visit the entire Everything® series at *www.everything.com*

THE
EVERYTHING®
GUIDE TO
CODEPENDENCY

Learn to recognize and
change codependent behavior

Jennifer J. Sowle, PhD

Adamsmedia
Avon, Massachusetts

I wish to dedicate this book to my son, Trevor,
who is an inspiration to me in many ways.

An Everything® Series Book.
Everything® and everything.com® are registered trademarks of F+W Media, Inc.

Published by
Adams Media, a division of F+W Media, Inc.
57 Littlefield Street, Avon, MA 02322. U.S.A.
www.adamsmedia.com

ISBN 10: 1-4405-7390-5
ISBN 13: 978-1-4405-7390-3
eISBN 10: 1-4405-7391-3
eISBN 13: 978-1-4405-7391-0

Printed in the United States of America.

10 9 8 7 6 5 4 3 2 1

Library of Congress Cataloging-in-Publication Data

Sowle, Jennifer J.
  The everything guide to codependency / Jennifer J. Sowle, PhD.
    pages cm
  Includes index.
  ISBN-13: 978-1-4405-7390-3 (pb)
  ISBN-10: 1-4405-7390-5 (pb)
  ISBN-13: 978-1-4405-7391-0 (ebook)
  ISBN-10: 1-4405-7391-3 (ebook)
1. Codependency. 2. Self-care, Health. I. Title.
  RC569.5.C63S69 2014
  616.86--dc23

                    2014008276

Cover images © gtranquillity/123RF.

This book is available at quantity discounts for bulk purchases.
For information, please call 1-800-289-0963.

Contents

20 Ending Codependency in Your Life / 283

Acknowledgments

I wish to thank my clients who have entrusted me with their innermost selves and have taught me about struggle and redemption.

I wish to thank Doreen for her loving care of our Ozzy during my many hours of writing.

I also wish to thank my writing colleagues, Trudy Carpenter, David Marshall, Patrick McMahon, and Marilyn Zimmerman. Special hugs to Trudy and Marilyn, who gave me extra time and support.

And finally, thank you to my nineteen-year-old cat, Conway Kitty, who, at the end of his ninth life, made for a cozy foot warmer and offered a comforting paw on my face as I wrote.

The Top 10 Ways to
Stop Being Codependent

1. Try to identify the *shoulds* that keep you from setting healthy boundaries for yourself.

2. Measure your level of resentment. Resentment comes from doing what you don't want to do, agreeing when you don't mean it, or expecting things from others without telling them.

3. Make sure your responses are not intended to control or manipulate another.

4. Take a look at your anger patterns. Do you get angry and defensive when others try to discuss a problem they have with you?

5. When you think you're being criticized, notice your responses. Do you react by being defensive, devastated, angry, crushed, incredulous, blaming, hostile, too fragile to handle it, etc.?

6. When you're asked for your opinion, don't immediately react. Take time to look inside for it, then share.

7. Respect others by allowing them to take responsibility for their own lives.

8. Identify what you have control over, and act on it. Let go of what you do not have control over.

9. Look at your current relationships and make sure you're being authentic. Speak your own truth without fear of another's judgment or reaction.

10. Look back at your family and see if you can identify codependent patterns there. This could help you become aware of your own unconscious patterns.

Introduction

CODEPENDENCY IS A STRANGE word. The prefix "co-" usually describes two or more components that exist in relationship to one another. And perhaps this word once made more sense back in the 1980s when it described the relationship between an addict and her partner. But that was then and this is now.

This book explains the concept of codependency in all its forms. You will discover that codependency can exist in your mind, as a part of your identity, without "co-depending" with anyone. And when codependent relationships are analyzed, it means almost all relationships, not just alcoholic ones.

If you went out on the street right now and asked ten people the meaning of codependency, they would likely have ten different answers, or they would have no answer at all! Codependency is one of those terms that everybody uses but few understand.

Codependency is obviously not a flash in the pan; it has endured beyond the fad and fashion of its time. It has cracked out of the shell of addiction and something new has hatched, something that undoubtedly touches you. When you've finished reading this book, you will know more about codependency than 99 percent of the population. You might even see your family, spouse, friends, and coworkers hiding in these pages. And odds are extremely high that you will see yourself!

This book will teach you about codependency and how not to get stuck in it. Here are some of the important ways you'll learn to change and move beyond codependency:

- You'll discover patterns in yourself and others.
- You'll find out how to use the results of the Codependency Quizzes.
- You'll develop non-codependent language and communication skills.
- You'll learn to journal and practice new skills at home.

- You'll engage your partner in change.
- You'll find a therapist.
- You'll break the spell of codependency and discover the real you.

The goal of this book is to give you some fairly weighty psychological stuff combined with a mix of personal growth and self-help. The mix is probably 1 cup psychological, 2 cups personal growth, and 2 cups self-help. Most people buy books like this one because they want to make their relationships better. If this is your quest, you've found the right book! You will briefly enter the lives of couples to see what codependency looks like. Then this psychologist will help you adjust your lenses so you won't miss the important parts. And that's how you'll learn about codependency.

This book is for you. Use everything in this *Everything*® book to learn about yourself. With your new insights, you can become your own mirror. Recognize your intrinsic value and embrace it!

CHAPTER 1

What Is Codependency?

Codependency is a pattern of thinking, feeling, and behaving. If you are codependent, you are unable to identify and follow your own needs, wants, and feelings. It's as if you have grown antennae, and you wave them as you move through life, straining to pick up vibes from others. If you are codependent, you are not powered from within; your quest for power is through controlling others. In fact, you're so focused on another, you may not even know how you feel or think.

How to Spot Codependency

Consider these pointers before you read the stories that follow. See if you can identify the codependent patterns in the relationships.

HOW DO YOU KNOW IF YOU'RE CODEPENDENT?

- You like to be in the helping role (which is the power role, by the way).
- You tend to surround yourself with needy people.
- You are too worried about pleasing others.
- You try to be all things to all people.
- You have a self-esteem that is connected to "doing."
- You have an overdeveloped sense of responsibility.
- You feel nagging anxiety, pity, or guilt when other people have a problem.
- You are afraid of making mistakes.
- You try to prove you're good enough to be loved.
- You worry about other people's problems.
- You have difficulty saying no and setting boundaries.
- You seek out chaos, and feel most alive when you're involved in it.
- You wonder why people don't do things for you.
- You feel victimized by the "selfishness" of others.
- You love to get involved in a crisis, and then complain about it.
- You are easily offended by others who you feel are cold, uncaring, or selfish.
- You get angry when somebody refuses your help or doesn't take your advice.
- You try to be perfect, and expect others to be perfect.
- You blame yourself and put yourself down.
- You must be in control at all times.

Codependents are not always passive, nurturing, and loving. The caregiver, the peacemaker, the guy who will give you the shirt off his back can be codependent. But so can those who are manipulative and angry, resentful and cranky. If you consider the core issue—a codependent person relies on the perceptions of others to tell her she is okay—you can see how vital another's opinion can be. Like Blanche DuBois in the play *A Streetcar Named*

Desire, the codependent relies on the kindness of strangers. What a powerless position this is.

ESSENTIAL

In 1987, Melody Beattie wrote the remarkable *Codependent No More: How to Stop Controlling Others and Start Caring for Yourself.* In her work, Beattie emphasized that alcoholism is a family disease, and she identified the codependent role played by the partner of an alcoholic. Since that time, the term has generalized to describe any person who focuses on another's life to the detriment of his or her own.

The following case studies will give you an idea of the many ways codependency can present itself. People with codependency come from all walks of life, are of all ages and lifestyles. You'll also see that codependency doesn't just exist in romantic relationships but occurs in many other types of relationships as well.

Alcoholic Brother: Joyce and Steven

Joyce is a successful teacher in a small town. Her older brother, Steven, is an actor in New York City. As far back as their teenage years, Joyce has been in denial about Steven's alcoholism. Over the years, she has made excuses for him. If he appeared drunk on stage, she explained that he was just tired from long hours. When he failed to show up for family gatherings, she said she understood because he was a very busy man. When Steven was getting divorced, she argued that his drinking was not the reason, and told family and friends that Steven's wife was having an affair.

FACT

When you are codependent, you don't have clear or firm boundaries. You don't know where you end and another begins. There is a joke about the codependent husband who reaches for a tissue and says, "Excuse me" when his wife sneezes.

When her brother starts calling Joyce and asking for money, she sends it to him and keeps her actions from her husband. When Steven is arrested for assault during one of his benders, Joyce tells her husband that her brother is sick and needs her. She takes a leave of absence from work and flies to New York City to help him. She borrows from her retirement fund and bails him out of jail. While out on bail, Steven steals Joyce's credit cards and leaves town. Joyce's marriage barely survives when her husband finds out what has happened. Joyce is codependent with her brother, Steven.

Unrequited Love: Bella and Baxter

Baxter meets Bella in college, and dates her off and on throughout his twenties. Baxter tells Bella from the start that he enjoys their sexual relationship and he likes her very much, but he isn't in love with her. He is very honest with Bella, admitting he doesn't want to settle down with her when he is ready. Despite Baxter's disclaimers, Bella falls in love with him and now waits for him to change his mind and fall in love with her. She refers to Baxter as her boyfriend to family and friends even though they aren't in an exclusive relationship.

Day and night, Bella's mind is occupied with what Baxter might be thinking. She is vigilant, searching for clues in Baxter's behavior and conversation that he loves her. Her only topic of conversation when she gets together with friends is Baxter. She shares conversations she has had with him and badgers her friends to agree with her that he obviously wants to be with her. Finally, her friends get tired of listening and stop calling her.

ESSENTIAL

Help versus enabling: If you offer help that has not been asked for, or interfere with a person facing the consequences of his actions, you are *enabling*. Offering help that is judged to be necessary by you, not the other guy, or helping a person who is self-destructive or harmful to others is *enabling*.

Over the course of two years, Baxter has had a pattern of showing up for a few weeks or months and then withdrawing from his relationship with

Bella. In the third year, the relationship diminishes to the point where it is little more than a few one-night stands, but Bella continues to hang on every word Baxter says and interprets them as a sign that he really loves her.

One day Bella is in the local bookstore when she spots Baxter having coffee. When she approaches, he greets her pleasantly and introduces her to Sarah, his fiancée. They talk for a few minutes about what a whirlwind romance Baxter has had with Sarah. The couple tells Bella how they met and that it had been love at first sight. Sarah shows Bella her engagement ring and tells her she and Baxter plan to marry next June.

Bella is in shock as she walks back to her apartment. As soon as she closes the door behind her, she becomes hysterical and rampages through her apartment breaking things and destroying any reminders of Baxter. Two days later, Bella is admitted to the hospital after she over-doses on sleeping pills. She's now in therapy to help her sort out her part in her own misery.

Helicopter Mom: Alice and Amanda

Alice is a single mother of sixteen-year-old Amanda. Alice often has said her daughter is "her life." Alice feels guilty that Amanda has only one parent, and she compensates for it by trying to make Amanda happy. When Amanda appears to be out of sorts, Alice enjoys doing things for her and giving her gifts. Even though she has a full-time job, Alice has been a classroom volunteer at school since Amanda was in fourth grade, was a scout leader until Amanda dropped out, and is now a volunteer for Amanda's cheerleading squad, driving the girls to the away basketball games. Alice loves hearing about Amanda's life, relationships, triumphs, and difficulties. She tries to give her daughter good advice and feels hurt if Amanda doesn't follow it.

Amanda has always been "the perfect daughter," but recently her grades have slipped. Alice panics and asks to meet with Amanda's teachers on a weekly basis to discuss her daughter's progress. She hires a tutor to bring Amanda's math grade from a B to an A. Alice already has sent to universities for catalogs and applications for Amanda.

When Alice makes an appointment with the principal to discuss what to do about Amanda's boyfriend breaking up with her, the principal uses the term "helicopter mom." Alice leaves the principal's office feeling angry and unappreciated.

Business Partners: Jim and Paul

Jim and Paul have worked for the same company for ten years when they decide to go into partnership together in their own clothing business. It seems like a match made in heaven. Jim has a head for finances and is able to see the big-picture growth of the company. Paul is the creative, gregarious partner who has a knack for selling, loves interacting with people, and is able to visualize clothing trends before they happen.

Each partner sticks to what he does best. Paul is not really interested in the nuts-and-bolts number crunching, and Jim loves fashion but he's not one for schmoozing with customers.

In their first year of business, a pattern starts to emerge. Whenever Jim tries to engage Paul in a financial discussion, Paul brushes him off by saying he trusts Jim, and whatever Jim decides is okay with him. Jim tries everything to get Paul engaged in the business end of things. He pleads, he gets angry, he starts making snide comments to Paul in front of their friends, and he even threatens Paul with dissolving the partnership. Nothing works, so Jim continues to do his best managing the finances by himself. Actually, he does a fine job, but he is so stressed, he begins to lose weight and develops intestinal problems.

In the third year, Paul wants to expand the business. Jim spends hours getting data to share with Paul so they can make a decision. Paul takes a look at the spreadsheets Jim has provided, but he doesn't really understand them, nor does he want to take the time to learn. Jim simply asks Paul if they can afford to expand, and when he says he thinks so, Paul starts looking at storefronts. He finds a building that is larger than they need, but he pouts or becomes angry when Jim suggests something smaller.

Jim gives in and they buy the building, hire three new people, and add an online store. Jim feels the pressure of such a large financial commitment, but Paul is excited and throws himself headlong into decorating the new store and going on buying trips to New York. With such an expansion underway, Jim wants regular weekly meetings with Paul to discuss finances. Paul meets with Jim a few times, but soon he is too busy, once again praising Jim for his business sense and handing the reins over to him.

Within a year after the expansion, Paul and Jim's business is faltering and Jim can't get Paul to sit down and figure out what to do. After a few months of Jim barely making payroll, Paul insists on hiring another employee. When Jim tells him it's impossible, Paul flies into a rage and accuses Jim of hiding things from him, maybe even embezzling from the company. Once Paul gets an attorney involved, the partnership and the business are over.

Aging Parent: Doug and Mother

Doug is the oldest of ten children. He grew up on a farm in Ohio. His father was a third-generation cattleman, inheriting the family ranch, expanding it to include crops. The entire family worked hard to make the farm a success. Doug was fifteen when his father was killed in an accident. His mother relied heavily on Doug to manage the farm. Losing his dad forced Doug to grow up fast.

Doug's brothers and sisters all leave home after graduation, but Doug stays on the farm, marries his high school sweetheart, Kathy, and runs the business. His mother helps raise his four children, and participates as best she can by tending the family garden, canning, and cooking. Doug's wife works a full-time job in addition to her farm duties. With everybody pitching in, the family makes it through lean times.

Doug's mother has a minor stroke when she is only sixty. Doug and Kathy take care of her at home until she recovers. Two years later, Doug's mother has another stroke. This time she is left with partial paralysis on her left side. Doug's sister, Jeannine, takes a couple of weeks off work to help care for their mother. The rest of the siblings chip in to help Doug and Kathy with the additional expenses of their mother's physical therapy.

More grief comes when Doug's mother falls and hits her head, leaving her unable to walk or talk. As usual, Doug volunteers to care for her in their home. As Doug's children grow, and eventually move out to attend college, it becomes more and more difficult for Doug and Kathy to care for his mother and run the farm. Kathy has been a trouper through all of their hardships, but now she feels Doug's siblings should do more to help. Doug doesn't want to bother his brothers and sisters, and he argues that his mother can't handle change.

ESSENTIAL

A codependent's defenses can shoot up like a firecracker if she senses disapproval. It can be excruciating for her to listen to complaints from another without taking it personally. For example, Mary's partner pleasantly asks her if she took the clothes out of the dryer. But Mary hears the question as a criticism and says, "You do the damn laundry if you're in such a hurry!"

As Doug's mother's health continues to deteriorate, Kathy tries to get Doug to talk to his family, but he won't. Out of desperation, Kathy goes to the local Commission on Aging for help. The therapist recommends a family meeting to discuss how siblings can contribute to their mother's care. When Kathy tells Doug about the plan, he becomes enraged and says he won't participate. At the therapist's urging, Kathy goes ahead and sets up the family session. Six of Doug's siblings agree to attend. Not wanting to inconvenience them for no reason, Doug grudgingly agrees to go.

The meeting goes well, with siblings agreeing to participate in their own way. Several of them want to take turns having mother visit for a month at a time, two siblings can afford to pay for mother's daily needs, and one sibling volunteers to take mother to all her medical appointments. Doug leaves the meeting feeling as if a giant weight has been lifted from his shoulders. He hugs Kathy, telling her how much he appreciates her intervention.

The first time one of his sisters says she can take mother for only two weeks, Doug says it's "No big deal." When his brother stops making his financial contribution, Doug tells Kathy he doesn't feel comfortable begging his brother for money. With Doug's inability to hold his siblings accountable, and his overwhelming need to take care of his mother, the participation plan soon falls through.

Doug became codependent with his mother at an early age. From there, it was easy for him to fall into a codependency pattern with his entire family.

Spendthrift Wife: Ron and Charlene

Ron marries Charlene right out of high school, and they have three children. Ron works his way up from a laborer to a foreman in a small contracting business. Eventually, he buys his own company, expands, and is now a very successful building contractor. Charlene stands beside him, raises the children, and manages their home. Ron's Achilles' heel has always been Charlene. She loves the lifestyle they worked so hard for. She entertains often, sets up family vacations, and makes sure the children have the finest things, including many cultural opportunities.

Ron and Charlene have had heated discussions over the years about her excessive spending. Many times Charlene has agreed to a budget, but continues to overspend, and Ron always manages to adjust for it. When the recession hits, Ron's company has little in reserve thanks to Charlene's financial demands. When the company starts to fail, he begs Charlene to stop spending, but by then it is too late.

Narcissistic Fiancée: Pam and Randy

Pam is a senior in high school, very popular, aspiring to become a doctor like her mother. Pam's boyfriend, Greg, is a straight-A student, hockey player, and yearbook editor. They are both on the fast track to college and plan to be married someday.

One evening during a hockey game, Pam meets Randy at the concession stand. They strike up a conversation, and Pam learns that Randy graduated from high school two years earlier and has a good job at a car dealership. Randy isn't handsome in the classical sense, but he is always well dressed and perfectly groomed, and has a dazzling smile and a twinkle in his eye. When they first meet, Pam tells Randy her steady is the captain of the hockey team, but he barely breaks stride in his attempts to impress Pam. Soon he is openly flirting with her.

QUESTION

What is self-esteem, and how can you increase it?
The beliefs that you are worthy and able to handle life situations with confidence are the main ingredients of self-esteem. Self-esteem increases every time you handle a difficult challenge.

The next day Pam gets a friend request from Randy on Facebook. Pam never turns down a Facebook request because she isn't one to hurt another's feelings. Once she friends Randy, he starts posting on her Facebook page. In no time, he establishes himself within Pam's social circle. He now has access into Pam's life and soon begins running into her frequently and chatting with her and her friends.

Over the months, Pam finds herself attracted to Randy. The attention he gives her is flattering, and finally she gives in to his charming ways and starts meeting him at the car dealership after school for coffee. Seeing Randy in his domain, how smooth he is and how his coworkers admire him, is the frosting on the cake. Just before graduation, she breaks up with Greg and starts dating Randy.

Against her parents' advice, Pam accepts an engagement ring from Randy the summer before she is to leave for college. When fall rolls around, Randy doesn't want Pam to leave. Pam's parents are concerned because they see things in Randy Pam obviously doesn't, like his selfishness, his spending habits, his constant dissatisfaction with how Pam spends her time. No amount of attention seems enough for him.

When Pam decides to go to Europe with her parents for two weeks, Randy flies into a rage and breaks up with her, calling her selfish and disrespectful of his needs. He accuses her of "using him" and says he never wants to see her again. Pam thinks he'll get over it, but when she returns, he's already dating somebody else.

Pam begs Randy to meet her for a talk. She apologizes for being so selfish and says she will try harder to be more considerate. After they reconcile,

Randy starts berating Pam about her appearance, the way she dresses, her weight, the color of her hair. On more than one occasion, he refuses to take her to dinner because he doesn't think she looks good enough. He says he is embarrassed to be seen with her.

Pam's parents are heartbroken to see their beautiful daughter changing to please Randy. At one point, she gets so thin that they are about to do an intervention. The more Pam caters to Randy, the more he criticizes her. She gives up on college and gets a job at the car dealership as a secretary. Seeing how charming and flirtatious Randy is around women customers, she is afraid to let him out of her sight.

FACT

Codependents can be very angry people because they expect others to change to accommodate their insecurities. And when others don't change, codependents have to face and cope with their own fears. Their anxiety often comes out as anger.

Three years into the relationship, Randy sells an expensive car to a wealthy married woman and eventually begins an affair with her. When Pam finds outs, she threatens to leave him if he doesn't break it off. Two years later, he is still promising to end the affair and Pam is still waiting.

Letter to the Psychologist

The following letter is taken from Here-to-Listen.com. Letters are written by visitors to the site and are answered by this psychologist. This letter helps highlight the difference between codependent behavior and helping.

Dear Doctor,
I've read about codependency on websites, but I'm still confused. What's the difference between being codependent and just being a mother? I think mothers should help their kids!

My son works hard as a server in a little restaurant downtown, and he has a roommate, but it's hard for him to make ends meet. When he has a bad week with low tips, he's really in a panic. He calls me when he needs extra money, and just last week his car needed new tires. He's doing his best, and I want to help him succeed. As a parent, isn't that my responsibility?

Val

Dear Val,

You've made some good points that will help clarify the thin line between helping those we love and codependency. It sounds like your son is taking responsibility for his own life. He's working hard, doing the best he can. Sometimes he runs into a snag. When he does, he calls you, and asks for help. Because your son is in the lead position, sees a problem, and asks for something, this puts you in the helping role. If you spend time checking on him, anticipating what he needs, and giving it to him without him asking, this is enabling behavior. This makes you codependent. In other words, you're taking responsibility for his life, deciding what he needs, and providing it. See the difference?

To speak to the last sentence in your letter, this sounds like a *should*. "Parents *should* be responsible for their children." Yes, they should when a child is a minor. But you are talking about an adult child. There is no *should* in this case. Some parents choose to help their adult children and others don't. It's a choice.

As a mother, how do you know if you're codependent with your son, or making a good choice? Check your thoughts and feelings. Thoughts: Are you responding to *should*? If so, you might be feeling guilty, or compelled to help based on a mistaken belief, like "Every parent should help their child no matter what." Feelings: Anger, resentment, or other negative feelings, like feeling taken advantage of, unappreciated, etc. If you check inside yourself, and find only positive thoughts and feelings, i.e., "I love my son, he is asking for my help, and I'm happy to give it . . . ," then you're giving freely when asked with only positive energy behind it. Resentment is the key. Don't help if you're going to be resentful later. This can only hurt your relationship with your son.

CHAPTER 2

The History of Codependency

The term *codependency* first showed up in the 1930s. Since then, the term has evolved through practice and usage to find its place in the common language of our culture. Like many other terms from the psychiatric literature that are part of our conversations these days—paranoid, dysfunctional, narcissistic, passive-aggressive—the meaning of codependency has become muddied as it has moved from the therapeutic community into the public domain. The concept of codependency has been shaped through seventy-five years of usage, so it's important to understand its history.

The Expansion of Psychological Theory

The 1960s brought great upheaval and change to established thinking. Ideas about how to help the mentally ill were no exception. During this time, beliefs about how psychosocial problems were identified, studied, and treated changed drastically. Previously, it was simply unheard of to include the family in mental health treatment plans. A psychiatrist or psychologist saw one, and only one, person in his office, and that person was the identified patient.

FACT

The term *codependency* started out as a part of the recovery literature, i.e., the codependent was the partner of an addict. Today it is widely used in the fields of psychiatry, psychology, and social work. Therapists *do* address codependency issues in therapy, but codependency is not officially part of the *Diagnostic and Statistical Manual of Mental Disorders (DSM)*, the book used by mental health professionals and insurance companies for diagnosing, treating, and billing mental illnesses.

This thing called codependency did not exist and could not exist without the expansion of psychological theory to include the elements of family systems theory, the recovery movement (Alcoholics Anonymous), assertiveness training, and the self-help movement. During this time of profound change, these elements provided fertile ground for new concepts to grow, mature, and become essential in the understanding of human behavior. Codependency is one of these concepts.

Family Systems Theory

Codependency is a term that describes a dysfunctional pattern of beliefs, emotions, and behaviors that develop from someone's interactions in her environment, most importantly within her family. Until the work of family system theorists, nobody even thought to look anywhere but inside the individual's own mind to see why she was experiencing psychological problems. This is why systems theory is so important.

Two major figures in the history of family systems theory are psychiatrist, researcher, and educator Murray Bowen (1913–1990) and educator, social worker, and family therapist Virginia Satir (1916–1988). In the 1950s, these innovators broke from the established medical model and proposed an entirely different way to look at human behavior.

ESSENTIAL

"Feelings of worth can flourish only in an atmosphere where individual differences are appreciated, mistakes are tolerated, communication is open, and rules are flexible—the kind of atmosphere that is found in a nurturing family." —Virginia Satir

In an article, "The Ten Most Influential Therapists of the Past Quarter-Century," published by *Psychotherapy Networker* in 2006, both Virginia Satir and Murray Bowen were cited among the top ten most influential therapists in a survey given to members of the American Psychological Association. Both Bowen and Satir are held in high regard for their work in family systems therapy.

Murray Bowen, MD

According to the Bowen Center, Murray Bowen began his psychiatric training at the Menninger Foundation in Topeka, Kansas, in 1946. Throughout his forty-year career, Bowen established a new understanding of human behavior, one that saw a person's behavior emerging from interaction with his environment. The Bowen Theory dramatically changed the way therapists worked with psychiatric patients.

ESSENTIAL

"That which is created in a relationship can be fixed in a relationship."—Murray Bowen

Virginia Satir

Virginia Satir is referred to as the "mother of family therapy." She worked in conjunction with Bowen while she was a member of the Human Potential Movement. Running a parallel course with Bowen during the 1950s through the 1980s, Satir was more hands-on in using systems theory in working with families. In her opinion, the issue bringing a person into therapy wasn't the real problem. Satir discovered that the problem was deeper and could best be identified and treated within the family. Since Satir focused on the family system and the connections among family members, it makes sense that she noticed codependent interactions and identified them early in her work.

FACT

A web article, "New Face of Codependency," reports that, "Virginia Satir, a key figure in family systems theory, studied more than 10,000 families and discovered that 96 percent of them exhibited codependent thoughts or behaviors."

In 1964, Satir published her first book, *Conjoint Family Therapy*, and subsequently published eight more. Her work was very important in shifting away from the illness model to a model of awareness and personal growth.

A Revolutionary Idea

The belief that a patient's psychological problems are connected to his family system was a breakthrough idea. As Satir pointed out, no matter who has the problem, it is the status quo of the family system itself that creates and perpetuates dysfunction. That was a startling notion. It truly changed the course of psychology and psychiatry in the treatment of psychological problems.

Think of the family system as a mobile, like the colorful mobiles hung over a baby's crib. Now assume our mobile represents an anorexic teenager and her family. Dangling from this mobile are the anorexic and her codependent mother, rebellious brother, absent father, and perfectionist older sister. Each of these pieces is firmly connected and perfectly balanced, but each has the potential to shift and move. Just poke one of the trinkets on a mobile and see what happens. When a therapist works with the family, he is poking the mobile. Through family therapy, the balance shifts, creating a space for healing, allowing the family members to reconfigure and achieve a new balance, one of recovery.

ESSENTIAL

"The overall goal [of counseling] is to help family members become 'systems experts' who could know [their] family system so well that the family could readjust itself without the help of an expert." —M. Bowen (*www.thebowencenter.org*)

Alcoholics Anonymous

Running alongside, albeit outside, mainstream mental health during that same time, Alcoholics Anonymous (AA) was the first group to identify codependency as part of the dynamic of alcoholism.

Throughout the 1940s and 1950s, AA Twelve-Step programs sprang up all over the United States and abroad. It seems clear that in the early years of AA, the focus was on the individual, almost as if the alcoholic lived in a vacuum. Maybe AA influenced family systems theory, or maybe family systems theory influenced AA—regardless, each reached the same conclusion: The family played a major role in recovery.

FACT

The Serenity Prayer, "God grant me the serenity to accept the things I cannot change; courage to change the things I can; and wisdom to know the difference" is recited at each AA meeting. It is a constant reminder to both alcoholics and codependents that they can only control themselves and how they react to their environment.

The realization that alcoholism was a family disease first appeared in the recovery literature in the early 1950s, but it was not until years later that Melody Beattie wrote her seminal book *Codependent No More*, published by the Hazelden Foundation in 1987. This book provided an in-depth exploration of the phenomenon of codependency within the alcoholic family in a way that was easily understood by the general population. Beattie's work also illuminated and expanded the concepts of enabling, letting go of control, and displaced anger.

The Recovery Movement

The distinctive handwriting of both family systems theory and Alcoholics Anonymous was on the wall, using different theoretical fonts but writing the same message. Both validate the role of family in the treatment of psychosocial ills, focus on interpersonal relationships and self-growth, and address the complicated interweaving of family relationships in maintaining disease or, conversely, in empowering recovery.

Today, what is known as the Recovery Movement encompasses not only the founding organization AA but its disciples, groups that share the common thread of empowering the individual to recover within a group of his peers. Such groups exist alongside professional mental health services and provide support for those dealing with abuse, eating disorders, gambling, depression, spending, grief, divorce, parenting, and so on.

Even though AA group meetings and the Twelve Steps sprang up as essential first-line treatment for the addict, AA now encourages family involvement for inpatient treatment. And as AA creates Twelve-Step groups for spouses, teens, adult children of alcoholics, and codependents, movement toward a family systems approach is apparent.

Today there is a strong network of recovery groups dealing with all kinds of mental health issues, each with their unique focus, but all follow the successful self-help format of AA.

Assertiveness Training

Assertiveness training presents a set of concepts and communication techniques that help in developing honest interaction between people. It emphasizes getting along with others while asserting your own needs and beliefs. Behaviorists Joseph Wolpe and Andrew Salter are credited with helping develop assertiveness training in the 1960s. Wolpe and Salter were colleagues and trailblazers in the development of behavior therapy, which has spawned many changes in the field of psychology, including assertiveness training.

FACT

In his book, *When I Say No, I Feel Guilty*, Manuel J. Smith issues a Bill of Assertive Rights. Two of them especially apply to codependents: "You have the right to judge your own behavior, thoughts, and emotions, and to take the responsibility for their initiation and consequences upon yourself. You have the right to be independent of the goodwill of others before coping with them."

In the heyday of the women's liberation movement in the 1960s and 1970s, assertiveness training was highly popular in helping women negotiate their way through an oppressive work environment and also gave them permission and tools to improve their personal relationships by expressing their needs in a productive way. Manuel J. Smith presented his systematic assertiveness techniques as a way to resolve conflict by finding the middle ground between passivity and aggression. His "Bill of Assertive Rights" fit the times and were especially helpful to women who were struggling with changes in social expectations. Of course, today assertiveness is seen as a helpful concept for both men and women. Smith spelled out how assertiveness can be used successfully in maintaining personal power and increasing self-esteem.

Because assertiveness was a new concept in the 1960s, structured programs emerged in the private sector, college courses, and political venues to help people learn the concepts and practice assertiveness techniques. By bringing these concepts to life in role-playing scenarios, participants in assertiveness training groups learned by doing, actually trying the techniques with each other in groups.

Today, assertiveness is less likely to be singled out and taught as a course or a workshop because many of the tenets of assertiveness are now well known. It's hard to believe that forty years ago, a person needed to work on her self-esteem before she could speak up on her own behalf. Today, assertiveness focuses more on communication skills. Role-playing difficult situations still may be part of the training, but over the years, the concept of assertiveness has been absorbed as an important component in business trainings, family and couples therapy, professional coaching, leadership training, and team building.

The Self-Help Phenomenon

There's no argument that the first enduring self-help group in America was Alcoholics Anonymous. For many years, AA stood alone against resounding criticism from the psychiatric community who believed that self-help groups would contaminate the purity of the medical model with nonregulated, untrained treatment for a very serious disease. For too long, mainstream medicine simply chose to ignore the fact that AA Twelve-Step programs worked in bringing about recovery. For many mental health professionals, AA just didn't fit the concept of "science," follow the hierarchy of medicine, or make a clear distinction between the healer and the sick.

ESSENTIAL

In the 1960s, many long-held beliefs were questioned, and people joined together to empower social change. The civil rights movement, the peace movement, and women's liberation challenged the status quo in America. During this time, it became clear that when people unite in a common cause, they can make big changes.

Expanded understanding of human behavior has now opened the door for other treatment modalities besides psychoanalysis. During the last thirty years, family therapy, group therapy, and relationship therapy came into practice. Ideas like personal growth, assertiveness, communication, and self-help moved psychology beyond the limited view that a psychological problem is an illness.

Social and psychological changes in the three previous decades created the right climate. The self-help phenomenon was seeded in the 1980s, and continues to grow.

FACT

Today you will be able to find a book, article, website, CD or video, television show, or documentary to educate you and offer you help for every psychosocial problem. There are community groups formed to support individuals in recovery. The boundaries of self-help and mental health are not as distinct as they used to be, nor are their differences as controversial. Today patients are leaving hospitals, treatment facilities, clinics, and therapists' offices with a list of recommended self-help books as a part of their treatment plans.

Letter to the Psychologist

The following letter is taken from Here-to-Listen.com and helps explain the differences between the types of dependency.

Dear Doctor,

I think I have codependency. When I asked my psychiatrist friend about it, he said dependency is just part of being human. We are born dependent, and what's wrong with that?

David

Dear David,

Your friend, who happens to be a psychiatrist, is absolutely right. Dependency is a relative term, i.e., babies are born entirely dependent on others for survival. As a child develops she is still quite dependent. Throughout childhood, she progresses toward independence, ultimately finding a healthy balance of dependency and autonomy.

Interdependency is a term that describes the balance an adult works toward in his relationships with others. It describes a state of mutual dependency between people. The term is often heard to describe the relationship between autonomous beings in the study of nature. An interesting example of interdependency is the crocodile and the plover. The crocodile sits in the sun with its mouth open. The plover flies in and picks meat out of the crocodile's teeth. It's win-win. The plover has dinner, and the crocodile has clean teeth.

If we were looking at codependency from a biological perspective, it probably would be described as a mutation of interdependency. It is one-sided. The codependent is looking to another to fill something inside himself he ought to be able to fill himself. The codependent has not achieved the balance between dependency and autonomy. He needs the reflection of himself in another to know he is okay.

CHAPTER 3

Is Codependency a Mental Illness?

Codependency isn't "officially" a mental illness. For something to be considered a mental illness, it must have identifiable symptoms that are part of the diagnostic criteria in the current edition of the *Diagnostic and Statistical Manual of Mental Disorders (DSM)*. In fact, the term *codependency* doesn't show up at all in the *DSM*. It is a pattern of behavior, emotion, and cognition that occurs predictably and consistently over time. The wheels of change in traditional medicine turn slowly, but it's clear to most social scientists that there is indeed a syndrome with identifiable symptoms that constitutes codependency. Clinicians are seeing it in their practices. People are identifying it in themselves and their loved ones. Whatever you call it, these patterns cause dysfunction in relationships, as well as distress and pain in people's lives.

The Mental Health System

In the United States today, we have a mental health system that is both private and public. It is based on the medical model, i.e., an illness model. Because of this, there must be an official diagnosis designating a mental illness. In order for individuals to be eligible for public services or reimbursed by insurance for private services, this diagnosis must be determined by a medical doctor, psychiatrist (specialist), psychologist, social worker, or other qualified mental health professionals, using the *DSM*. This is the universally accepted way in which people receive inpatient and outpatient treatment.

ALERT

According to the Psychiatric Archives, a feature of *JAMA Psychiatry*, an estimated 26.2 percent of Americans age eighteen and older—about one in four adults—suffer from a diagnosable mental disorder in a given year.

Psychiatry

Psychiatry is a medical specialty focusing on mental disorders. A psychiatrist is a trained medical doctor (MD or DO) who has completed a three- to four-year residency in psychiatry. Because she is a medical doctor, the psychiatrist is the only mental health professional who can prescribe medication and, more specifically, is an expert on prescribing psychotropic drugs in the treatment of psychiatric problems.

FACT

All the professionals mentioned in this section—psychiatrists, psychologists, social workers, marriage and family therapists, and perhaps others like counselors or pastoral counselors—can do psychotherapy. Usually licensed clinicians in these fields are eligible for insurance reimbursement, which means you can use your health insurance for your therapy.

Prior to the early 1800s, the mentally ill were seen as hopelessly lost, dangerous, or possessed by the devil. "Lunatics" were housed in deplorable conditions and given the barest of necessities, doomed to a lifetime of captive misery. As the field of medicine advanced, a new possibility of treatment and care for the mentally ill emerged. At that time, the medical specialty of psychiatry appeared.

The International Encyclopedia of the Social Sciences points to the evolving status of psychiatry: "Although the strictly biological and medical approaches were pursued early, it was late in the nineteenth century before hypnosis, introspection, psychotherapy, and psychoanalysis placed the emphasis on deeper levels of mentation rather than on behavior, and the focus centered on the psychology of the individual. It is worthy of comment that the psychologies and sociologies that took significant hold in psychiatry were those developed by psychiatrists themselves."

According to the U.S. Department of Labor, Bureau of Labor Statistics, May 2012, there were 25,210 psychiatrists practicing in the United States.

Clinical Psychology

Clinical psychology is a branch of psychology that uses research and a tried and tested set of clinical skills to help diagnose and treat people with psychological disorders. The clinical psychologist is a PhD, not an MD, so he cannot prescribe medications. However, clinical psychologists hold a very important position in mental health services, because they are the only social scientists who can administer and interpret certain psychological testing and do psychological evaluations of all kinds.

A Princeton Review article, "A Day in the Life of a Psychologist," says, "Despite potentially grueling schedules and emotional demands, psychologists report great satisfaction in their jobs; the gratification they receive from helping others keeps them in the field. Wrote one psychologist, 'the best thing about this job is that people open up their lives to you—that's a great responsibility but also an honor.'"

More than any other social science, psychology has contributed to the understanding of human behavior because it is the most research-based discipline in the field of mental health.

Social Work

Social work had a completely different start than psychiatry and psychology. It began as part of child welfare. Social work started as a volunteer activity among wealthy women who wanted to help those less fortunate. Because social work provided services to the poor, and agencies were funded by churches and donations, the profession was not always regarded as highly as the other fields.

The profession of social work developed during the nineteenth century. Admittedly, professional social work had difficulty achieving status among the helping professions because of the lack of professional training required. Many of the early social workers were "grandfathered in" without a degree, working and developing in the trenches.

In the 1960s, social work finally achieved status through the creation of social work programs in a number of colleges throughout the country, starting with fifteen universities offering advanced degrees in social work in 1964.

FACT

According to the US Department of Labor, Bureau of Labor Statistics, in 2012 there were 607,300 jobs in social work, divided into two categories: direct-service social workers who help people solve everyday problems in living, and clinical social workers who diagnose and treat mental, behavioral, and emotional issues.

For the vast majority of licensed social workers, the master's degree in social work, MSW, is still the most common degree. The PhD or DSW typically is pursued by those who wish to teach at the college level or wish to take a supervisory role over other social workers.

In *What Is a Social Worker?* Tara Kuther, PhD, writes, "Social work is a helping field. A social worker is a professional who works to help people.

Most often he or she is a professional who works with people and helps them manage their daily lives, understand and adapt to illness, disability, and death, and obtain social services, such as health care, government assistance, and legal aid."

Social workers are employed in public and private agencies, clinics, hospitals, schools, and private practices. They must meet the requirements for licensure in the state in which they work. Clinical social workers make diagnoses and do psychotherapy like clinical psychologists, with the exception of administering certain psychological testing.

Marriage and Family Therapists

The profession of marriage and family therapy began in the mid 1960s as a result of the research done in family systems theory. In the early years, professionals previously trained as psychologists and social workers added additional training in marriage and family therapy to their existing degrees. Eventually, colleges and universities designed curricula and began training programs for the master's degree in MFT.

Dawn Rosenberg McKay in *Marriage and Family Therapist: Career Information* reports that "[M]arriage and family therapists help their clients overcome or manage their disorders or illnesses which can include anxiety, low self-esteem, obsessive-compulsive disorder, depression, and substance abuse. They take into account the effect a client's family has on his or her mental health by evaluating family roles. They also help clients resolve interpersonal problems within relationships."

FACT

According to the Department of Labor, in 2012 there were 166,300 marriage and family therapists employed.

Not all states require separate licensing in MFT, but most do. The minimum educational requirement is a master's degree. A PhD in marriage and family therapy is usually held by university professors and those who have high positions as supervisors or directors of clinics or training institutions.

Similarities and Differences in Mental Health Professionals

Following is a short list of the differences between the mental health professionals you may encounter:

- **Psychiatrist:** Is an MD or DO physician with a specialty in psychiatry, is the expert on psychotropic drugs, and has the ability to prescribe medications.
- **Psychologist:** A PhD who can work independently with a full license, can do psychotherapy, psychological testing, and evaluation. Master's level: Can do the same clinical work with supervision.
- **Clinical social worker:** Provides counseling and helps individuals navigate the social welfare system. Master's level practitioners can do the same clinical work as psychologists with some limitations.
- **Marriage and family therapist:** Handles the same clinical work as other disciplines, and uses family systems theory to treat couples and families.

Community Mental Health

It wasn't until 1946 that President Harry Truman signed the National Mental Health Act, which called for the formation of the National Institute of Mental Health (NIMH). In 1961, a governmental program, *Action for Mental Health*, assessed mental health conditions and resources throughout the United States "to arrive at a national program that would approach adequacy in meeting the individual needs of the mentally ill people of America."

In 1963, President John F. Kennedy, who had a mentally disabled sister, gave the first presidential message to Congress on mental health issues. Congress quickly passed the Mental Retardation Facilities and Community Mental Health Centers Construction Act of 1963 (P.L. 88-164), beginning a new era in federal support for mental health services. NIMH assumed responsibility for monitoring the nation's community mental health system.

Community mental health is now a national system funded and administered at both state and federal levels. This system provides no-cost or low-cost mental health services for those who qualify.

The *Diagnostic and Statistical Manual (DSM)*

The American Psychiatric Association issued the first edition of the *Diagnostic and Statistical Manual: Mental Disorders (DSM-I)* in 1952. It contained a glossary of descriptions of the diagnostic categories and was the first official manual of mental disorders for practical use. The manual went through two editions, *DSM-I* and *DSM-II*, before it was revised to include specific diagnostic criteria in the *DSM-III*. Because of the discovery of inconsistencies, the *DSM-III-R* was published in 1987. In 1994, after a comprehensive review of the literature and the work of over a thousand psychologists, the *DSM-IV* was published. After almost twenty years and thousands of research papers, the most recent revision, the *DSM-5*, came out in April 2013.

In its six revisions over a sixty-year period, the *DSM* has added diagnoses and has also eliminated them. The formulation and approval of a diagnosis takes years of research and deliberation by experts in order to be included in the *DSM*, but that doesn't guarantee permanency. As is everything else, the *DSM* editions are a product of the times in which they were revised. Research is ongoing, and the *DSM* must consider new discoveries in its revisions.

Social conditions also impact diagnoses. A key example of this is the fact that homosexuality was once listed in the *DSM* as a mental illness. It was dropped in 1973. Another example of the influence of social change is the inclusion of gambling disorder and hoarding disorder in the *DSM-5*.

Will Codependency Ever Be in the *DSM*?

Since the term *codependency* describes a pervasive pattern of thought, emotion, and behavior occurring consistently over time, it comes closest to a personality disorder.

In the *DSM-5* significant and controversial changes were proposed for the category of personality disorders. At one point, it was recommended by the work group that the number of distinct personality disorders be dropped from ten to six, but the APA Board of Trustees did not approve this proposal.

The American Psychiatric Association explained the changes in the identification of a personality disorder by clarifying that "Critically, a person must have significant impairment in the two areas of personality functioning—self and interpersonal. Self is defined as how patients view themselves as well as how they identify and pursue goals in life. Interpersonal is defined as whether an individual is able to understand other people's perspectives and form close relationships. The scale by which these will be judged ranges from mild to extreme."

To quote Andrew Skodol, MD, the work group's chair and a research professor of psychiatry at the University of Arizona College of Medicine: "The importance of personality functioning and personality traits is the major innovation here. In the past, we viewed personality disorders as binary. You either had one or you didn't. But we now understand that personality pathology is a matter of degree."

As reported on the Family Practice News website, Mary Ellen Schneider (3/2010) comments on trends in psychological practice by saying, "The categorical model and criteria for the ten personality disorders in the *DSM-IV* will remain the same in the new manual. However, to encourage further study on how personality disorders can be diagnosed, the *DSM-5* will include a separate section with new trait-specific methodology."

One can make the case that a departure from the "either-or" concept to a "matter of degree" notion could provide an opening for the inclusion in the *DSM* of a codependent personality disorder.

ALERT

In order for a treatment to be reimbursed by insurance, the diagnosis must be included in the gatekeeper, the *DSM*.

In 1986, Dr. Timmen Cermak, board certified in Addiction Psychiatry, proposed diagnostic criteria for Codependent Personality Disorder. According to the Serene Center website, "Timmen Cermak, MD, suggests that codependency is a personality disorder. His reason is that when specific personality traits become excessive and maladaptive and cause significant impairment in functioning or cause significant distress, this warrants a personality disorder diagnosis."

Is a Person Born Codependent?

Many people wonder if a person is born codependent. Unfortunately there is no definitive answer. The temperament is present at birth. Babies, even newborns, can exhibit traits like calmness or activeness, boldness or shyness, sleepiness or wakefulness, fussiness or complacency, sullenness or happiness, etc. In that sense, temperament can be a precursor to personality, but not always. Some of these early traits fade; parents may say the baby has "outgrown them."

We all have a personality, which is a configuration of traits learned in childhood and pretty much set by the end of adolescence. The personality is thought to be quite fixed and pervasive throughout adulthood, i.e., a person is likely to behave, think, and emote in the same way across most situations and interactions.

Most experts agree that the personality is learned by a child's interaction with his environment, with some biological influence. That is why parenting is so crucial in the forming of personality. Also important is birth order, sibling relationships, extended family, social status, trauma, religion, schooling, and all the factors present in a child's life as he grows up, and grows into his personality.

Codependency and Relationships

First of all, human beings do not exist outside of relationships. Even if a child is separated from parents at birth, he still requires caretakers and is relating to those caretakers as he develops.

For example, if a child is abandoned at birth and left at the doorstep of a police station, from the moment that child is picked up, he is relating to someone. He starts to develop his perceptions and view of the world. He learns how to get basic needs met; if he cries, someone will attend to him. Or, unfortunately, in some cases if he needs something, nobody will come.

If the abandoned child is placed in a foster home, awaiting adoption, he is moved again, learning to adapt to change, perhaps forming a fear that he will be left again. The family who adopts him will become his family of origin and will interact with him continuously as he develops. So, in that sense, codependency does not exist without a relationship because personality traits are developed as a child interacts with his environment, i.e., people.

However, there may be another way to relate to this question of codependency and relationships. When your personality is fully formed, as an adult, can you be seen as codependent if you live alone and have no primary, important relationships? The answer is still yes. While codependency traits can be seen most clearly as they occur in your primary relationship, codependency patterns exist in your head, in the way you think, your beliefs about yourself and others, and the emotions you feel.

Codependent Behavior, Thoughts, and Feelings

Codependency describes thoughts and feelings that may or may not be manifested in behavior. Here's an example. Judith's husband, John, divorces her when he falls in love with someone else. Judith is devastated and starts psychotherapy. During the period of her therapy, approximately four months, Judith has cut off contact with friends and family, and barely leaves her home. She certainly doesn't want another relationship because she is still emotionally attached to John.

During therapy, Judith learns about codependency, gains insight into how she had catered to John, almost always had deferred to him, and then resented it. She was afraid to voice frustration when John wanted to spend more time away from home. She felt powerless and afraid, but instead of telling John how she felt, she grew sullen and withdrawn. When he reached out to her intimately, she made excuses. She was angry most of the time, and when John asked her if there was anything wrong, she said, "No." With this codependency pattern, the marriage began to slip away.

While Judith is in therapy, she shares with the therapist how she felt during the time she was married to John. At first, she breaks down and cries often in her sessions, wondering why John doesn't love her when all she wanted was for him to be happy. She no longer sees John at all, but her codependent thoughts and feelings are very much alive in the therapy sessions.

Gradually, with insight and guidance from her therapist, Judith begins to change her thoughts and feelings. She takes baby steps toward assertiveness with her family and friends. Whether or not Judith will be codependent with her next partner is still unknown, but she is likely to be less codependent the next time around.

The point is, during therapy, Judith is still codependent with John even though she no longer has any contact with him. Codependency is a pattern of thought, behavior, and emotion. Even when it is not expressed in your behavior, it still exists within you as perception, values, ideas, and feelings.

Codependency and the Disabled

Spouses and family members may be called upon to provide help in the case of a loved one's disability, whether that may be mental or physical. This situation is an especially daunting road to navigate because the loved one truly does need help. Even so, your resentment meter must be your guide. Perhaps you believe you *should* take care of a loved one. If you can provide that care without resentment, and you can set boundaries within the commitment, you would not be codependent in providing care. However, you can see this decision going horribly wrong when you look at the occurrences of elder abuse, the abuse of the disabled, and in codependents who give up their entire lives while secretly wishing their loved ones would die so they could be free.

FACT

In an interdependent relationship, couples take turns helping one another through rough times. But in the codependent relationship, one person is always the helper, in fact, his identify depends on it. This is the person who ends up feeling resentful and victimized by the problems of his partner, yet he finds it almost impossible to leave.

The beginning of a relationship like this can be seen with Vaughn and Katie, who meet during a French cooking class at a local college. What starts out as a connection around a shared interest evolves into a friendship. Vaughn is fifty-three and was married to his high school sweetheart until she died three years ago. Vaughn has two grown children. Katie is forty-eight and has no children. She has had three serious relationships, but she has never been married.

Through the summer, Katie and Vaughn become closer; they share many activities together—boating and biking, movies, long walks, and a love of cooking. Vaughn is pleasantly surprised to find he's falling in love with Katie. After Katie joins Vaughn for a family Christmas with his children, Vaughn asks her to marry him. Katie is reluctant, pointing out that they've known each other less than a year and there is something she needs to talk to him about.

Katie shares with Vaughn that she has had periods of depression all her life and she takes medication for it. When Vaughn looks troubled by the news, Katie assures him that she is doing very well now. He asks her a few questions and finds out she was hospitalized a couple of times when she was younger and has been under the care of a psychiatrist ever since. Vaughn is worried, but Katie again reassures him that she's fine. They agree they will date until summer, and if everything goes well, they will get engaged.

The relationship is going smoothly, but by May, Vaughn starts to notice small things about Katie's behavior. He notices she can be moody and withdrawn sometimes. When he mentions it to her, she always seems to have a reason for her mood shifts. Her explanations seem reasonable to Vaughn, who is now very much in love with Katie.

In July, Vaughn asks Katie if she would like to take a food and wine trip to France. As the trip draws near, Katie seems stressed and asks Vaughn to plan the trip by himself. He agrees, but often when he comes to Katie to share his plans she seems dismissive. When he asks her if she still wants to go, she emphasizes how excited she is about it. The trip is everything Vaughn hopes for. Vaughn and Katie return from France engaged.

Shortly after their return, the couple gets into their first argument, which quickly escalates with Katie yelling and throwing things. Vaughn tries to calm her down, but Katie finally ends the fight by throwing his keys at him and screaming for him to get out. When Vaughn arrives home, he is so upset he calls a friend. His friend tells him that these things happen and he should just wait until the next day and talk to Katie.

Vaughn can't sleep. He spends all night running past behaviors through his head and worrying about Katie's emotional health. At the same time, he discounts his thoughts and rationalizes that it's probably just him, overreacting. When Vaughn calls Katie's house in the morning, there's no answer. He leaves numerous messages, and continues to call her throughout the day with no response. By dinnertime, he's beside himself with anxiety. He waffles about it, but decides to go over to Katie's condo. She answers the door looking refreshed and calm. She has no explanation for her behavior except that Vaughn made her mad.

Vaughn is bothered all week by Katie's temper tantrum. The next time they are together, he tries to talk to her about it. Again, she becomes enraged, calling Vaughn all kinds of names and throwing the engagement ring at him. He bends to pick it up from the floor, and when he does, Katie kicks him. He leaves in tears, ring in hand.

The next day, Katie calls and apologizes. Vaughn asks her if she would go to a couple's counselor, and she agrees. In the course of their therapy together, Vaughn makes it clear that he loves Katie, but he sometimes feels abused by her behavior. He tells her in front of the counselor, Dr. Banks, that if it doesn't stop, he will have to break off the relationship. Katie appears to understand, but when they leave the office, Katie grabs Vaughn's car keys and drives off in his car, leaving him at the curb, bewildered.

In the next session, Katie again apologizes and says she loves Vaughn. She asks for the engagement ring back, and Vaughn gives it to her. Dr. Banks works with Vaughn and Katie on anger issues, communication, and conflict resolution. They each practice their skills and seem to be catching on by the end of the session.

That weekend, Katie tells Vaughn she has never married because she has never loved anyone as much as she loves him. She is sure she has made the right choice in Vaughn, and she wants to get married right away, fly to Vegas to one of those darling wedding chapels. Vaughn agrees that getting married right away is a wonderful idea, but he wants his children to be there. Katie gets up from the table in the restaurant and throws her wine in Vaughn's face. She hurls the ring at him and shrieks that she won't play second fiddle to anybody. As Vaughn leaves the restaurant, he hears Katie screaming that the relationship is over.

Vaughn is heartbroken. He keeps the appointment with Dr. Banks, and continues to see him. Dr. Banks helps him realize that he's codependent with Katie, who is mentally ill. Vaughn is plagued with guilt, because it isn't Katie's fault, and she needs him. Through the course of his therapy, Vaughn sees that it's okay to consider his own needs, even if Katie's ill. He has a right to choose the life he wants. Dr. Banks keeps reminding Vaughn that the only life he has responsibility for, and control over, is his own.

The Psychologist's Opinion

When you're codependent with someone with a mental or physical illness, it is especially hard for you to choose yourself and your own well-being. There is tremendous social pressure for you to become a caretaker because that person legitimately needs help. Vaughn is in this situation. He feels like a bad person because he just doesn't want to sacrifice his own life for Katie. He must do a lot of soul-searching to realize it's okay for him to consider his own needs, even if his partner needs him. Otherwise, he will spend the rest of his life in an abusive marriage.

Letter to the Psychologist

The following letter is taken from Here-to-Listen.com and helps explain how some characteristics of codependency may overlap with *DSM* diagnoses.

Dear Doctor,

I just started therapy a few weeks ago, and I'm excited about making changes in my life. During my first appointment, I told my therapist I was there for codependency. Last week, my psychologist said he billed my insurance for my treatment, and I would be receiving a report in the mail. I asked him what my diagnosis was, and he said I had an anxiety disorder and a dependent personality disorder. I thought we were working on my codependency. I don't get it.

Robert

Dear Robert,

Codependency has not yet been approved by the American Psychiatric Association in the *DSM-5*. Therefore, your therapist cannot make a diagnosis of codependency. Your therapist made the diagnosis of anxiety disorder because you met the diagnostic criteria for it. This diagnosis is likely to be right on target since codependency and anxiety often coexist. Insurance will reimburse for this diagnosis. Let's look at dependent personality disorder and see how it is similar to and different from codependency.

A personality disorder must be present since early adulthood. Both codependency and dependent personality disorder fit this criterion.

But the diagnostic criteria for DPD are different from codependency. For example:

- Dependent personality disorder patients have a hard time making decisions on their own. (This is **not** a dominant feature of codependency.)
- They want others to take care of them in most areas of their life. (This usually is **not** true in codependency.)
- They won't disagree with others out of fear of disapproval. (This can be true of codependency.)
- They have trouble initiating things on their own. (This typically is **not** a major feature of codependency.)
- They fear being alone. (This is **not** a feature of codependency.)
- They feel desperate to find someone to care for them in another relationship when their current relationship ends. (Codependents seek out another relationship, but usually not to care for them.)
- They fear being left to take care of themselves. (This is **not** a feature of codependency.)
- They go to great lengths to get support and nurturance from others. (In codependency, they seek approval.)

Your psychologist evaluated your symptoms, and based on his assessment, he determined that you met at least five of the criteria for dependent personality disorder and that's why gave you that diagnosis.

CHAPTER 4

Can Codependents Be Happy?

When professionals talk about codependency, they have a certain shared understanding of what characteristics make up this syndrome. Once these characteristics have been identified and validated as items on a test, codependency can actually be objectively measured. An example of this is the Holyoake Codependency Index. Similarly, components of "happiness" can also be isolated and validated as items on a test like the Oxford Happiness Questionnaire, which measures psychological well-being. But if codependency is unhealthy, and happiness is healthy, how can they coexist? In order to understand this apparent discord, it is necessary to first understand the concept of normal.

Normal

The term *normal* is a scientific term. It is not based on moral judgment and it's not arbitrary. Simply put, if you are in the majority, no matter what the measure, you are normal. If you are in the minority, you are abnormal. Take weight, for example: It has been determined that the normal weight range for women of 5'6" in the United States is 120 pounds to 159 pounds. If Ellen weighs 90 pounds, she has an abnormal weight. By the same token, if Janet weighs 193 pounds, she also is in the abnormal range.

You can also see this in the field of psychological research. Early in the development of psychiatry, people who were "insane" were locked in institutions. The majority of U.S. citizens were not in mental institutions and were therefore normal. The minority were in mental institutions and thereby considered abnormal. This is when the first research was conducted to investigate mental illness.

ESSENTIAL

When a person reads self-help books or comes to therapy, he wants to know if what he is experiencing is normal. He is wondering, "What is causing my misery? Is it normal to act or think or feel this way?"

Using a captive research population, researchers entered the asylums to observe the patients. From those rudimentary clinical observations, distinctive mental illnesses were eventually identified. For example, researchers observed that a certain number of patients had hallucinations and delusions, paranoid and grandiose thoughts, and a break with reality. This cluster of behaviors was eventually labeled as a mental illness called schizophrenia. As psychiatry has evolved, psychological research has advanced to include valid and reliable psychometric tests that provide detailed diagnostic impressions regarding schizophrenia and other mental illnesses.

What if there was a psychological test that measured results on two scales: the Codependency Scale and the Happiness Scale? Each of these scales has passed reliability and validity criteria, and the test is found to accurately measure the two variables. But what if a person scores high on the Codependency Scale and also scores high on the Happiness Scale?

Since happiness is equated with healthy and good and codependency is equated with unhealthy and bad, how can you explain these results?

FACT

Helping professionals value the role of testing when they consider diagnoses and develop treatment plans. The term *psychometric* simply means a test used for this purpose. The term *psychometric* or *psychometrics* is used interchangeably with *psychological test*.

Thoughts Match Behaviors and Feelings

One possibility for understanding a positive correlation between happiness and codependency is the absence of conflict. Instead of the inner and outer conflict most codependents feel, there is congruence. An inside/outside match creates a sense of psychological well-being (happiness).

For example, let's take the case of Grace. Grace grew up in a large family in the hills of Kentucky. Her father worked in the mine and her mother and siblings tended goats and chickens, gardened, and pretty much lived off the land. Grace was the oldest of eight children. Her mother was definitely in charge, bearing the brunt of the work and the care of her children. Being the oldest, Grace fell into a position like most of the oldest girls in her community. She tended her younger siblings when her mother was working and went to school in her neighborhood. She was well-liked and valued by her family, church, school, and community. Girls in her small town married young; when Grace turned sixteen she married a boy from her village who rejected the miner's life and became a farmer down in the valley.

Grace has four children now, works hard in the fields with her husband, supports him emotionally in his decision-making, tends to his sore muscles when he works too hard, and tries to fix good meals to keep up his strength. She sometimes helps her kids with their chores because she knows how hard it is to work and never have any time for play or fun. She'd rather stay up a couple of hours later to get her work done than expect the children to give up their childhoods.

Grace is a beautiful singer and loves to make up songs while she's working in the fields. When her kids join her, she teaches the songs to them and they all sing while they work. Grace and her family are poor, but the love is great.

"Happiness is when what you think, what you say, and what you do are in harmony." —Mahatma Gandhi

The Psychologist's Opinion

Grace has many of the characteristics defined as codependency: She puts her own needs last, is subservient to her husband and children, doesn't ask for much, and doesn't feel she deserves much. On the surface, many would think Grace is living a barren life, but she's not. This is because her thoughts, feelings, and behaviors all match. Grace actually finds joy in the mundane work of her life. She doesn't mind sacrificing for her children because there just isn't enough to go around and she accepts that. She is focused on her husband because she loves him and she know that he is working hard, many times too hard, to support the family. She truly wants to help him in any way she can, and she knows he feels the same way about her.

Grace's choices are also normalized and supported by social expectations. Grace is following the norms of her farm community. All the women work in the field, support their husbands, and raise the children. In a different environment, Grace might feel angry, thinking she's being taken for granted, or victimized in some way. But not here.

Codependency and Traditional Roles

The same matchup, or congruence, applies to the case of Elizabeth. She also is happy with her life even though others might consider her codependent.

Elizabeth grew up in a very sheltered environment. Her father and mother run a food co-op and have brought Elizabeth to work with them since she was a baby. Because Elizabeth had a difficult birth, she suffers from mild brain damage. Her parents have been very involved in Elizabeth's development and have mastered the thin line between protecting her and challenging her.

QUESTION

Can you be codependent and not know it?
"Not knowing it" simply means lack of conscious awareness. If you are experiencing an authentic feeling of well-being, or happiness, you don't have a problem with codependency.

Elizabeth attended Montessori school through high school. Because every child is taught at her own learning ability and pace, Elizabeth fits in well there, and is outgoing and friendly. After graduation, Elizabeth begins working in the food co-op with her parents.

Elizabeth meets Felipe in the store. He brings produce to the city from the outlying farms to sell at the co-op. After a long friendship, the couple starts dating, and eventually marries. They have a very traditional marriage, pretty much patterned after their own parents. Felipe is the breadwinner and Elizabeth is a stay-at-home mother.

ALERT

Resentment is anger left unresolved. If anger can be seen as mud that occurs after a storm, you can visualize it washed away while it is still soft. If that mud isn't washed clean, it can harden. Each hardened piece of anger can build, one piece upon another, until it forms a wall. Walls of resentment can keep you isolated from those you love.

Felipe and Elizabeth value family above all else. They are both hands-on parents, but Elizabeth is the primary caretaker of the children. Elizabeth likes to sew, cook, and spend time with the kids. Felipe works hard, but also enjoys family time when he's not working.

Elizabeth, like Grace, would very likely score high on the Codependency Scale, but she would also score high on the Happiness Scale.

The Psychologist's Opinion

If an outsider observed her life, he might evaluate Elizabeth as codependent. He might even think Elizabeth is vulnerable because of her disability and that Felipe is taking advantage and keeping her at home to raise his kids and clean the house. But Elizabeth wouldn't agree. She would say she enjoys her role as a wife and mother. She feels comfortable and happy at home. Her thoughts and actions are congruent.

Again it's an inside-outside match. She harbors no resentment toward the life she has chosen. Elizabeth feels loved and content in her family situation; she has the support of her extended family and her community.

Codependency and Religion

Certain religious sects are almost islands unto themselves. For example, the Mennonites and their Amish offshoot here in the United States have their own distinctive way of life. Although the Mormons and Jehovah's Witnesses do interface with the secular community, their beliefs also are quite rigid. Within strong religious communities like these, it may not be accurate to label certain behaviors as codependent, even though they may fit the criteria.

If you consider the Amish family, for example, the women might be seen as subservient to the men. This gender role stereotyping would not be acceptable in our culture as a whole, and women who adhere might be seen as exploited or "second class." If Amish women went down a checklist of codependency traits, they'd likely score high. But these women may not feel oppressed. In fact, Amish women hold an esteemed position in their own sphere of influence, the home and family. Some also extend these talents outside the home by owning businesses like quilting, horticulture, and food products.

Amish children are raised in a world that has rejected the secular life. They do not use electricity or motorized vehicles, and they selectively use modern conveniences like phones, computers, and the like. The Amish are self-contained in that they raise their own food and seldom interface with the greater culture. The women wear long solid-color dresses with capes and white or black bonnets. Amish men wear dark vests and pants, often with suspenders, and white shirts and straw or black felt hats; older or married men wear beards. Children are miniature, somewhat more colorful versions of their parents in appearance.

ALERT

> Some of the more fundamental religions provide their own counseling using tenets of the church in their work. But even in secular settings like mental health clinics and private practices, spiritual well-being is seen as an important dimension of happiness.

The Amish have strict cultural and religious rules that may vary slightly from location to location. Those who do not follow the rules are excommunicated or shunned. There is a very strong pressure toward conformity in these communities, and because of this, individuals do not experience the same type of inner conflict that forms resentment and anger.

The Psychologist's Opinion

Codependency traits are not as likely to be seen as problematic in certain religious communities because many of these traits—like self-sacrifice, subservience, hard physical labor, and deprivation—are seen as admirable and desirable traits that will get you through the gates of heaven.

This does not mean codependency couldn't exist in such communities. Again, if resentment is building inside you when you follow the rules and customs of your community, something is wrong. You could stay and be codependent and unhappy, but a healthier choice would be to change the things in your life you are resentful about. In this case, you may have to leave the religious community you were born into and find congruence elsewhere.

Codependency and Culture

Historically, America has been called a melting pot because of the ethnic diversity of the immigrants who came to this country to build a new life. However, some distinctive nationalities have not melded as thoroughly as others, and have maintained their own distinctive cultural and familial rules and norms.

For example, in the Muslim population, which has increased significantly in the United States since 1965, it would neither be useful nor wise to apply exclusively Western standards to analyze the Muslim experience of happiness. In the article "The Muslim Family, Predicament and Promise" in the *Western Journal of Medicine* (November 2000), authors Sangeeta Dhami and Aziz Sheikh caution helping professionals against overlooking the distinctions of the Muslim culture. For example, the family is the center, the extended family structure being the most common constellation for Muslim families. Women who are "protected" by their husbands do not necessarily view their position as lower than those of men. A Muslim woman interviewed in this article felt her husband respected and valued her.

ESSENTIAL

Educational test bias is explained on the Glossary of Education website under *Multicultural Education* (last updated 8/29/13). This explanation also applies to psychological tests. "Educational tests are considered biased if a test design, or the way results are interpreted and used, systematically disadvantages certain groups of students over others, such as students of color, students from lower-income backgrounds, students who are not proficient in the English language, or students who are not fluent in certain cultural customs and traditions."

It is obvious that a Western analysis of happiness and codependency would need to be modified to account for cultural differences in the case of these minority cultures living in the United States.

The Codependent and the Narcissist

If there were such a thing as a pathological "match made in heaven," it would be the codependent and the narcissist. Gill, the narcissist, believes the world revolves around him, and Bryan, his codependent partner, also believes the world revolves around Gill.

Gill and Bryan have been in a committed relationship for seven years. They met when Bryan visited Pebble Beach for the PGA National Pro-Am Golf Tournament. Gill was playing in the tournament, and Bryan was there with a group of friends standing on the sidelines when he caught Gill's eye. Later that night, Bryan was at a pool party when Gill asked him to dance.

After seven years, Gill is still a major player in the PGA. For the first couple of years of their relationship, Bryan kept his job as a prosecuting attorney and Gill did his own thing traveling around the country for tournaments. But Gill increasingly misses Bryan and insists that if the relationship is to continue, Bryan will have to quit his job and travel with Gill.

Bryan wants to talk about alternatives, but Gill has made up his mind. Afraid of losing the relationship, Bryan gives his two weeks' notice, closes up the house, and becomes Gill's constant companion. For the first year, it's fun. Bryan keeps busy handling Gill's schedule and keeping up with all the busywork associated with competitive golf, like press releases, public appearances, scheduling time off for Gill, etc. Bryan also enjoys traveling to new places, meeting new people, and learning new skills.

By the third year of their relationship, conflicts begin to arise around Gill's needs and Bryan's dissatisfaction with Gill calling all the shots. Every time they try to problem-solve, Gill eventually just says he's sorry Bryan is unhappy, and maybe they should just break up so Bryan can find somebody else.

Every time this happens, Bryan is devastated. He loves Gill and wants to work on the relationship, but he is powerless to get his needs met. To Gill, "It's my way or the highway." Bryan continues to try to be indispensable to Gill. He knows there are many young men out there who are attracted to his partner, and he's afraid Gill might leave him, especially since he threatens it when he doesn't get his way.

The fourth and fifth years of the relationship are smoother because Bryan has stopped asking for his needs to be considered. Every time he brings something up, Gill either gets defensive, or reminds Bryan he's a top player who has to keep his mind clear and his emotions calm. If ever Gill loses a tournament, he blames Bryan for upsetting him with his petty problems.

In their sixth year, Gill begins an affair and doesn't tell Bryan about it. He requests that Bryan resume working and only travel with him to the top tournaments. Bryan is confused, but that's what Gill wants, so Bryan moves back home. Rather than return to a public position, Bryan figures he will have more flexibility to be with Gill if he's self-employed. Unfortunately, Gill pretty much stops asking Bryan to join him. He's home periodically, and the rest of the time he's traveling.

Now that Bryan and Gill are in their seventh year, Gill decides he wants his freedom. Juggling between two partners is too hard on him; he feels that the stress is interfering with his game. Instead of ending the affair, he breaks up with Bryan.

The Psychologist's Opinion

It's clear that neither partner in this couple would score high on the Happiness Scale, but their friends and family might score them high. They don't fight, they seem to have an ideal life, both doing what they like to do and working out the logistics of their respective careers. When they're together, they seem very much in love, their sexual relationship is good, they love to laugh, and they seem to enjoy the same things, like vacationing, dining out with friends, and socializing together.

The difference between this couple and the others in the chapter is that with Bryan and Gill, the outside does not match the inside. Both are codependent. Gill's codependency manifests in narcissism. He seems selfish and egotistical and he is, but he also needs that mirror of Bryan's adoration and the worship of others to feel okay. Bryan is more easily identified as codependent because he has literally given up his own life for Gill's. Over the course of their relationship, anger and frustration have built up because of their inability to talk to one another. From there, Gill starts abusive behavior like threatening to leave if he doesn't get his way. Bryan capitulates to Gill's demands because his identity depends on it.

On the outside, it looks like Bryan is the devoted partner and Gill is the selfish one. But they are both codependent in their own way. Inside they feel the same thing—resentment, anger, despair, and loneliness.

Letter to the Psychologist

The following letter is taken from Here-to-Listen.com and helps explain that you are responsible for your own happiness.

Dear Doctor,

My wife just read a book on codependency, and she says it fits me to a T. I am so sick of her telling me what's wrong with me. She's always bugging me to go to marriage counseling or read this article or that book. I would be just fine if she'd stop nagging at me and expecting me to talk to her about my feelings. When she does this, I just stop talking to her and eventually she gets over it. Why would I go to marriage counseling when the problem is definitely her?

Vern

Dear Vern,

You don't sound very happy in your marriage. It's hard to feel blamed by your partner, but I'm not sure clamming up and waiting for it to pass has enhanced your sense of well-being. Do you feel content with yourself in this situation? First of all, stop reacting to your wife and ask yourself if you are happy with how you are handling the communication issues in your relationship. Why not go to therapy? You just might end up with a happier marriage.

CHAPTER 5

Is Codependency a Social Illness?

The term *codependency* encompasses a number of characteristics, many of which have been viewed in the past as particular to women. It raises the question as to whether codependency is a women's problem. Are women *socialized* to be codependent? When you read about gender bias in this chapter, you will see that it still exists, but it may influence codependency in a different way than you think. Both men and women can be codependent, but perhaps codependency behaviors in men look different than those of women because of gender bias in our culture.

Are Girls Socialized to Codependency?

As you mature, you look out into your world to understand what it means to be a girl or a boy. The term *gender role* appeared in the late 1950s. During the 1960s, gender studies exploded and social scientists conducted thousands of studies. Academics wrote many articles and books investigating the differences between traits in girls and boys, and why they exist. It was about nature versus nurture. Studies showed that many of the characteristics unique to each gender were rooted in social expectations.

Many studies have been done in the last thirty years on gender differences; the vast majority of these studies agree that the differences between boys and girls are socially learned. In an article published in 2010 in *Scientific American*, "The Truth about Boys and Girls," Lise Eliot concludes that, "Experience itself changes brain structure and function. Most sex differences start out small—as mere biases in temperament and play style—but are amplified as children's pink- or blue-tinted brains meet our gender-infused culture."

If social expectations were the same now as they were in the 1960s, when gender was first studied, girls would be expected to be quiet, pleasing, fragile, and delicate. They would have tea parties and invite all their dolls and stuffed animals, and use Easy-Bake Ovens to make cakes and serve them to their parents. Girls would play with dolls, feed them and change their diapers, dress them in pretty clothes, and pretend they were getting married. Girls would be "pretty" and "cute," would cry and be comforted when they were hurt. They might learn to knit or sew, help mother with housework, and learn to cook.

Girls are socialized to be passive and look to others for their sense of self. As girls play, they practice being responsible for others. They play dress-up, pretend to take care of a home, husband, children. In other words, girls are trained and programmed to be caretakers. Girls learn that happiness is found in a relationship, having a boyfriend, a husband, children, family.

Expectations for Girls Then and Now

After forty years of change, gender behaviors for girls are not nearly as limited as in the previous three decades. But maybe on a deeper level things haven't changed all that much. Dottie, who is now sixty, had an Easy-Bake Oven when she was a child; she bought one for her daughter, who is now forty, and her daughter bought one for her daughter, who is now fourteen. The Easy-Bake Oven hasn't changed. Like the oven, maybe the expectations for girls really haven't changed either.

Reviving Ophelia

In her groundbreaking book, *Reviving Ophelia: Saving the Selves of Adolescent Girls* (1994), Mary Pipher addressed the question of the socialization of girls in our culture. Through her clinical work with a number of troubled adolescents, Pipher provides a conduit for these girls to reveal the truth about their lives.

ESSENTIAL

Some psychological charts suggest that adolescence extends to age twenty-seven. Be patient with your adolescents while they are trying to find themselves.

While it is clear times have changed since the 1960s, the surprising message of the book is that girls were still struggling to find themselves in a gender-biased world in 1994. Often, formerly confident girls reach adolescence only to discard their true selves in a desperate attempt to fit in. By this time, the reference group shifts to peers who are in the same boat.

Pipher found that girls felt less important as they realized effects of sexism in their world. As they considered their future, they saw that men remain in most of the power positions in government and industry. In a 2013 article, "Benchmarking Women's Leadership in the United States," Dean Lynn M. Gangone says, "It is the twenty-first century and the fact that this report shows that women remain, on average, less than 20 percent of positional leaders across 14 sectors in the United States is unconscionable." Given this reality, is it any wonder that girls may still feel discouraged about the lack of possibilities in their lives?

Given social scientists' understanding of the adolescent stage of development, by junior high, being popular may be the most important goal. So much so that girls hide their true identity and construct a malleable false identity in a desperate attempt to be accepted. During the crucial time of adolescence, just as they are preparing to jump into adulthood, the rug is pulled out from under them. And where do they look to find themselves? Their peers are in the midst of the same identity confusion. This elusive identity that will direct their destiny is not yet set. They must look to others to tell them they are okay. Losing touch with their internal point of reference, codependency traits are reinforced. This evolving identity becomes an image reflected off the opinions and judgments of others.

Now here is the good news regarding social influences on codependency. If codependency were strictly biological, it would be seen as fixed, unchangeable. Scientists would be researching a physiological intervention like drugs or brain surgery. If it involves the way children are socialized, then it is learned. What is learned can be unlearned or remediated; perhaps we can control the learning process from the start.

Swimming with Sharks

Sobering statistics on teen pregnancy and suicide validate the stories told in *Reviving Ophelia*. This book was published twenty years ago, but it is still relevant today. In fact, it is used in many schools as recommended or required reading.

On the surface, the waters of gender role stereotyping have smoothed since the 1960s. Young girls are encouraged to be all they can be. The awareness of inequality for girls is there; "gender neutral" is the slogan. But deeper in the psyche of the adolescent girl, there are sharks, remnants of years of gender bias still below the surface. These leftovers may not be as obvious, but they very well may be more dangerous.

Are Boys Socialized to Codependency?

If we look at socialization through the same lens as we just did with girls, we see that the boys of the 1960s were expected to be rough and tumble, adventuresome, brave, strong, stoic. They played with army men, climbed trees, and went swimming in the creek. They fought with each other, but never cried. They'd play sandlot baseball and go fishing and hunting with their dads. They were curious to see how things worked, maybe asked for an Erector Set or a chemistry set for their birthday. They loved trains and trucks. Boys who dressed up would be in football or baseball gear or have a tool belt or a gun and holster around their waist, wear a cowboy hat, a football helmet, or an army uniform. The boys of the 1960s were expected to be "all boy."

Expectations for Boys Then and Now

Boys also have benefited from changes brought about by studies done on gender role stereotyping. Boys don't have to be pigeonholed into athletics, hunting and fishing, playing army, or lifting weights. For boys, as with girls, the gender roles have loosened up, giving all kids all choices. And yet, it appears that there is still a pretty clear delineation between expectations for boys as compared to girls. As it relates to codependency traits, our culture does not expect boys to be caretakers. Boys are expected to be active and competitive, sports stars or heroes, tough and manly, leaders and saviors, and warriors who show no mercy for their enemies.

ALERT

Suicide is the third leading cause of death among adolescents and teenagers. According to the National Institute for Mental Health (NIMH), about 6.5 out of every 100,000 teenagers committed suicide in 2007.

Adolescence is no walk in the park for boys. Culturally, they must swallow their own kind of poison. In some respects, adolescence is even more difficult for boys than girls. The judgments can be even more severe for boys who step out of stereotypical behaviors. Let's face it—it's still more acceptable for a girl to be a "tomboy" than for a boy to be deemed a "sissy." It's rough for boys to struggle with identity issues amidst all the expectations they must meet.

The Difference Between Codependent Boys and Girls

Since the 1980s, codependency has been seen as a women's disease. While it has been identified in women, and women tend to self-describe as codependent, this belief has recently come under question. Some researchers speculate that codependency exists as frequently in men as it does in women.

In an Australian study, the Holyoake Codependency Index was used to test a mixed sample of male and female college students to identify traits of codependency. The index was distilled to a thirteen-item instrument measuring three aspects of codependency and was reliable by retest validation criteria. In other words, the test was able to reliably measure three aspects of codependency: external focus, self-sacrifice, and a sense of being overwhelmed by another person's problematic behavior (termed *reactivity*). To simplify the results: Men responded similarly to the women in endorsing attitudes defined as codependent.

FACT

Adolescence is a tough challenge for both sexes. In the article, "The Gender Paradox in Suicide" by Canetto and Sakenofsky, girls think about and attempt suicide about twice as often as boys, and tend to attempt suicide by overdosing on drugs or cutting themselves. Yet boys die by suicide about four times as often as girls, perhaps because they tend to use more lethal methods, such as firearms, hanging, or jumping from heights.

When we consider that boys can experience feelings of abandonment, confusion about their identity, and assaults to their self-esteem, why wouldn't they emerge from childhood with the same wounds as girls display? Codependent feelings and thoughts surely emerge from these conflicts.

What is extremely important to understand is that boys react to their vulnerability and fear differently than girls do. Girls react with typical codependency behaviors: primarily the caretaker and peacekeeper behaviors, with tentativeness, attempts to please, passive-aggressiveness, passivity, and secondarily anger and detachment. Boys don't overtly react this way. Why? Because boys have not been socialized to express themselves this way, they aren't likely to self-identify as codependent, nor are they likely to be described as codependent by observation.

Many boys do not hear from their fathers, male coaches, peers, and teachers about how to maintain an intimate relationship. They come into adulthood able to attract a partner, but they have no cultural expectations to be good at it, nor do they have a clue how to maintain it. The shame and isolation they feel within a relationship they do not know how to handle gives them little recourse in figuring out what interdependency really looks or feels like. This, together with residual prohibitions against men seeking help or appearing weak, fuels anger and frustration that may be based on codependency but is expressed as narcissism or rage.

FACT

In her piece "Blame-Storms and Rage Attacks Common to Border-lines, Narcissists," published in *Psychology Today*, Randi Kreger points out, "The anger of narcissists . . . can be more demeaning. Their criticism evolves from their conviction that others don't meet their lofty standards—or worse, aren't letting them get their own way. 'Narcissistic injuries,' or wounds to the ego, often pave the way for narcissistic rages, which can be passive-aggressive or planned out, as well as sudden."

A man's codependency thoughts and feelings are often expressed as narcissism. Believe it or not, this inflated narcissist has low self-esteem. He needs the attention of others, most especially his wife or partner, to mirror back his value. He has a hole he needs to fill. His own identity isn't enough, he needs to create a blown-up picture of himself. When he doesn't get the admiration he needs, he reacts with manipulation, anger, indifference, isolation, and sometimes rage and violence. These responses are honed by socialization. Just like women, men are codependent, but they are programmed to express it differently.

One Piece of the Codependency Puzzle

To summarize the answer to the questions asked at the beginning of this chapter: "Are women socialized to be codependent?" and "Is codependency a women's problem?" The answer seems more and more frequently to be no. Codependency is not exclusively a woman's problem. Socialization is just one puzzle piece for both women and men. And behavior is only one observable component of codependency. As a group, codependent men behave differently than codependent women because of the influences of socialization.

Letter to the Psychologist

The following letter is taken from Here-to-Listen.com and helps explain the identity crisis of adolescence.

Dear Doctor,

My son is sixteen now and he's changed so much I hardly recognize him. He was always such a sweet boy, telling me all the time he loved me and laughing and talking with me or watching TV with me and talking about the shows. I thought my son was going to grow into a sensitive man who respected women and shared his feelings, and cared how others felt.

Yesterday, Michael called me a "bitch." I just couldn't believe it. He is surly and short-tempered, moody. I can't stand him. What can I do?

Julie

Dear Julie,

Try not to panic; your son is going through adolescence. Your goal during this time is to ride out the storm. The things you have valued in your son are still in there. Try to keep the communication open. Sit down with him when he's calm and tell him you understand being a teenager isn't easy. But that he cannot be disrespectful of you just because he's feeling crummy about himself. Give him some options for dealing with his anger, like going out for a run or leaving the house for a half hour until he cools down. Try to plan a few things together to keep the relationship close, but realize it isn't cool to be seen with your mother at his age. Don't take it personally. Humor is a great way to relate to him now.

CHAPTER 6

Codependent Relationships

Codependents are often angry, depressed, and anxious. They may feel misunderstood, wounded, unloved, disappointed, slighted, and abandoned. They often feel like a victim of the person they love the most. It's as if your spouse holds the magic mirror that changes your image from a toad to a princess. Powerless to transform yourself, you must make sure that he is nearby, mirror in hand, to make you see how beautiful you are. It becomes a desperate and debilitating need.

Will This Relationship Survive?

When a couple goes to relationship counseling, it is the job of the therapist to see the layers of dysfunction in their relationship and guide the couple toward change. At each point along the way, the therapist evaluates the strategy as the process unfolds. There are points of change that the therapist must be able to identify to help the relationship improve. Here are several case studies of couples that are in trouble. As you read the stories, look for signs of codependency. Compare your impressions against the psychologist's opinion that follows each story.

The Recovering Addict: Beverly and Linda

Beverly and Linda have been in a committed relationship for seven years. Linda is a recovering alcoholic and drug addict who has been clean and sober for four years before she meets Beverly. Beverly is a successful professional, and Linda is a hard worker in a blue-collar job. After several years, Beverly suggests that the couple start a business. Linda is reluctant, but Beverly convinces her that the side business will give them more money to travel and enjoy life. Without consulting Linda, Beverly gets a second mortgage on her home and announces to Linda that they are going to buy rental properties. They buy several fixer-uppers in the same town where Linda works, with the idea that Linda will manage them. Before long, Linda is complaining about the extra work. Bev feels badly for her, and agrees to do all the cleaning when tenants move out. When a house becomes vacant, Bev spends two solid weekends of backbreaking work to get the house ready for the next tenant. Linda does not offer to help her. The new business is an ongoing source of stress for the couple.

FACT

"You don't develop courage by being happy in your relationships every day. You develop it by surviving difficult times and challenging adversity." —Epicurus

After about a year, Beverly comes home to find Linda crying and upset. She asks her what is wrong, and Linda says she has to move out and "see what she wants in life." Beverly is caught totally off guard and is devastated; she begs Linda to reconsider, but eventually has no choice but to let her go.

In the meantime, Bev works the business on her own. A month later, she receives a call from the bank that the business account is overdrawn. After meeting with a bank official, she discovers that Linda had been funneling money out of their business account for some months before she left. She suspects Linda has been gambling at a local casino. When Beverly finally reaches her, Linda denies gambling and minimizes the theft, but agrees to reimburse the account. A couple weeks later, Bev finds out from friends that Linda is seeing another woman she met at the casino. After two small checks, Linda stops paying Beverly back. Will this relationship survive?

The Psychologist's Opinion

There is not much hope for this relationship. Linda has a history of addictive behavior. Although she has been clean and sober for some time before she commits to Bev, she is vulnerable to reacting to stress with a relapse. She doesn't want to start a business, but she isn't honest with Bev about it. She lets Bev go ahead and get a loan, and then just sits back and lets her do most of the work. Obviously, Linda has been secretive about her feelings for some time. By the time she decides to talk to Bev about it, she is ready to leave. Not talking is definitely a red flag for relapse for an addict.

Bev is the codependent in this relationship because she is the one who made the move to start the business in order to "help" Linda be more successful. Instead of asking Linda if she wants to do this, she tries to control the whole project and then is resentful when Linda isn't appreciative. Bev falls in love with a blue-collar worker and then tries to change her into an entrepreneur when that's not who Linda is. Bev feels she's helping Linda, but what she doesn't realize is that she is trying to remake Linda because Linda doesn't meet Beverly's expectations.

When the business starts to flag, Linda isn't equipped to deal with it in a direct way with her partner. Alcoholics are extremely adept at rationalizing destructive behavior. It's unclear what Linda has been telling herself about betraying Bev, but by the time she begins to steal money from her, there is a very strong chance she has started drinking, drugging, or gambling. This is the point where she is in a complete relapse, and it is only a matter of time before she will be found out.

The negative prognosis for the relationship reflects the fact that, even after she is found out, Linda makes no attempt to be honest, apologize, or take responsibility for her actions. She resorts to addictive behaviors like rationalization, minimizing, and more lies. Bev's need to believe she is taking care of Linda—making sure she is happy, mortgaging her home to help her—blinds her to what is really going on. As a codependent, she never sees it coming.

FACT

According to the American Psychological Association, marriage and divorce are both common experiences. "In Western cultures, more than 90 percent of people marry by age fifty. Healthy marriages are good for couples' mental and physical health . . . However, about 40–50 percent of married couples in the United States divorce. The divorce rate for subsequent marriages is even higher."

Bev should move on and deal with her own codependency issues around this relationship and realize that she cannot control what is happening with Linda. Linda will continue to run the course of her relapse. Hopefully, she will get back into recovery before she hurts anyone else. Beverly can take steps to stay out of the codependency role by being completely honest about Linda's behavior to family and friends. To do otherwise would be a continuation of caretaking, "protecting" Linda from having to face the consequences of her actions.

The Emotionally Abusive Relationship: Dirk and Gloria

Dirk and Gloria have been together fifteen years. They have three children under the age of ten. Gloria is a successful attorney at a large law firm, and Dirk is a stay-at-home dad. Dirk is working when he meets Gloria, but injures his back several years into their relationship and is out on disability for a year. Once he recovers, Dirk decides not to go back to work. Since Dirk is staying at home, the couple decides to start their family, with Dirk as the primary caretaker for the children.

After their first child is born, Dirk develops a close relationship with one of the mothers in the neighborhood. They spend a lot of time together drinking coffee and talking while their children play together. When Gloria questions Dirk about the friendship, he becomes angry and accuses Gloria of being possessive and unreasonable. Gloria drops the issue, but months later she finds a receipt for an expensive bracelet Dirk has given his friend. Dirk continues to deny any relationship other than friendship with the neighbor. Gloria knows she is in a losing battle, so she keeps her mouth shut and seethes inside. Over time the friendship with the neighbor cools.

From the beginning of their relationship, Gloria's friends and family observe how controlling Dirk is. He monitors everything Gloria does and complains when she has to work overtime or go on a business trip. He reminds her constantly that she isn't spending enough time with the children. This controlling behavior is obvious to their friends because Dirk says these things in front of them. If they are out for dinner, for example, and Gloria orders dessert, Dirk tells her she doesn't need it. If Gloria wants to buy a new pair of shoes or a suit for work, Dirk calls her a selfish spendthrift and says that the budget won't allow for it. It is painfully clear to everyone who knows them that Dirk is controlling in every way. Even in parenting, he is strict with the children and often contradicts Gloria in front of the kids when she is more lenient and fun-loving.

Three years after their last child is born, Dirk again becomes close with a woman he meets at the kids' soccer games. They begin to spend more and more time together since their kids play on the same team. They go out to lunch with the kids after soccer, and sometimes, when Gloria is out of town or working late, they spend time together taking the kids to the movies or other activities.

Gloria confronts Dirk on his apparent attachment to his new woman friend. Again, Dirk becomes outraged and accuses Gloria of being a hypocrite. He reminds her of her friendships with the male attorneys at work and that she has lunch with them or even travels with them on occasion. Gloria backs off, because she believes Dirk has a point; maybe she does have a double standard. When Gloria notices credit card charges for items she knows she hasn't purchased for women's apparel and jewelry, she again confronts Dirk. He is matter-of-fact about buying his friend some gifts because her husband is struggling financially and she needs some new clothes. He is just helping out a friend.

FACT

Bestselling author and Harvard psychology researcher Daniel Gilbert, PhD, says, "It's not marriage that makes you happy, it's happy marriage that makes you happy. Married people are happier than unmarried ones, perhaps because the single best predictor of human happiness is the quality of social relationships. Marriage seems to buy you a decade or more of happiness."

Gloria cries herself to sleep that night as she has many nights before. This time she makes a lunch date with a friend and confides in her about how unhappy she is. Her friend is outraged at Dirk's behavior and thinks Gloria is being taken advantage of. Gloria's friend feels Dirk is lying and spending too much time and money on his friend. Besides, she says, Gloria's relationship with Dirk has never been a healthy one. Dirk bosses her around, humiliates her in front of people, and controls every aspect of their relationship together. Gloria's friend encourages her to give Dirk an ultimatum about his friend and start getting a backbone and standing up to Dirk's dictatorship. Will this relationship survive?

The Psychologist's Opinion

This relationship can be saved only if Gloria stands up for herself and finds her self-esteem. To allow Dirk to control her every move, humiliate her in front of friends, and dictate what she can and cannot spend or how she does her job is completely unacceptable. This relationship is abusive. One person is trying to control the other, primarily through bullying and humiliation. This dynamic is very destructive to the relationship and is a terrible model for the children.

FACT

> According to the Huffington Post website, "Very few people who have experienced a broken relationship even try to reconcile. Even U.S. statistics on separation and divorce show that almost 87 percent of separated couples proceed to obtain a divorce. The remaining 13 percent reunite after separation."

Like many women, Gloria is extremely capable and successful in her professional life, but on a personal level she can't stand up for herself. She likely is working out childhood issues here. When someone's behavior seems out of character and the picture seems clear to others, there is a good chance that some of the deeper issues are out of Gloria's awareness. She is not financially dependent on Dirk. In fact, he is dependent on her. So, we have to assume that she is codependent with Dirk. This is the key issue in this marriage. Dirk is emotionally abusive and Gloria is allowing it.

The second issue is that Dirk is giving what little supportive and positive energy he has to women other than his wife. Certainly, men and women can be friends, but Dirk's relationships with these other women are fulfilling needs that should be met in the marriage—for example, the need for companionship, going out and having fun, and mutually enjoying their children. Dirk bestowing expensive gifts on these women and hiding this from Gloria is a great big red flag. Perhaps Dirk is trying to compensate for not being a wage earner by giving these gifts to assert his masculinity. The major issue with it, though, is that he's lying to Gloria (by withholding the information). This is a betrayal that Dirk is not willing to address. Instead, he gets defensive and tries to shift the blame onto Gloria for being a hypocrite. This signals real problems in their communication.

The relationship can survive, but the point of change is with Gloria. Dirk will not propose they seek marriage counseling because, underneath his righteous indignation, he knows he's behaving in a way that is dishonest and self-serving but he has no motivation to change. Gloria needs to set a boundary with Dirk. Either he participates in marriage counseling or she will have to seek therapy on her own. This will be a threat to controlling Dirk because he won't like anyone else having an influence on Gloria.

The therapist will have his hands full with this couple. If Dirk agrees to participate, he may soon drop out as he sees the therapist as an adversary. At this point, Gloria must continue in therapy herself to understand her codependency with an emotionally abusive man. There is hope, but it will require a lot of change from each of them.

The Mutually Codependent Relationship: Robin and Carlton

Robin and Carlton's marriage has been a roller coaster since they married twenty-five years ago. The pattern of their ups and downs has been a push-pull of unresolved conflict and unmet needs. Carlton is a workaholic who focuses on his law practice to the detriment of his home and marriage. The couple has no children. Robin also works hard as an engineer and is ready to retire. In the last ten years, Robin and Carlton have drifted apart and each has found other interests outside their relationship. Carlton enjoys golf and playing poker with his buddies. Robin is an artist and spends most of her time in her studio upstairs.

Robin had high expectations when she met Carlton. She came from a family in which her parents were unavailable and quite distant. She longed for someone like Carlton who is attentive and loving. She didn't want to feel lonely and rejected in her marriage, like she did when she was growing up. By the same token, the first time Carlton said no to Robin, she felt as if she'd been abandoned. She expected, and expects, him to be there for her whenever she needs something.

Carlton loved the fact that Robin came from a wealthy family. He respected Robin's dad for being a self-made man, and Robin's mother for being a traditional wife who takes good care of her husband. He saw Robin as that kind of partner in the successful life he had planned.

Over the years, a pattern of codependency develops. Robin asks for Carlton's help with the lawn, grocery shopping, and planning trips, but he seems uninterested in domestic responsibilities. He might agree to replace the lock on the back door, but he never quite gets around to it. Robin finds herself in a Catch-22. The more she reminds Carlton, the more he complains that she is nagging him and the more resistant he becomes to her demands. She feels powerless to get Carlton to follow through on his promises. She feels that if Carlton loved her, he would do these simple things to please her. She becomes more and more resentful and feels like she does everything and Carlton does nothing.

FACT

The work of personality theorist Dr. Erik Erikson outlines eight levels of psychosocial development, each stage building on mastery of the previous stage. Stage six is Intimacy vs. Isolation. This is the stage from age nineteen to about forty where a person seeks to connect intimately with another person. The reward for mastering this stage is love. Failure to connect results in isolation.

As Robin becomes more frustrated and feels more unloved, she withdraws her affection from Carlton. Carlton longs to be physically close to Robin, but she rejects him. With this stalemate, Carlton and Robin grow more and more distant. Soon they are almost completely emotionally detached. Will this relationship survive?

The Psychologist's Opinion

This is a couple that each once thought a partner could make up for unmet needs carried forward from childhood. Although these expectations are unconscious, they play out in their adult relationship. Robin wants the unconditional love she didn't get from her parents. When Carlton was intensely focused on Robin during their engagement, Robin felt loved and cared for.

Carlton wants to be successful, to prove to his parents that he is a capable, talented son. Once he marries the perfect wife that goal is met, and he moves on to focus on his career. He resents Robin's requests for him to help out at home because he truly feels it is her job to care for him. Over the years, Carlton feels punished and lonely.

Both Robin and Carlton want the same thing. They want to feel special, loved, and cared for in their relationship. At this point, neither knows how to get it. When they try to talk about it, neither of them will risk being vulnerable, so all they do is attack and defend, each trying to be heard and understood by the other. It seems they are mutually codependent.

Typically, they will continue to do the same things and expect a different result from their partner. However, the relationship could be saved through therapy where the therapist will bring new insight and direction for the couple.

First they must learn communication skills. No conflict, big or small, can be resolved without a healthy way of discussing it. As they each feel heard and validated, trust will begin to develop again. This trust will provide the safety they each need to share their hurts and fears. This is when intimacy will be restored and the potential for them to have a new relationship will show itself.

The question is: Can hearts iced over by years of disappointment and anger melt, revealing the love that still exists between the two?

ALERT

An intimate relationship gives you an opportunity to reach your full potential by examining your own ego strengths and weaknesses in the pursuit of love. If you leave a relationship without exploring your own ego issues, you're likely to have the same issues in your next relationship.

All of the couples presented here have issues with codependency. Hopefully, you were able to see where they went wrong, and what they might do to help mend their relationships. Many times, the individuals in a couple are in so much pain, they just cannot muster the emotional energy required for counseling. Sometimes one or both partners is incapable or unwilling to do the necessary work to make the relationship better. A relationship is supposed to enhance one's life, and when it doesn't, leaving may be the only answer. A person should never sacrifice their true identity for a relationship.

Letter to the Psychologist

The following letter is taken from Here-to-Listen.com and helps explain how codependency can look like helpfulness, but it has strings attached.

Dear Doctor,

I'm dating this girl who I really like. She is sweet and kind and is always doing little special things for me. She's even cleaned my apartment when I'm at work. I always thank her when she does these things. The problem is now she's seems mad at me all the time because she thinks I don't appreciate what she does for me. She says she would never treat me like I treat her. I'm not sure what she means except I don't do for her all the time, but I surprise her with gifts and take her out to special places, and I'm very nice to her. Really!

I appreciate what she does for me and I always make a big deal about it. I tell her I don't expect any of this attention and she shouldn't feel like she needs to do all this stuff. But she keeps doing it. I'm telling you, I dread to see what she's going to do next "for me." Is this codependency?

Patrick

Dear Patrick,

Looks like it. Why does your girlfriend feel compelled to do things for you? Is she trying to prove she's a good girlfriend? Even if she did these things with no strings attached, it's going to create an imbalance in your relationship. But, there are strings attached. She's really working overtime to please you and then resents it when you don't do likewise. It's not clear exactly what she expects, but my guess is you will not be able to deliver to her satisfaction.

CHAPTER 7

Codependent Children

It's hard to think of children as being codependent. But children develop psychosocial problems in childhood; they respond to their surroundings and their caregivers beginning in infancy. Arguably, children are still developing personality traits until adolescence, so perhaps it's more accurate to say that early programming may result in codependency traits later in life.

Childhood Patterns

Erik Homburger Erikson was a developmental psychologist and psychoanalyst known for his theory on psychosocial development of human beings. Erikson's first four stages of psychosocial development include Trust vs. Mistrust (Birth–two years), Autonomy vs. Shame and Doubt (two–four years), Initiative vs. Guilt (Preschool, four–five years), Industry vs. Inferiority (five–twelve years). In this context, you can see how certain patterns in childhood may be precursors to codependency.

Mother's Little Helper: Crystal

Crystal is six years old and is "mother's little helper." She wants to help her mother with housework, cooking, and taking care of her younger sister, who is eighteen months old. She gets a lot of thanks from her mom and dad for her helping attitude. Often she basks in the praise as her mother tells her friends and acquaintances how much she appreciates Crystal. "I just couldn't do it all without Crystal's help," she says. Sometimes she lets Crystal help serve refreshments to the women at card club. Then Crystal sits quietly in the living room while the women play cards.

Crystal's dad is a busy man. When he comes home, Crystal helps him take off his shoes and then she hoists his legs up on the ottoman. She hands him the paper and brings him a beer from the refrigerator. He always smiles and gives her a kiss on the cheek. "That's my girl," he says with a sigh as he leans back in his chair and opens his paper.

The Psychologist's Opinion

It seems obvious that there is a pattern that signals the development of caretaking behavior. Six-year-old girls should be playing with their friends, and focusing on themselves. It is normal for children to be self-centered.

Of course, it's good for girls of this age to spend time with their parents—playing a game, reading, talking about school, playing the piano, sports, etc. But the balance is off kilter in this dynamic. Crystal is taking care of her parents' needs when they should be taking care of hers.

QUESTION

Are beauty pageants for young kids as depicted in TV shows okay? There may be a connection to codependency, because these pageants promote pleasing, sexual manipulation, judgments about being worthy, etc. And another danger would be using a child to fulfill the narcissistic needs of the parent. A 2007 report by the American Psychological Association found that the hypersexualization of young girls is strongly associated with eating disorders, low self-esteem, and depression.

Fortunately, Crystal does begin to outgrow her caretaker role with her parents. But when she starts to separate and wants to spend time with friends, her mother pouts and says, "Who will help me with the baby?" This is the second phase of Crystal's programming. She isn't rewarded for being a normal kid. She is made to feel guilty if she does not consider the needs of her mother, sister, and dad. When she does focus on them, she is praised and appreciated, which is more fuel for the codependency fire. Now Crystal is beginning to believe that the needs of others are more important than her own needs.

Coming out of childhood into adolescence, Crystal is anxious and worried about how she is perceived by others. She is a pleaser, a "teacher's pet," and continues to be compliant to her mother's needs. Crystal will grow up to be a caretaker, taking responsibility for others' happiness and putting others' needs before her own. Soon her resentment will build as she gives up herself to please others.

The Star: Jake

Jake starts playing T-ball when he is three years old. As he advances up through the baseball ranks, his mom and dad want to support his interest in baseball. They attend all his games. As he gets older, his dad starts coaching his team. Then Jake makes the All-Star team, traveling around the state in addition to participating in the baseball season at his school. Going into junior high school Jake often is named most valuable player. He is definitely a standout.

Jake's dad encourages Jake, and engages him in all things baseball. They've been attending major-league baseball games since Jake was a little kid. Most weekends, you can find Jake and his dad either outside throwing balls and pitching, at a local baseball game, or catching a couple of games on TV. Sometimes they manage to juggle all these activities in one weekend!

In ninth grade, Jake's skills begin to wane. He is lagging behind the other players in size and strength, and he is becoming discouraged and depressed. Jake just knows his dad is disappointed in him, and he doesn't want to let his dad down. In fact, he's terrified he'll lose his close relationship with his dad.

It's been awhile since Jake's been the star of the team, and he notices that his dad wants to practice more with him out in the yard. Sometimes, after dinner, it's almost dark and Jake has homework, but he wants to make his dad happy. He keeps a close eye on his dad to make sure he isn't depressed. Jake is sure that if his dad is "down" it will be because Jake isn't doing well in baseball. Jake is afraid to talk to his dad because he's afraid his dad will get mad. Or worse yet, his dad might be terribly unhappy. Jake fears his dad will be devastated if he quits baseball. If truth be told, Jake is drawn to acting, and he would like to try out for a school play, but he knows he can't. His dad wouldn't understand.

The Psychologist's Opinion

Here we have a child who truly is a baseball star during his grade school years. But we already know his days of being a big frog in a small pond are limited. As he grows, he just doesn't have the size and strength to remain a top player. It is hard to sort out whether his dad molded him into the son he wanted, the son who enjoyed baseball just as much as dad did. We do know that at three years old, Jake wasn't able to make this decision himself. Kids this age still count heavily on their parents as a home base, and parents should encourage them to explore independently within reason.

At age three, Jake is trying to master the psychosocial stage of development, Autonomy vs. Shame and Doubt. If parents expect too much too soon, children can be afraid to explore and fail, recover, and explore again. Parents should encourage and not directly steer young children into a limited way of expressing themselves. This is likely what happened with Jake.

ALERT

When it's time for a child to take that next step, e.g., joining a traveling team in baseball, be sure it is not a step over the skill level of a young player. This can affect his self-esteem and cause him to lose interest. Observe the emotional tenor of the child as he talks about his interests, and make sure the desire is coming from him and not you.

For most of his childhood, Jake willingly participates in baseball, a sport that makes his dad proud and happy. Because baseball is his life, he isn't concerned about losing his dad's approval. But when Jake approaches adolescence, he sees that he can't maintain the level of play that he thinks his dad needs. The fact that he is no longer a top-notch player could free him up to look at other interests, which would be a healthy response. But Jake is already feeling codependent with his dad, so when he finds himself interested in acting, it isn't a joyful discovery. It is a change he dreads because he is taking responsibility for his dad's happiness. That's a pretty big burden for this junior high kid.

Fortunately, Jake's misery about baseball comes to an end when his dad gets home from work early and finds Jake crying in his room. Jake is anguished about possibly losing his dad's love, but he's so unhappy, he is finally forced to confront the issue. When Jake tells his dad he doesn't want to play ball anymore, his dad doesn't reject him. He loves him anyway. Dad puts his arms around Jake and tells him everything is okay.

The Perfect Child: Penny

Penny is eleven and she is perfect. Her room looks like something out of a magazine, as if her bedroom has never been used. She makes her bed every morning and picks up her stuff before she goes to bed every night. Penny has her own alarm clock and does not need anyone to wake her for school. She is so anxious about missing the bus that she usually wakes up an hour or so early. She is an A student, participates in several clubs at school, goes to Sunday school and church every Sunday, and is a member of the youth group at church.

Being perfect is very difficult. Penny is filled with anxiety most of the time. She is trying very hard not to make her mother sick. Penny's mother has been sick with back problems ever since Penny can remember. This causes Penny's dad to worry all the time about Penny's mother. Penny has worried every day since she was about five years old that her mother will die. She knows stress is not good for her mother because her dad keeps asking her mother if she feels stressed, and if her back hurts and how badly.

Penny's mother used to be a teacher until she went on disability, so Penny knows how important it is to her mother that Penny does well in school. She hopes she never brings home a report card with less than an A in every subject because it might create stress for her mother and worry for her father. Penny has perfect attendance; if she is sick, she keeps it a secret and goes to school anyway.

As soon as she returns from school, Penny checks out the emotional climate in the household. If her mother is in pain, Penny tries to make her happy by telling her stories or getting her an ice pack or the heating pad. Sometimes Penny rubs her mother's back. When her dad gets home, Penny's antennae go up to see if he is "down" or "nervous." She listens carefully to her parents' conversation to make sure everything is okay.

Now in this scenario, it is clear that Penny will continue to feel responsible for her parents. Their needs come first. Penny's parents are not directly reinforcing codependency in Penny. Penny is reacting to her home situation, which happens to include a chronically disabled mother and an anxious and depressive father. Her mother is physically ill and her father is psychologically challenged. This environment fosters codependency in young Penny.

The Psychologist's Opinion

If they knew how, these parents could mitigate the situation at home with proactive, direct messages to Penny about being a kid. They could emphasize that they are the parents, and they will take care of each other and Penny. Penny's parents could develop a plan, maybe afterschool fun times for Penny so she wouldn't feel so responsible. Give Penny time with friends, away from the stress of home. The parents could more closely monitor their conversations in front of Penny. Awareness of what is going on with Penny and measures to get her away from the caretaking role would go a long way toward helping Penny get out from under the weight of codependency.

The Fearful Child: Nicholas

Eight-year-old Nicholas is a fearful child. Ask his parents and they'll tell you that Nicholas is afraid of everything! They are at their wits' end trying to figure out what is wrong with Nicholas. They have had him evaluated for autism spectrum disorders, and the findings were negative for autism.

Nicholas was a fussy baby. He reacted to the slightest noise by startling and crying. He cried when trying new food or being introduced to a new toy. In fact, he was restless and agitated a lot of the time. His parents referred to him as a "sensitive" baby, and asked grandparents and others to keep their voices down and pick him up slowly so he didn't freak out. The TV and radio were kept low, the ring on the phone was turned down, and the front doorbell was turned off. It seemed as if Nicholas had magical powers to change his parents' entire world.

Nicholas's parents respond to their fussy baby by becoming overprotective. As Nicholas grows, his parents are watchful, making sure he isn't exposed to any frightening stimuli. As a result, Nicholas loses the ability to know what is dangerous and what is not. So, at age eight, Nicholas is fearful of a whole host of things. He has never stayed overnight with anyone, including his grandparents. He has never gone to daycare nor had a babysitter. Neither of his parents will try to leave him because seeing how frightened Nicholas becomes is heartbreaking to them.

Nicholas is afraid of getting his hands dirty; he's afraid of carnival rides and loud cars and trucks; he's afraid of all animals, especially dogs that bark loudly. He's afraid of the dark and of storms and other bad weather; he's afraid to ride a bike or go on a swing or go into water. He will not participate in gym at school or engage in sports. He will eat only two foods. He has an excuse from the doctor to skip recess and lunch hour. He brings his own lunch, alternating between the two foods he likes, and eats in the classroom.

A child as fearful as Nicholas has not developed his own internal point of reference. His attention is directed outward, looking for danger at every corner. He has not yet learned how to soothe himself, so the only option he has is to expect that his environment or people will change so that he will feel comfortable.

The Psychologist's Opinion

Infants may start out with a tense temperament. From there, how parents react to that temperament forms traits that might be with that child for the rest of his life. A child who is overprotected is much more likely to develop an anxiety disorder later. People with anxiety are "other directed," continuously reacting to perceived danger. This is another way of saying that Nicholas may grow up to be codependent, with the resulting anxiety of trying to control things and people he has no control over.

ESSENTIAL

Once your child has developed unreasonable fears, don't scold or force her into fearful situations. It's not too late to work with her patiently and gradually toward the fear. For example, with fear of animals, start with an animal the child is not afraid of; let her get completely used to that animal, then move on to another. Move forward as she overcomes her fears.

The Angry Child: Eric

Eric is one of those kids who is just plain angry. It seems he came out of the womb mad as a wet hen. That's his temperament, and it appears that he has inherited a predisposition to anger from his dad.

How much of Eric's anger is biology and how much is socialization is especially unclear here because Eric's dad demonstrates anger every day. Dad grumbles about the weather, politics, the economy, work, and other people randomly. He is the type of person who is likely to have road rage or yell at a store clerk, his wife, or the kids. Eric's dad was a "hothead" as a teenager, and he spent some time in jail for assault.

The Psychologist's Opinion

Eric has learned to do as he's told and stay clear of his dad's anger. This is where the codependency pattern shows itself. Eric is afraid of his dad, so he is constantly assessing his dad's moods. He's become so good at it, he can see a conflict coming a mile away and gets away from his dad by going outside or up to his room. Eric believes he can control his dad's anger. He believes he can keep his dad calm by anticipating situations that might trigger anger in his dad and then trying to head them off at the pass. While he is still a child, this codependent pattern Eric has developed is a matter of survival.

Here are a few things you can do if you have an angry child. Make sure you are not modeling rage or anger. Maintain a connection with your child; it reduces his or her anxiety. Like the teapot, anger is the steam that anxiety lets off. Use humor as often as you can. Lighten up on your perfectionism. Spend relaxed, fun time with your child.

However, there is another side to this coin. Eric is also being taught from his dad that if you just get angry, people will back down. It is a false sense of power and control. So when Eric is at school, playing sports, or just hanging out with his friends, he can be a bully. His anxiety gets expressed through angry outbursts just like his dad. And like his dad, he picks on others who are weaker than he.

It would be unusual for Eric to remain codependent once he reaches adolescence. With the self-consciousness that sometimes comes with being a teenager, his anger will undoubtedly escalate. He still may fear his dad, but he is just as likely to challenge his dad at some point. Eric has learned that anger rules. Anger will become Eric's biggest obstacle in achieving and sustaining healthy relationships. When Eric finds a partner, he is apt to be the abusive one, and his significant other the codependent.

The Abused Child: Carmen

A child who grows up in an abusive environment learns very early to keep her eyes open, her mind alert, and her intuition sharpened. Carmen is such a child. Never in her thirteen years has she felt safe and secure. She is now in foster care. Her caseworker describes her as "thirteen going on thirty."

When Carmen is born, her teenage mother abandons her. As an infant, she is given to her mother's older sister, Frieda, to raise. Frieda is a single mother and already has three boys, but she agrees to do her best to raise Carmen. Frieda works nights. She can't afford childcare, so she leaves her nine-year-old son in charge while she's working. She doesn't leave until the children are all tucked in and asleep for the night, and she returns before they wake the next day.

FACT

According to the Children's Defense Fund, there are close to 16 million latchkey children. The Census Bureau found that 15 percent were home alone before school, 76 percent after school, and 9 percent at night. Presumably, the 9 percent have parents who work night shifts.

But the new baby complicates things for oldest son Steve. When the baby wakes during the night, crying, Steve tries to comfort her. Failing that, he takes baby Carmen down to the basement. With the door closed, the other children can sleep through the night. Early the next morning, Steve retrieves his baby sister from the laundry basket in the basement before his mother gets home.

As Carmen grows up, her older brothers tease her unmercifully. When alone with Carmen, they slap her and choke her and make her wait on them hand and foot. Like most abused children, Carmen is afraid to tell because she believes her brothers when they threaten to kill her.

Carmen is seven when Frieda marries Tom, a man she met at work. Tom joins the family with his whip cracking. Steve is now sixteen and leaves home. The other two boys are fifteen and thirteen, and Tom doesn't really like them. He is very strict, beating them when he's angry with them, which is often. The more Tom abuses the boys, the more they abuse Carmen. It is a sort of pecking order for abuse.

Finally, Carmen's teacher notices bruises on Carmen's arms and calls Protective Services. Carmen is placed in foster care. Frieda blames Carmen for getting Tom in trouble. She fears her kids will upset Tom and he will leave her. When it's time for Carmen to come home, Frieda tells the authorities she's not Frieda's biological or legal mother. She abandons Carmen to the foster care system, where she remains.

The Psychologist's Opinion

Carmen has been powerless since birth. She is an unwanted child sent into a dangerous situation. Her brothers abuse her, leaving her powerless and afraid. Her mother is not there to protect her. Children are extremely limited in their choices. In the case of physical abuse, becoming codependent is one of the few survival skills a young child has. Carmen developed radar to assess the dangers in her environment. This codependency pattern develops in the relationships Carmen has with her abusers. In addition to this, Frieda has modeled a very strong and persistent codependency with her husband, Tom. And because of it, she has neglected her children.

Letter to the Psychologist

The following letter is taken from Here-to-Listen.com and helps explain how the parents' reaction to their child's temperament can remediate the development of codependency.

Dear Doctor,

My son is almost three and he is very shy and is easily startled. My husband is getting very frustrated, and almost angry with him. Yesterday, he called him a sissy. I don't want my son growing up to be codependent, worrying about being yelled at or ridiculed, catering to how everybody else thinks he should be. My husband says that's ridiculous. His fear is that our son will not be of strong character.

Jan

Dear Jan,

Kids come in all shapes and sizes, colors and temperaments. All children must be made to feel that they are accepted just the way they are, especially if they are anxious. Don't get angry with this little guy for being who he is, and reacting to his environment. It's very important for you two parents to get on the same page with your son. Start with exploring what each of you may be doing to contribute to your son's anxiety. He's in an important developmental stage. He needs to feel safe to explore at his own pace in order to develop a sense of autonomy. Don't yell at him for being shy.

CHAPTER 8

Codependent Adolescents

The fifth stage of psychosocial development is adolescence. The current estimates by professionals on the age spread for this stage is anywhere from age twelve to twenty-eight. The developmental task for this stage is Identity vs. Role Confusion. During adolescence, a teen is not only struggling with how she fits in; she's actually trying to figure out who she is. She is developing close ties with friends, trying out ways to interact with the opposite sex in more intimate ways, and is thinking more seriously about moral issues. She's not a child, and she's not an adult. The developmental task for the adolescent is to move through role confusion to establish her identity.

In Search of the Self

Some teens move through adolescence unscathed, but for most it is an emotional roller coaster. Hormones rage and bodies change and emotions can feel scary and out of control. Because this is a crucial time for the development of a young person's identity, there is a lot at stake. Often the confident, well-balanced child seems to disappear and some stranger shows up. Parents are at a loss, wondering where their son or daughter went and lamenting the arrival of this surly, emotional, moody adolescent. For teenagers, they may feel the same way on the inside. "I hate myself." "What's the matter with me?" "Who am I?"

The Perfectionist Teen: Rob

Rob lives in a rural town that's big on team sports. Rob, however, just doesn't match up with how his town views the "All-American Boy." He is thin and fragile and has worn glasses since he was four years old. In grade school, he was taunted and teased by the other kids. When the neighborhood kids play baseball or gather for outside games, Rob stays inside playing video games and drawing. He also enjoys reading and collecting coins.

FACT

Brain studies of adolescents done in the last ten years have shown that the frontal lobe of the brain is not yet fully developed. This part of the brain has to do with impulse control and the ability to see long-range consequences of choices. This suggests that teens are just not yet capable of making the kind of sound decisions we expect from them.

Rob's parents try to encourage him to be more active, get out more with other kids. So when Rob turns twelve, his parents give him a membership with the local YMCA. Rob isn't pleased with his birthday gift, but he doesn't want to hurt his parents' feelings so he agrees to try swimming.

After a few nervous visits to the Y, Rob is surprised at how he enjoys the solitude and repetition of doing laps in the pool. Since he wears a snorkel, the rhythm of his breathing relaxes him and pushes him to do more. Over the summer, he begins to rely on swimming for a sense of well-being. The few times he misses, he just doesn't feel right. Before long, he is using a stopwatch to time his laps.

Toward the end of the summer, one of the junior high coaches notices Rob in the pool and invites him to try out for the eighth-grade swim team. Rob feels awkward and uncomfortable being singled out. The thing he likes most about swimming laps is trying to achieve his personal best like he does in everything else.

Almost despite himself, Rod gains muscle as his swimming improves. The stronger he gets, the better swimmer he becomes. The coach approaches Rob again and asks him if he is interested in some pointers. Rob is still uncomfortable, but since it will be one-on-one coaching, he agrees. That is the start of Rob's all-star swimming career.

FACT

Cliques are a part of the adolescent quest to fit in, to belong. According to San Diego high school student Karen Ceballos in *Conquering Cliques in School*, "There are the anime lovers, the hip hop dancers, the gamers, the metal rockers, the skaters, the surfers, the honors kids, the drama kids, the emos, and many more."

By the time he starts high school, he is wearing contact lenses so he can see when he's swimming, and he's grown close to six feet tall, lean and muscled. He's getting a lot of attention from the girls. Rob is suddenly like a fish out of water, literally. Although he is now confident on the swim team with his teammates, he is terrified around girls. He doesn't know what to say or how to act around them. When he sees a girl coming toward him, he panics. He's concerned about how he's dressed, whether his hair is neat and his breath clean, or whether he has something in his teeth. His perfectionism about his physical appearance is escalating to the point where he showers a lot, spends too much time in front of the mirror, and yet wonders if he could do more to make sure he's looking his best. He often turns down invitations to just hang out with his friends because he's worried that he might not look good enough if they run into girls.

Rob's awkwardness and fear of being judged are tearing him up inside. He watches the other boys interact with girls to see how they behave. He pays special attention to how his friends talk about girls, what they like about them, and how they feel. When girls talk to Rob, he tries to be funny or flirty like his buddies. Rob is desperate to fit in, to be like the other guys. He longs to have a girlfriend, and despite how he looks on the outside, he's painfully insecure about his developing sexual feelings and whether he will be good enough to date somebody.

On the outside, it looks like Rob's swimming medals have gone to his head. His friends tease him about being "too cool" or "too good for" the girls. To the girls, he appears to be aloof, conceited, unapproachable, and superficial.

Rob's situation illuminates the connection between narcissism and codependency. To observers, Rob may appear to be narcissistic. His uncertainty might come across as having no feelings and a "don't care" disregard of the feelings of others. His worry about his appearance could seem to others as self-centered or egotistical. Because of his star position on the team, others assume Rob has an inflated ego. Because Rob doesn't talk much, their perceptions go unchallenged.

Rob is so ill-equipped and so painfully awkward and uncomfortable coming into adolescence, he cuts off from his feelings. He really wants to fit in with his buddies, feel like they do, think like they do, and behave like they do. By taking on an identity more similar to his friends', Rob finds his anxiety decreases. He now knows his role.

The Psychologist's Opinion

Rob's story illustrates a point. Presenting a list of how to spot a narcissist might be helpful on one level, but behavior alone is not enough to make this determination. Would Rob's behaviors such as his preoccupation with his appearance, aloofness, sports star self-centeredness, and apparent disregard for the feelings of others be on a list of narcissistic characteristics? Of course they would. But identifying Rob as a narcissist would not be accurate.

On the inside, Rob longs to fit in, express himself freely, and be popular with girls, but that's not who he has been. Coming into adolescence, Rob was a quiet, introspective boy, compliant, and very much a loner. He was lacking in the kind of social skills that come with interacting with others, belonging to a team or a group, or navigating the world of childhood with his peers. The day he was noticed in the pool by the coach was a turning point for Rob. As he becomes more visible as a swim star, develops physically, and becomes more attractive to the girls, he is forced to relate to people in a different way. It is hard for him to adjust to the attention, but later he enjoys it and wants more.

His previous identity from childhood no longer feels right, but he is caught between the two. His interest in being popular is heightened, but he hasn't learned the skills necessary to easily adjust. Although he appears to be a stand-off egotistical guy, his psychology more closely resembles that of codependency. On the inside he is insecure and desperately needy. You can see in the case of Rob that codependency tends to show itself differently in boys. As you know, the process of merging his insecure inside with his misperceived outside will continue through adolescence; during that time, he will continue to look outside himself for direction.

The Sexually Precocious Teen: Crystal

Crystal is fifteen and is a sophomore in high school. She began puberty earlier than most of her friends. By thirteen, she is fully developed. All of a sudden, Crystal looks much older than her age and finds herself the target of much attention from boys, and even men. At first Crystal is mortified. She still feels like a kid on the inside and is bewildered by this unwanted attention.

As a child, Crystal learned to work for the attention and approval of adults to the detriment of her own needs. Crystal has come into adolescence a "pleaser." Her self-esteem depends on noticing, identifying, and tending to the needs of others. It started with her parents and later generalized to teachers and other adults.

With her beauty and physical development, she now finds herself in a new position to please—sex. Crystal isn't even all that interested in boys in her sophomore year; what she really wants is to fit in with the popular girls in her class, but they have rejected her. On the other hand, the boys seem to like her and enjoy hanging out with her. If they need something from her, she feels compelled to give it to them. Through her sexual encounters with boys, Crystal finds what she thinks is approval and affirmation. It is only afterward that she feels shame and guilt.

Unfortunately, Crystal's attempt to gain approval turns back on her in the judgments of her peers. She soon realizes that there is no hope now that she'll ever be accepted by the popular crowd. Now Crystal is in a serious identity crisis. Despite her attempts to be accepted and liked, she finds herself mirrored back as bad and unlovable, the very thing she tried so hard to avoid.

ALERT

To see today's teen fads, browse Youtube.com to find videos of the current crazes: sexting, condom snorting, biting, smacking, rainbow parties, ingesting weird substances, drinking hand sanitizer, car surfing, the choking game. With social media, dangerous fads can spread quickly, playing on a teen's poor impulse control and attraction to risky behavior.

Crystal has no internal compass for direction at this point, and the external judgments are damning. Crystal is really in trouble. Her self-esteem continues to plummet. Feeling hopeless, she attempts suicide and ends up in the Adolescent Psychiatric Unit at the local hospital.

The Psychologist's Opinion

The good news is that Crystal is alive, and where there is life, there is hope. With an early intervention before her personality is solidified, she may be able to move forward in her life without the burden of codependency.

The road back from rock bottom is a long one for Crystal, but with the help of her treatment team, she is able to see how she has sabotaged herself. Her insights are the first step toward finding her authentic identity and moving through adolescence to begin her life as an adult. After a suicide attempt, the only answer for Crystal is professional help.

The Passive Teen: Melody

Melody has always been a loner. She grew up outside of town on fifteen acres. She has horses to ride, trees to climb, woods to explore, and a creek to swim in. Melody is involved in 4-H, and wins medals at the state fair for her goats, sewing skills, flower arrangements, and barrel racing with her quarter horse, Jimmy. She is often reluctant to try new things, but when she does, she's successful. Melody's real love is music. There is nothing she enjoys more than playing her guitar and singing with her dad.

Melody has always been quite timid, almost afraid of people. She seldom makes eye contact when she does say a few words. If she wasn't so afraid of hurting her parents' feelings, she never would have joined 4-H. She likes the activities with the animals, but has high anxiety when she competes. When she's riding she tells herself that it is Jimmy who is competing, and she's just along for the ride. Melody has earned many ribbons, but she is still painfully uncomfortable when she is called to go up and receive her award. If she wasn't so afraid of disappointing her parents, she wouldn't even attend the ribbon ceremony. She attributes her many accomplishments to her parents pushing her. Actually, her favorite fantasy is riding her horse across the fields and sitting around the campfire playing sad songs on her guitar. She is most comfortable when she is alone.

Melody is especially shy in school, where she feels judged by the other kids. Melody is smart, but would not raise her hand or speak up in class. To Melody it feels like a big light is being shined in her eyes, and people are prying into her private world. She's like her dad that way; he doesn't talk much unless he has something really important to say. They both would rather express feelings in their songs.

Now that Melody is a teenager and developing sexually, she's even more awkward and self-conscious. She feels like the ugly duckling, gawky with braces on her teeth. She barely smiles and walks to class with her head down for fear someone will try to talk to her. She was quiet before; now she barely speaks. Melody struggles every day with her self-esteem. If she does well in school, she knows she pleases her parents, and that feels good. But what she really wants is friends. Try as she might, she just can't figure the girls out. At this point, she has given up.

It's hard for teens like Melody to push through adolescence. Much of her day is spent trying to figure out what other people want. When she gets home from school, she goes to her room, lies on her bed, and cries. When her mom checks on her, she says she's studying. The only time Melody feels confident is when she's away from people, playing her guitar or riding Jimmy through the woods. It's hard to see how Melody is codependent with people because she actually fears any contact with them. But inside, she longs to fit in. She is looking to please, looking to find the key to friendship.

If you're a loner in high school, will you always be a loner?
Adolescents may try out an identity or two in high school; because of the pressure to conform, the choices are limited. If it isn't ambushed by drugs, abuse, codependency, risky behavior, depression, or the like, in the mid to late twenties, the true identity can be experienced.

Melody is very talented and has had many opportunities in high school to perform, but she has never been able to overcome her anxiety. Finally, in her senior year, Melody finds her niche. She starts out working after school shoveling horse manure at a local stable. After graduation, she begins training as an equestrian and becomes quite well known in the horse circuit. By her mid-twenties, Melody is already an excellent trainer.

The Psychologist's Opinion

Because she is doing a job, Melody is in a role that has specifically defined requirements. Therefore, Melody's role as a teacher frees her from social anxiety in interacting with her students and their parents. Her codependent traits, like focusing intently on another, figuring out what people need, and concern for how she presents her suggestions, have actually helped her professionally. Melody has a leg up in insight and in understanding what makes her young riders tick.

This is a good example of how a person who is codependent can pursue a career that makes good use of traits that are usually seen as negative or codependent in personal relationships. Other professions like this are nurses, trainers, doctors, occupational and physical therapists, and all of the helping professions. If Melody can channel her codependency into work, she may feel less codependent in her close relationships. The closer the relationship, the more difficult it may be for Melody. It is never black and white when we talk about human behavior.

The Runaway or Throwaway Teen: Carmen

Carmen is one of the many children who are born into abusive families. Not every runaway child is growing up in a seriously dysfunctional home. Nor is every throwaway as seriously abused as Carmen. Carmen entered the foster care system when she was still very young and now she is an adolescent.

FACT

Studies have shown that when he is part of a group, an adolescent may do things he normally wouldn't do. Peer pressure, undeveloped impulse control, attraction to risky behavior, tests of masculinity, group initiation, and codes of behavior can influence the levels of teen violence and aggression.

Carmen is placed in foster care when her family disintegrates and her "mother" (who was actually her biological aunt) gives her up to the system. The combination of neglect and abuse culminating in Carmen being thrown away shattered her identity.

Carmen remains in foster care for a year before she runs away. On the street, she is soon recruited into prostitution. Carmen's codependency makes her an easy target for pimps. In one sense, it feels comfortable for her to please one person, her pimp, and for that, she receives the protection she needs on the street. As a child, she had already given up so much, and yet she had never been protected. Ultimately, she was discarded by her family like yesterday's garbage.

Carmen is an adolescent, yet her peer group is other teen prostitutes, and the adult figure giving her guidance is her pimp. Carmen survives her situation by trying to make herself invaluable to Jackson, her pimp. She knows how to anticipate his needs and meet them, she is adept at caretaking the other prostitutes, and she has no self-esteem. This makes her a valuable commodity and assures a place for her in Jackson's stable of prostitutes. For Carmen, this false sense of security is better than nothing.

The Psychologist's Opinion

Carmen represents the population of children who grow up in severely dysfunctional families. She is a child of abuse and neglect who is trying to make the best of an impossible situation. What she is looking for is belonging and protection. Is becoming a prostitute the best answer for Carmen? Of course not. But not every child is given the same opportunities in life. She has found a way to survive. And until she finds a way to break the victim cycle, she is surviving the best way she knows how.

The point is often it is impossible for a child to avoid codependency traits that have developed in childhood as a means of survival. Growing into adulthood, these children continue the pattern because they cannot see themselves as worthy of a good life.

The Failure to Launch Teen: Jason

Jason is nineteen and is scheduled to graduate from high school in a few months. He has quite a lot to accomplish before then. He has yet to finish up a couple of Incompletes from last year, he has a fifty-page paper due, and if he misses one more day of school for any reason, for the third time he will not graduate. He's been told by the principal, in front of his parents, that he holds the record for the number of near-graduations at his high school.

FACT

The codependent relationship of Romeo and Juliet was so strong it became more important than their own lives. Riding an emotional roller coaster, teens are easy targets for unhealthy relationships. The codependent adolescent doesn't seem to have an identity, is emotionally unstable when he is not with his girlfriend, and cuts himself off from family and friends.

Jason had his first serious girlfriend in his sophomore year. He did everything he could to please her. He even quit football so they could spend more time together. Despite all his attention to her needs, she cheated on him. A sensitive kid, Jason was deeply wounded and blamed himself. He pleaded for her to give him another chance. When she refused, Jason became very angry and threatened to post nude photos of her on Facebook. Once he calmed down, he thought better of it. But the next day, he confronted the boy whom his girlfriend cheated with and broke his nose. Jason was arrested for assault, which his attorney plea-bargained to several weekends in the county jail.

When Jason met Jill, he was upfront about what had happened in his previous breakup. He was very apologetic about his behavior, and swore that nothing like it would ever happen again. He seemed genuinely remorseful. Jason entered the relationship with Jill vowing that he would do better this time. Again, he started trying to please. Despite the great inconvenience, he offered to pick Jill up for school and take her home. He surprised her with a cell phone so that they could talk more; he fixed her car and computer. This time, he wanted to be the perfect boyfriend so Jill wouldn't cheat on him, wouldn't leave him.

FACT

> According to Kim Parker in her article, "The Boomerang Generation," "If there's supposed to be a stigma attached to living with mom and dad through one's late twenties or early thirties, today's 'boomerang generation' didn't get that memo. Among the three-in-ten young adults ages twenty-five to thirty-four (29 percent) that have been in that situation during the rough economy of recent years, large majorities say they're satisfied with their living arrangements (78 percent) and upbeat about their future finances (77 percent)."

He was so wrapped up in his relationship with Jill that he dropped his other friends. In the evenings, he spent hours talking on the phone with Jill instead of doing schoolwork. As his grades fell, so did his self-esteem. He began having frequent arguments with his parents about his need to buckle down. The first time he failed to graduate with his class, he wasn't that upset because that put him in Jill's graduating class. The second time he failed, Jill graduated and moved on to college—and Jason didn't. He tried everything to get her to change her mind about college. After she left, he would drive sixty miles one way to visit her on campus several times a week. At this point, Jill became disgusted with him and broke off the relationship. She called him a loser.

When Jason finally does graduate, he doesn't go on to college. He feels so insecure and so down in the dumps, he can barely get out of bed. His dad is on his back to either go to school, go to work, or move out. Jason starts lying to his parents about all the job applications he is submitting and all the colleges he is checking out online. Every week it seems that he is going to major in something different. He makes a lot of promises to his parents, but he is so afraid of failing, he doesn't follow through. Jason spends most of his time online or working on his car and going out drinking on the weekends looking for someone to love him. Now he is working part-time at a carwash and living with his parents.

The Psychologist's Opinion

Jason is a painful example of how codependency at its worst can render a person helpless. He lacks the emotional stability that is gained from a strong sense of self. He sought an ego mirror in his girlfriend and attached himself to her much in the same way a parasite attaches to its host. Needy and lacking direction, he sought his identity through pleasing his girlfriend who he then counted on to reflect him back as a good guy. Because of this codependency, he became a slave to her needs, doing things that eventually pushed her away and disgusted her.

Jason began his codependency in his family, and he's still lying and rationalizing his behavior to his parents while at the same time expecting them to rescue him. He's lonely and depressed, defeated in love and defeated in life. Jason needs to get help to get out of this vicious codependency cycle. Unfortunately, he is more likely to find another girlfriend and start the codependency patterns all over again.

Letter to the Psychologist

The following letter is taken from Here-to-Listen.com and helps explain how parents sometimes role-model codependent behavior.

Dear Doctor,

I can't stand what's going on with my daughter, Erin. At sixteen she says she's in love with Jordan who's a year older than she. It's like he's taken over her life. I heard them arguing over the phone and I heard him call her a bitch. Now that's it! I told her she needs to break up with this guy immediately. I'm not even going to tell my husband about it; he would blow his top.

If Erin doesn't come to her senses, I'm going to lock her up! She just wasn't raised to be acting like this. Jordan, the boyfriend, is bringing this out in her.

Karen

Dear Karen,

If your daughter is codependent, it didn't just start with Jordan. Somewhere she learned that another's needs are more important than hers. Now let's apply this to the current situation. She says she loves Jordan. This means that she has a need to date him. You don't like Jordan, so your need is to intervene and save her from him. You fully expect your daughter to bend to your will without even discussing your concerns with her. I know she's only sixteen, but if you want to be an ally for her in navigating adolescence, you need to be approachable. Your immediate and strong reaction to Jordan's comment suggests that you are better at laying down mandates (and so is Erin's dad) than discussing this with Erin. Unless you perceive that she is in danger, try to be present, but not intrusive. With your support and guidance, she needs to start handling her own relationships.

CHAPTER 9

Codependent Parents

Codependency can be passed along from generation to generation. As you know, if an unhealthy pattern exists on an unconscious level, it can never be changed. How can you change something when you don't know it's there, what it is, and what to do about it? It is very important as you move through this awareness process that you not feel guilty or self-deprecating when you realize you may have inadvertently role-modeled codependent behavior for your children.

Gaining Awareness Is Key

With a dysfunctional pattern like codependency, you may not realize it's lurking below the surface of your parenting. Until you gain this awareness, you cannot parent in a different way. Only after you gain this awareness can you use it to illuminate your parenting methods (warts and all), and translate that awareness into real day-to-day changes in your life.

As a parent, you want to give your children the best environment within which to grow and mature into healthy adults. Parenting is an awesome responsibility and a daunting job. You know that there is no such thing as a perfect parent. As you work on your own codependency, there is no doubt you will improve your parenting skills. Your children, present and future, will benefit too.

The Emotionally Needy Parent: Dawn

Dawn becomes pregnant when she is only fifteen. The pregnancy is the result of a one-night stand, and Dawn chooses not to tell the father. The news of Dawn's pregnancy is especially hard on her mother, who became pregnant when she was only sixteen, quit school, and married. To think her daughter will be destined for the same hard life breaks her mother's heart.

As it turns out, Dawn has the baby, continues to live with her parents, and finishes school. Dawn is an attentive mother to her new baby, Dylan. She comes directly home from school every day to care for him. It is an admirable choice, but as a result, Dawn misses out on school activities, dating, friends, and the social life a teenager should have.

When Dylan turns five and it's time for him to start school, Dawn decides she wants to establish her own family. Dawn's family loves Dylan and doesn't want him to leave, but Dawn is determined to separate from them and get settled with Dylan before he starts school.

Dawn moves into a studio apartment on the other side of town from her parents. On her own, she isn't able to afford all of the things Dylan is used to, but she does the best she can. With Dylan in kindergarten half-days, Dawn is able to work full-time. Her mother picks Dylan up from school and keeps him at her house until Dawn gets out of work.

Now Dawn is twenty-one years old, the mother of a five-year-old son, and employed full-time as a dental hygienist. She is so busy, she really has no time for a social life. She's missed out on making friends, dating, and being part of a peer group. If you ask Dawn, she would say her only friend is her son, Dylan.

According to Robert Firestone in his article, "Emotional Hunger vs. Love," contact with an emotionally hungry parent leaves a child impoverished, anxiously attached, and hurting. The more contact between this type of parent and the child, the more damage the parent does to the child's security and comfort.

With her busy schedule, Dawn goes to bed early with Dylan. In their studio apartment, Dylan sleeps with Dawn. His mother lets him fall asleep while she reads. She enjoys cuddling with him, and when she wakes, Dylan is right there next to her.

Once Dylan is in school all day, Dawn arranges her schedule so that she can take him to school and pick him up every day. Dylan sometimes asks if he can go to a friend's house after school or join an afterschool activity, but Dawn just hugs him and says she'll miss him. Soon Dylan stops asking because he doesn't want to make his mother sad.

The Psychologist's Opinion

There is no doubt that Dylan feels loved by his mother, but the love is beginning to feel confining, guilt-producing. He wants to do things with friends, but he doesn't want to hurt his mother's feelings. In a healthy mother-son relationship, Dawn would encourage Dylan to make friends and spend time with them. It is her job to support her son's interests and encourage him to try things on his own.

It appears that Dawn is trying to meet her own needs for intimacy, companionship, and friendship through her son. A child should not be expected to meet the emotional needs of a parent. Although she doesn't realize it, Dawn is too enmeshed with her son. She is not focused on Dylan's need to develop autonomy; she's more concerned with her own need to feel loved.

But it is not Dylan's job to be a friend to his mother, nor is it okay for Dawn to put her emotional needs on him. Unfortunately, Dawn is codependent with her son, and is also fostering codependency in him.

The Neglectful Parent: Janice

Janice married Jim right out of high school. They settled down and had two children. Janice revolved her life around Jim, moving across the country for his job, losing touch with her family and friends. She thought she was living the American dream. But Jim had other plans. The next time he was promoted, he didn't take his family with him.

When meeting potential dating partners, be upfront about the fact that you are divorced (or single) and have children. You are looking for a relationship with somebody who will fully accept and appreciate your children, so you don't have to downplay the importance of being a mother.

Left with two kids to support and no job, Janice felt abandoned and depressed. She eventually found work at a local retail store, but she didn't earn enough to support her family. It didn't take long for her to use up savings from her divorce settlement. Janice had no choice but to sell the house and move to an apartment. Living as a single parent working six days a week for minimum pay wasn't where Janice expected to be.

After two years, Janice resolves to find a new husband. She wants someone to share the burden, help support and care for her children, and love her. She hires the teenage girl down the hall to come over after school to watch the kids. After work each night, Janice stops for a drink. She always looks her best, sits at the bar, and smiles at strangers. Before long, she begins meeting men and going out on dates.

What starts out as a short-term plan turns into a lifestyle for Janice. She enjoys the single life, dating and dancing and being treated to dinner at upscale restaurants. It is almost as if she is leading a double life. She never tells her dates she has children. Still in her twenties, Janice fits in with the young single crowd. The problem is that Janice isn't a young single. She is the mother of two children, paying a teenage babysitter to take her place with the kids.

When Janice meets Alex, he seems to be the perfect match, but he tells her on their first date that he doesn't really like children. Janice decides to wait and see if they fall in love before she tells Alex her secret. She figures he will eventually accept the children if he loves her enough. For almost a year, the kids barely see their mother. She leaves early for work, and the babysitter comes after school and puts them to bed at least three nights a week. On the weekends, Janice has started to travel with Alex. She leaves after work on Friday, and does not return until late Sunday night, after the kids are in bed. On the weekends, the kids are with their weekend sitter, an older woman who also lives in their building.

The Psychologist's Opinion

First Janice's children were abandoned by their father and now they have lost their mother. One of the most difficult things for them to deal with is the daily uncertainty. They listen to their mother's phone conversations to see if she's making plans or hiring a sitter. They beg her not to go out so much, and she hugs them and tells them she loves them, but then she's off on another adventure. What the children hear and what they see do not match up.

Janice's codependency in her first marriage kept her from investing herself in a meaningful way with her husband. She was so concerned about pleasing him by being whoever he wanted her to be that she had no idea who she really was and neither did he. After the divorce, her manipulative, cater-to dating behavior continues this codependent pattern. Janice wants a man, so she's willing to mold herself into whatever she thinks he wants. The fiasco with Alex is about to come to a head. Janice has managed to hide her kids for months while Alex falls in love with her. She can't pretend to be somebody else forever. Soon Alex will find out and he'll wonder who he's in love with. The tragic part of this story is the negative effect it is having on Janice's children.

The Adult Child Parent: Mark

Mark grew up in an alcoholic home. He doesn't drink, but he carries the legacy into his own parenting. To his credit, Mark has been attending Adult Children of Alcoholics (ACoA) meetings through his local AA on and off since he was in his early twenties. At this point, Mark undoubtedly is more prepared to parent his children than many others from alcoholic families.

Mark can't remember a time when his dad hugged or cuddled him, and he's vowed he will shower his kids with affection. It's easy for Mark to cuddle baby Ian. What surprises Mark is that when Ian cries, he feels anxiety and anger. Mark hands the crying baby to his wife, and says he needs to take a shower.

Instead of talking with his wife about it, he is overwhelmed with shame and feelings of inadequacy, codependency feelings he felt daily in his alcoholic home. Intellectually, he wants to do things differently with his family, but now he finds himself unable to talk about it. Mark has slipped into the "don't talk rule" of the alcoholic family. Mark knows what it felt like to be the victim of harsh, inconsistent behavior. Old messages about not being good enough, or not being brave enough, press down upon him.

FACT

Adult children of alcoholics have trust issues and damaged self-esteem. They also are unclear as to what a "normal" family dynamic is. This can make them quite insecure in their role as a parent.

Mark's son is an easy baby, but when Ian hits the "terrible twos" he is a handful. Mark knows he should encourage his son to explore. He knows he should want to play with Ian, help him learn about his world. But the more independent Ian becomes, the more anxious Mark is. Instead of just relaxing into his authentic self, it becomes clear that Mark doesn't really know who he is as a parent. He has a million *shoulds* in his head about being a good parent. The more tense and self-recriminating he becomes, the more he withdraws from Ian. It's almost as if Mark needs to get away from his father role because it's too painful for him to be a failure in something he considers so important.

One day in the spring, Mark and his wife take little Ian to the park. They are having a great time, watching Ian explore the playground. When Ian's mother leaves to use the bathroom, Ian discovers the jungle gym, and is playing on the bottom rung. Mark wants him to explore, but he's keeping a close eye on him. Mark is distracted briefly when his wife returns, and Ian falls. He's only startled, not hurt. He lies crying under the play equipment.

This is normal kid stuff, but to Mark, this momentary distraction on his part is unforgivable. All those codependency feelings of being bad wash over him. But instead of comforting Ian, he yells at him and calls him a "bad boy." When his wife tries to talk to him, he clams up.

When they get home, Mark's wife confronts him. At first Mark is defensive, and tries to blame his wife for the incident. The idea that he could not protect Ian is intolerable in Mark's perfectionist, black-and-white thinking. His wife is the mirror, and right now Mark sees himself mirrored back as a bad father. He pulls out all the stops arguing with her about the issue. This is codependency at its worst. Mark looks in the mirror (his wife) and sees himself as unlovable. The only thing he knows to do is force a change in the image. Codependents can use defensiveness, blaming, intimidation, denial, name-calling, putdowns, and even violence to bully the mirror into changing.

The Psychologist's Opinion

There are three very favorable signs that Mark will work through his codependency issues in his effort to be the father he longs to be. First of all, Mark has a history of seeking help. Through his participation in ACoA he has learned to accept his faults and to acknowledge his powerlessness over them. Even though his first response is to get defensive when his wife confronts him, he knows he is wrong and will quickly begin to shift his direction to one of self-discovery. He has learned these important lessons in personal responsibility from his ACoA work.

Secondly, the will or desire for change cannot be underestimated in reaching a successful outcome. Mark hadn't realized that at a deep level he still had some issues to work on before he could be the dad his father wasn't. Once he accepts that he has work to do, he will do it.

Third, Mark has a very strong ally in his wife. Fortunately, Mark's wife is not codependent. She knows who she is and she knows how to set healthy boundaries. She leaves the room and waits until Mark cools off, then she gives him a choice. Either they get family therapy or she will consider asking Mark to leave. She gives Mark a week to make his decision. She stays attached to Mark in a loving, if distant, way during that time. Mark goes to an ACoA meeting every day for a week. At the end of that time, he makes an appointment with a therapist recommended to him at a meeting.

The Hovering Parent: Jasmine

Jasmine did quite well when her two children were young and needed a lot of supervision and guidance. But now that the children are older and it's time for them to become more independent, Jasmine won't let them.

At around five, children typically learn to navigate the new world of school. Sometimes this change is scary. Each of Jasmine's children threw a fit when it was time to start school, crying and screaming and clinging to their mother. This is hard for most parents, but it is important for them to reassure their children and encourage separation. As each of Jasmine's children started kindergarten, they looked up at their mother, and she was crying and obviously tense and worried. What she is affirming to her kids with her own anxiety is that school is indeed a scary place. After all, look at Mom—she's a wreck.

FACT

Instead of rigidly controlling your children or trying to be their friend, try this technique. For example, to a twelve-year-old fussy eater: "I can make spaghetti, pork chops, or chicken for dinner, which would you prefer?" You set the boundary, and from within that boundary, allow him to make a choice. Use this with everything, and be 100 percent consistent.

It is very frightening for the codependent parent to allow her children the space and independence needed to successfully master all the developmental stages. Jasmine is the parent now called "the helicopter mom." She hovers over her children, making sure that she has control over every aspect of the children's lives. A hovering mom continues to do for her child long after the child is capable of doing for himself.

In Jasmine's mind, her life's work is to make sure her kids turn out right. Her identity as a stay-at-home mother depends on it. To Jasmine, this means keeping them happy all the time. When her kids are sad, mad, or disappointed, Jasmine can't stand it. As a result, she's a pleaser, unable to follow through and allow the kids to experience natural consequences.

Every morning, Jasmine makes the kids breakfast and packs their lunches while the kids play video games. She checks their homework and lays their clothes out for them. After following them around making sure they brush their teeth and comb their hair, she gathers up their belongings and has them in backpacks by the front door. All the other kids in the neighborhood take the bus, but Jasmine's kids don't like the bus, so she drives them to and from school.

After school, the kids grab their video games or watch TV or make plans with friends. Jasmine is a great cook and makes dinner each night for her husband Frank and the kids. If the kids don't like what she's preparing, she makes something else for them. Each night she sits down with them for homework time. Sometimes, if they are frustrated, she does their schoolwork for them.

Parenting is a source of constant conflict between Jasmine and Frank. Frank wants the kids to be better behaved. He's willing to make a plan and stick to it because the household is always in such chaos. Frank feels Jasmine does too much for the kids and is wishy-washy in her discipline. Frank is right. But for Jasmine it's not as easy as simply making rules and sticking with them. With her codependency issues, she just cannot tolerate seeing her kids unhappy, so she caves in at the first sign that they are upset. Kids will find power where they can, and with Jasmine's inconsistency, they are in control.

The Psychologist's Opinion

On the surface, it may look like Jasmine is the perfect mother. Look at how well she takes care of her kids. If this were the case, Jasmine would be content, relaxed, and happy. But she's not. She's resentful, frustrated, angry, worried, and miserable. Her codependent feelings are directly connected to her children's moods. If they're happy, she's happy. Because of her codependency, Jasmine becomes the wishy-washy, easily manipulated parent. Instead of having rules and limits that are consistent, Jasmine crumbles at the slightest sign of distress from her kids. The more she allows the children to call the shots, the more out of control they become. Now she can't get them to go to bed and she can't get them up for school. She can't get them to do simple chores. If she asks them to stop watching TV or to put down the video games, they whine, throw a fit, or cry. At this point Jasmine backs off or starts bargaining with them.

Jasmine's codependency issues have set her up to fail as a parent. Her children are out of control and she is powerless. Frank has withdrawn from discussions about the kids because Jasmine bristles at the slightest suggestion or help he gives. Frank is the mirror for her failure and she resents him for it, gets defensive, and attacks him.

In short, Jasmine is heading for a major depression. She feels like a failure as a parent, and she's stressed-out all the time because she has allowed the kids to walk all over her. Because of her codependency, she can't hear Frank's parenting ideas as a support. All she hears is criticism, even though Frank is trying to help. Finally, he gives up trying to co-parent and withdraws. Now Jasmine is alone in the worst self-esteem quagmire she can imagine. The one thing she devoted her heart and soul to was her mothering, and she's sinking fast and won't take Frank's hand to help pull her out.

The Narcissistic Parent: David

David grew up in a wealthy family and lived a privileged life. He attended college then dabbled in some businesses, and married his wife Emma in his early thirties. David wanted a child right away and hoped it would be a son. The couple had difficulty getting pregnant, and when Christopher was born, they were delighted. Emma thought all their dreams had come true. But it turned out that David's idea of parenthood was a little different from hers.

David loves the high life, traveling, partying with friends, and pursuing his many interests. In the first week after Christopher is born, David insists that Emma start interviewing for nannies for the baby. He is sick of staying home all the time and needs a vacation. Emma doesn't want to leave the baby, but David hints that he could leave without her if she doesn't want to go. The couple compromises and hires a nanny, who accompanies them on a three-week trip to Europe. When they return home, David surprises Emma with a personal trainer who will come to the house and help her "get back in shape." He also gives her a beautiful emerald ring, Christopher's birthstone. He hosts a party for the new mother and their new son, inviting all the most important people to their home.

FACT

Particularly damaging to the child of a narcissist are the two faces she wears, one for the world and one at home. This duplicity affects a child's sense of reality, safety, and love. Why is it that everyone loves his or her mother, when she is so mean? What's wrong with me that I don't trust her?

In a couple of months, David is ready to travel again. This time he wants to sail around the Canary Islands for two weeks. He explains to Emma that the vacation isn't really suitable for the baby. Again, they compromise and Emma reluctantly agrees to go with David for one of the weeks and leave the baby at home with the nanny.

By the time Christopher is a year old, Emma has decided not to travel for a while, but that doesn't stop David. He agrees not to be gone more than two weeks at a time if possible, and Emma agrees to accompany him on several trips during the year. Every time David comes home, he showers little Christopher with elaborate gifts from all over the world. While he and Emma are home together, David wants to continue their lifestyle of theater, parties, and dinners out, a social event almost every night.

When Christopher is about five, David begins an affair with a woman he met in Barbados. It is easy for him to pull it off, since he is away from home so often. Emma is thrilled when she gets to stay home with Christopher and doesn't really focus on what David is doing. She would like another baby, but David's sexual interest in her seems to have waned.

David appears to be the doting father. He enjoys spending time with Emma and Christopher. He sees his family as a perfect unit. His wife is beautiful, intelligent, outgoing, quick to laugh, and fun to be with. Everybody loves Emma. The older Christopher gets, the more David wants to take his family out with him. He's amused by his son and can see already that he is going to be a handsome young man with an outgoing personality. "Like his father," Emma says.

The Psychologist's Opinion

Because David is a narcissist, he loves the outside trappings of being a father, since having the perfect family reflects favorably on him. But he certainly doesn't expect to make any sacrifices for them or change his lifestyle. He is indulgent with Christopher, but at the same time he is emotionally neglectful. David doesn't know how to give unconditional love to his son, because being a father is all about David trying to fill a void in himself. As long as Emma implicitly agrees to feed his narcissistic needs without really expecting much back, David is happy. Now he's found a mistress to fill in for Emma when she's at home with their son.

Narcissus was pursued by many, but he loved no one. Once his need for admiration was met, he scorned his admirers. The gods, fed up with his selfish behavior, put a curse on him. They wanted him to know what it was like to love one who would never love him back. When Narcissus gazed into a pond, he saw his image and fell in love with it. Narcissus could not break his gaze on it and died there.

Sons of narcissistic fathers tend to develop some of the same traits when they mature. Christopher doesn't have much of a role model for being a man with feelings and depth, capable of being in healthy, interdependent relationships. What he has learned from David is to expect everybody else to cater to his needs. Christopher doesn't know that men can be empathic, affectionate, feeling human beings.

Emma tries to compensate for David's inability to focus on their son by becoming enmeshed with Christopher, loving him too much, giving too much, and catering to his needs beyond what is healthy for him. What she is teaching him in the process is that his needs come first and he can expect people, especially the women in his life, to sacrifice for him. Emma cannot teach her son what he needs to learn from David.

Parent of Grown Children: Bill

Bill's wife died four years ago when his son, Jason, was seventeen. Jason grieves the loss of his mother and seems to recover quickly. He graduates from high school, gets a part-time summer job, and then heads off to college in the fall. Bill e-mails and phones his son often, and Jason comes home on holidays and for the summers. Jason hasn't let his dad know this, but he has been struggling in college. When it's time for him to graduate, he has to come clean and tell his dad he doesn't have enough credits. Now Jason wants to stay through the summer to complete his degree. Bill and his wife had saved to provide money for Jason to graduate in four years. At this point, Bill dips into his retirement fund and agrees to pay for the extra schooling.

Halfway through the summer, Jason changes his mind and tells his dad he's moving home. This is a big adjustment for Bill, who is now getting out more and wants to entertain friends in his home. Jason stays up into the wee hours and sleeps half the day. He eats a lot and leaves dirty dishes in the kitchen. Bill's home looks like a frat house with Jason's stuff thrown all over the place. Jason insists he's looking for a job and asks his dad for spending money until he finds one. Bill finds himself looking at the want ads in the local paper and bringing them to Jason's attention. When he asks Jason if he has called on a job, Jason always has a reason why he didn't.

The weeks roll by and Jason is still sleeping until midafternoon and asking his dad for spending money or to use his car. This pattern continues to the point where Bill is arguing with his son almost every day. Bill is becoming more and more resentful and angry that Jason isn't doing what he said he would.

In the fall, Jason wants to attend a different college out of state that has a program perfectly suited for him. Bill is at his wits' end, but agrees to help his son with the tuition. After two months, Bill receives a credit card statement with a large balance. When Bill calls about the bill, Jason says he misunderstood his dad. He thought the card Bill had given him for a dire emergency meant he could use it for living expenses. Jason says he can make the minimum payments, but Bill doesn't want his son to start a career with a big debt hanging over his head. He offers to pay off the balance just this one time.

Bill is worried that his son is not turning out the way he and his wife wanted. He feels guilty, then angry, then resentful, then guilty, then worried and afraid. One night he sits in his room and cries and talks out loud to his dead wife, apologizing for letting her down and for failing so miserably as a father.

The Psychologist's Opinion

In 1959, Erickson defined adolescents as ages thirteen through nineteen; however, most modern psychologists designate the adolescent stage as somewhere between the ages of twelve and twenty-eight. Jason is still in the adolescent stage, but he is also considered an adult by societal expectations. Bill enables his son to stay stuck by agreeing to Jason's demands even though Jason is not doing his part. Now Bill's so angry and fed up that it's ruining his relationship with his son.

Boundaries that appear obvious to everyone else are not clear to Bill because he's codependent. Before she died, Bill's wife was the mirror through which he saw himself as a good guy. When she died, his son became his mirror. Now Bill feels Jason's failures are his fault. Bill thinks he's helping his son, but he's really trying to prove to himself that he's a good father. The best thing Bill can do to help Jason is to respect him enough to treat him like an adult. Bill can continue to love his son and maintain a healthy relationship with him, but he has to stop enabling. The development task for this psychosocial stage is Identity vs. Role Confusion. To enable a young person to remain dependent on the parent does not allow this stage to be completed successfully. Bill won't let Jason grow up.

Sometimes birds, especially adult birds, need to be pushed from the nest. The gift Bill will be giving his son is the opportunity to fly.

Letter to the Psychologist

The following letter is taken from Here-to-Listen.com and helps explain that you can be a successful parent without giving up your identity.

Dear Doctor,

I love my kids, but I don't want to spend all day with them. Before we started our family, my husband and I agreed I would be the stay-at-home parent until the kids were in school. I thought it would be easy for me to give up my career, but that's not the way it's turned out. My husband has no idea how I feel, and I'm thinking I should just bite the bullet for three more years. But, honestly, being at home with the kids is making me crazy. I tried to talk to my sister about this, and the judgmental look she gave me made me clam up. She is the perfect princess mother, and I'm a frog, I guess.

Ronda

Dear Ronda,

Don't wait another minute to talk to your husband about this. You may not realize it, but it's probably occurred to him that you're not happy. If feelings are not spoken directly, they are likely to come out sideways in a number of ways. If you feel you can be a better, more relaxed, and happier mother by working, then do it. Unless your husband is rigid and lacks empathy, he is likely to respond to your feelings and be willing to consider the alternatives.

By the sound of your letter, it is you who cannot accept that you don't want to be a stay-at-home mom and you're projecting it on others. At the end of the day, you are the only one who can judge how you're doing and what changes you need to make to empower your own happiness.

Don't suffer silently for another three years and make everybody miserable in the meantime. Do what you need to do.

CHAPTER 10

Codependent Friendships

Codependent feelings and thoughts may be experienced only in our most intimate relationships, or in all of our relationships. These feelings and thoughts can result in subtle codependent behaviors or intense, crippling codependent patterns. Codependency may show itself often or intermittently depending on how pervasive it is in a person's make-up. Here are examples of how codependency can show itself in friendships.

Signs of a Codependent Friendship

A trained therapist is governed by a set of ethical principles that define her role. These principles make clear that a therapist is not a friend. The therapist is a helper and the client or patient is someone who seeks help. The relationship is not mutual because it is not defined and constructed that way. Conversely, and for the same reasons, a friend is not a therapist. Here are signs of a codependent friendship:

- The codependent is in a therapy role; the friendship is not mutual.
- The codependent shares little of her inner world.
- The codependent talks little while his friend goes on and on about himself.
- The codependent often is disappointed by the lack of caring from a friend.
- The codependent can feel trapped or overwhelmed by a friend's problems.
- The codependent tries to figure out what a friend should do.
- The codependent agrees to do a favor and then resents it or "forgets" to do it.
- The codependent avoids a friend altogether because he can't be honest with him.
- A codependent takes pride in being "the one" that everybody talks to about problems.
- The codependent can feel held hostage by a friend's neediness.
- The codependent can't say no.

Of all these signs, the most important is the first one, because it is the key question to ask yourself. If you are playing the therapist, you know you're not in a friendship. If one person is always the helper, and the other person is the one with problems, that simulates the therapy relationship but it's not one—it's a codependent relationship.

The Bully and Cindy

In the adolescent stage, you shift from family influences to peers. In the midst of identity confusion teens and young adults develop friendships as a kind of trail-and-error in discovering themselves. Probably at no other time in your life will the friendships you develop carry as much weight in the development of your personality.

This case of Anna points out just how important a friendship can be in the development of identity. Anna attends Catholic school in a small town. Ever since fourth grade Anna has longed to be in with the popular girls in her class. Anna has identified Cindy as the leader of the popular girls, so she sets out to make friends with her. She starts out by doing favors for Cindy, and by junior high she has become part of Cindy's group.

FACT

Psychosocial studies have shown that there is a connection between crowd behavior and violence. Most social scientists would agree that individuals will do things as part of a group that they would not do on their own. Codependent kids are especially prone to this influence.

In seventh grade, Cindy emerges as a bully, constantly in trouble for teasing or taunting other kids. One day when Anna is at lunch with the girls, Cindy is discussing a plan to torment Beth, a smart but timid girl in their class. She orders Jill, Katie, and Emma to wait until Beth is outside waiting for the bus, then they are to come up behind her, pull her hair, push her down, and say Cindy is out to get her. The other girls carry out the plan without a hitch while Cindy observes from inside the school door. For the next few weeks, Cindy comes up with increasingly more threatening plans to scare Beth. Beth is afraid to tell her mother or her teacher; all she can do is steer clear of Cindy and her mean girls.

Anna laughs along with the girls as they talk about bullying Beth; she even starts to make suggestions for mean things they can do. The more Anna participates in the "mean girl" conversations, the more she belongs. Now the others are asking for her opinions and ideas. As a bonus, Anna finds she is quite talented at making funny mean comments about Beth to make Cindy laugh.

By the end of the school year, the big plan is to lock Beth in the storage room in the basement of the old school. They will wait until Friday afternoon when Beth is alone in the biology lab, cleaning up for the teacher. It is the most elaborate plan yet, carried out at the end of the day so Beth will be locked up until somebody discovers her missing.

When Friday comes, Emma is out sick. An emergency meeting is called and Cindy refuses to cancel the plan, and she doesn't volunteer to take Emma's place. Instead, she expects Anna to fill in. Anna is not a mean-spirited girl, despite her efforts to appear like one to the others. But now the day of reckoning is here. Anna immediately agrees, and then stews all afternoon, rationalizing why this really isn't so wrong, that Beth deserves it, that she'll do this just one time, then Emma will be back to reclaim her spot.

Around four o'clock, right on schedule, Beth does her "teacher's pet" duties in the biology lab while Jill removes the light bulbs in the storage room. When Beth leaves the lab and is alone in the basement hallway, Anna, Jill, and Katie grab her and push her into the dark storage room, pull out the doorstop, and lock the door. Mission accomplished.

ALERT

Any child can be bullied, but codependent children are easy targets because of their lack of assertiveness and poor self-esteem. Children onlookers can play a significant role in stopping bullying, but they must be encouraged to step out of the crowd and break their own codependency with their peers.

Anna's adrenaline level is soaring and so is her sense of belonging and approval. When the girls meet up with Cindy after school, there are hugs and accolades all around. Cindy invites the girls over to her house Saturday morning to see how the plan is going.

On Saturday, the girls are talking in Cindy's bedroom when the police show up. Anna keeps her mouth shut and watches Cindy finesse the police. After the police leave, Anna is crying and wants to confess. She has never been in trouble in her life, and she's scared, guilty, and filled with dread. At this point, Cindy threatens her. She tells Anna that she could easily replace Beth as the target of their bullying.

All of Anna's efforts have paid off. She's an important part of the group she admired and now Cindy is her friend. But Anna is having a deep identity conflict. She knows what she has done is wrong, yet she doesn't want to give up her friendship with Cindy because she sees Cindy as the gatekeeper for her social standing and happiness at school. She believes she needs Cindy's approval in order to be popular.

The Psychologist's Opinion

It is clear that Anna is in a codependent friendship with Cindy. It is a codependent friendship of the worst kind because Anna has given up her identity for it. Anna is at a real crossroads here. She can choose to come clean about the bullying and worry about picking up the pieces later, or she can make this her identity for her entire adolescence. She will be one of the "mean girls," a girl who looks to Cindy to define who she is.

The Addicted Friend and Krista

Brain studies have shown that the part of the brain that controls impulse is not yet fully developed in adolescence, making teens particularly vulnerable to risky behaviors like substance abuse. Addictions formed in adolescence may be deeply entrenched and dependency may last a lifetime. Krista has found herself in a codependent friendship with just such an adolescent, Macy, an addict.

Krista is sixteen and very responsible for her age. She plays volleyball in the winter and softball in the summer. She has close relationships with her parents, and she even likes her thirteen-year-old brother. Krista is the steady rock in her group of friends. If anyone has a problem, they know they can talk to Krista. Krista has had a best friend, Macy, since grade school. They hang out at each other's house and play sports together. They say they're like sisters, traveling on vacations with each other's family, borrowing each other's clothes, double-dating.

In the early part of her sophomore year, Macy unexpectedly ends up in the hospital after an overdose. Macy's mother is extremely distraught and asks Krista why Macy did it. It seems to have come straight out of the blue for Krista; she has no idea. Krista visits Macy to offer her help as soon as the doctor gives the okay. But Macy brushes her off, saying she doesn't know why she took the pills. When Macy gets back to school, Krista notices that she seems moody and short-tempered. When Krista asks if there's anything wrong, Macy says no. Through their sophomore year, Macy pulls away from Krista, drops out of sports, and starts dating someone from another school. Krista is losing touch with her best friend, and she's worried.

The friends don't see much of each other over the summer because Macy isn't returning any of Krista's calls, texts, or e-mails. When junior year begins, Krista is shocked to see her friend. Macy is thin and pale, has dyed her hair black, and has a nose ring. Krista tries to talk to her, but she just doesn't seem interested.

FACT

With the best of intentions, adolescents enable their troubled friends to continue destructive behavior. It is especially difficult for teenagers to know the difference between enabling and help. Along with attempts to help, a teen may feel frustrated, resentful, and angry about how he is being treated by a friend. This is a sign he may be engaged in enabling behaviors.

One night when Krista is studying, she gets a call from Macy asking if she could pick her up on a corner downtown. Krista agrees and drives down to pick up her friend. When she gets there, Macy is obviously high, her mouth is bleeding, and she's hysterical. She still won't tell Krista what has happened; she lies and says she's high because somebody put something in her drink. Krista offers to take her home, but Macy wants Krista to call her mother and tell her she is staying with Krista. Krista wants to help her, so she does what Macy asks.

The next morning, Macy is still sleeping when Krista leaves for school. Krista lets her sleep it off without telling anyone in the household she is there. She even writes out a fake excuse, signs Macy's mother's name, and turns it in at the principal's office.

A week later, Krista hears Macy is in the hospital again. Krista goes to the hospital only to be screamed at by Macy who calls the nurses, telling them she hasn't given permission for Krista to visit. Krista is asked to leave. She feels powerless and frustrated. Why doesn't Macy want her help? Is she confiding in somebody else? What has she done to make Macy hate her?

The next week at school, the rumors are flying that Macy has left for a rehab facility. Soon after that, Krista starts getting letters, then phone calls from Macy. She tells Krista that she is sorry, it was the drugs. She thanks Krista for standing by her and begs her to come visit her. Krista is thrilled that she has her best friend back.

The morning of the visit, Macy calls and says she needs her iPod and would Krista pick it up from a friend and bring it to her. After a three-hour drive to the treatment facility, Krista waits for two more hours before Macy comes out, arms outstretched for a big hug. She smiles and tells Krista she loves her, and thanks her profusely for visiting. She whispers in Krista's ear, asking about the package. While they are sitting there talking, Krista passes the iPod to Macy. Very shortly after that, an aide comes in and says it's time for Macy's group therapy. After the long drive and waiting, Krista is with Macy for about forty-five minutes. She is happy to call Macy's family on her drive home and report that Macy is doing great.

When Macy's mom answers, she is furious. She has just received a call from the treatment center that Krista has smuggled drugs in to her daughter. She screams at Krista to stay away from Macy or she will turn her in to the police.

The Psychologist's Opinion

So this is the thanks Krista gets for trying to help her friend? The answer is yes, because Krista isn't helping, she's enabling. Krista is codependent with her addict friend, Macy. She has enabled Macy to treat her like dirt, take advantage of her, and then set her up to bring her drugs. Krista has interfered with Macy facing the consequences of her addictive behavior by bailing her out and lying.

Krista thinks she's being a loyal friend, trying to help Macy through rough times. But now that Macy is an addict, she's in a relationship with drugs and will do anything to keep using. She has stopped caring about Krista as a friend. Krista is simply a mark she can use to enable her to stay high. Until Macy truly is clean and sober, she cannot be a friend. Krista needs to move on and learn from this experience.

The Angry Friend and Colleen

Colleen has not seen her friend Haley since high school, but now Haley e-mails Colleen and says she's recently divorced and relocating to Pittsburgh where Colleen has lived for twenty years. Haley expresses how afraid she is to move to a big city. Colleen volunteers to help Haley get adjusted to Pittsburgh and sets up a lunch date with her the week after she relocates.

FACT

"The glory of friendship is not the outstretched hand, not the kindly smile, nor the joy of companionship; it is the spiritual inspiration that comes to one when you discover that someone else believes in you and is willing to trust you with a friendship." —Ralph Waldo Emerson

Colleen is waiting at her favorite restaurant when Haley bustles in. She gives Colleen a quick hug, sits down, and starts complaining about the traffic. She's angry with the crowds in the downtown area, and wonders why Colleen didn't suggest a restaurant closer to her neighborhood.

Colleen knows the server and greets him warmly. When he brings their orders, Haley is dissatisfied with her salad. She says it is too "skimpy." The server asks if he can bring more bread or a cup of soup, but the more polite he is to Haley, the angrier she gets. Finally, she asks him to take the salad back and bring her a hamburger. She eats the burger even though it is "undercooked." Through a two-hour lunch, Colleen hears about what a jerk Haley's ex-husband is and how badly he has treated her, story after angry story to make her point.

From that day on, Haley calls Colleen almost every day asking for recommendations for grocery stores, dentists, doctors, dry cleaners, hairstylists, pharmacies, massage therapists, etc. The next time they get together for lunch, Haley complains to Colleen about her suggestions. She's mad at Colleen because the dental hygienist made her gums bleed. Another long lunch of complaints leaves Colleen tense and uncomfortable.

Against her better judgment, Colleen invites Haley to her holiday party. The next day Haley calls to complain to Colleen about her party guests, how rude they were to her, and how attacked she felt. Colleen listens for over a half-hour, then makes an excuse to end the call. Over the next few weeks, Colleen screens her phone calls to avoid Haley. Each time the phone rings, Colleen jumps a little. She asks her husband not to pick up if it's Haley. Bob tells Colleen that he is starting to resent the constant negative presence Haley has in their life.

Colleen knows Bob is right, but the next time she sees Haley at the grocery store, she is full of excuses and feels compelled to spend time with Haley so Haley won't see her as a bad friend. When she has lunch with Haley the following week, Colleen doesn't even tell Bob.

FACT

It's hard for most people to be direct when they are delivering bad news, especially if they anticipate anger. Although face-to-face is always best, a short note or e-mail is better than not saying anything.

The Psychologist's Opinion

It seems to be impossible for Colleen to set a healthy boundary with Haley. She doesn't even like Haley at this point, yet she is being held hostage by codependency. Colleen can't relax in her own home because she startles every time she hears the phone ring. She knows Bob is right about Haley, so now the problem is interfering with their marriage. Colleen feels judged, and is withholding from Bob when Bob is just the messenger with the bad news. And that bad news is that Haley is an anger junkie and Colleen is hopelessly codependent with Haley and just can't seem to break free of it.

The Dismissive Friend and Janet

Janet and Kim met when they were young mothers living next door to one another. Janet's husband, Robert, worked at the local fishery, and Kim's husband, Charlie, had just started his career at the bank.

Janet and Kim have coffee together every morning and usually eat lunch together with their kids during the week. They plan joint activities for their kids during the summer, and a couple of times the two families rented a cottage for a week. Janet and Kim trade off childcare so that one or the other can have a night out with her husband. On the weekends, both families enjoy spending time together. Robert and Charlie get along well and like to fish and play poker together.

When he gets his third promotion, Charlie feels it's time for the family to move from their working-class neighborhood to a larger home on the other side of town. Janet is heartbroken that Kim won't be right next door anymore. But the city isn't large, and they commit to continue their friendships as before. Charlie and Kim usually invite Janet and Robert and their kids to their home because there is more room for the kids and they have a swimming pool.

FACT

If you find yourself disappointed in the lack of consideration you're getting from your friends, look inside yourself for signs of codependency. Ask yourself if the friendship is mutual or if you are the giver and the other the taker.

Over the next few years, Kim joins the country club and plays tennis there. Through tennis she connects with some new friends. When she gets together with Janet, she often talks about her other friends and social activities she's been involved in. She keeps saying that she must have the girls meet Janet, but she doesn't do it. During the holidays, Kim invites Janet and Robert to a party. When Janet arrives, she feels awkward there. The guests are dressed so elegantly, and obviously have money. Janet and Robert really don't know anyone, and neither Kim nor Charlie make a point to introduce them.

By the time the two couples are approaching fifty, Kim and Charlie move again, this time to an exclusive community in the hills outside the city. They invite Janet and Robert to the housewarming party and then ignore them. Robert says he understands that he and Charlie just don't have as much in common anymore. Janet, on the other hand, is crushed.

Later that summer, Kim calls Janet. She is crying so hard, she can hardly speak and asks Janet to come right over. When she arrives, Kim tells her that their oldest boy has been killed in an accident. Janet drops everything to be there for her friend. She uses up her precious vacation time and spends long hours helping Kim with the funeral arrangements, listening to Kim's grief, comforting her whenever Kim needs her. She encourages Kim to see a therapist, but Kim says all she needs is Janet.

A long six months after the funeral, everybody gets back to their lives—everybody but Janet. She calls Kim every day to see how she's doing, stops over to sit with her, does errands for her, and generally focuses all of her energy on her friend. Finally, Kim begins to heal. Often when Janet calls, Kim isn't there. She's playing tennis, lunching with her friends, and has planned a trip away with Charlie.

As her relationship with Kim becomes increasingly one-sided, Janet breaks down and tells Robert how unimportant she feels. How she feels Kim has dismissed her just because she doesn't have the right clothes. She can't believe she's being treated so badly. What has she done to deserve this? Robert is kind and wants to fix things, but Janet knows he really doesn't understand. She feels betrayed by someone she loves deeply, someone for whom she has just sacrificed so selflessly. Janet is so depressed, she makes an appointment with a therapist.

The Psychologist's Opinion

When Kim and Janet were raising their young families together, they formed a strong bond. To outside appearances, it looked like a very healthy give-and-take friendship. On the inside Janet was already codependent. She sought approval from her husband and tried to make sure all his needs were met. She sacrificed for her children and gave up her social life, except for her friendship with Kim. In the process, Kim took on way too much importance in Janet's life.

After several months in therapy, Janet begins to realize she has set herself up for Kim's dismissive behavior through her own codependency. The level of her despair over the changing relationship highlighted the power Kim's friendship had over her. Kim was constantly in Janet's thoughts, and when Kim needed her, she was right there, many times neglecting herself and her family while she tried to anticipate Kim's every need and fulfill it.

Taking care of her friend was Janet's codependent attempt to raise her esteem in Kim's eyes, thereby increasing her own sense of worth. If she could be Kim's savior when her son died, Janet surely must be the friend after whom you could throw away the mold. Being Mother Teresa to Kim would surely make Kim realize how badly and unjustly she had treated her. What appeared on the surface as devotion to Kim was really Janet's codependency. When Kim didn't respond with accolades and love, Janet was destroyed.

After therapy, Janet now knows better than to attach herself to a friend in such an unhealthy way. She still sees Kim, but she doesn't allow her to take advantage of their friendship. She has set a boundary that they will only get together with Kim and Charlie as they used to, just the four of them.

Janet now feels she is in control of her friendship with Kim. She hasn't cut Kim out of her life, because she still loves her. But now she is more honest with Kim, she says no to Kim, and she lets Kim know what she needs from a friend.

Letter to the Psychologist

The following letter is taken from Here-to-Listen.com and helps explain why codependency can exist in only one rather distant relationship.

Dear Doctor,
    There is only one friend I think I'm codependent with. All my other relationships seem pretty healthy. Is it possible for a person to be codependent with only one friend?

Ron

Dear Ron,

It's possible, but uncommon. Maybe you have worked through codependency in your life and this friend is a residual. Perhaps this person's personality or mannerisms trigger feelings in you that are connected to somebody you knew as a child, deeper feelings that aren't often reached. Codependency is on a continuum of pervasiveness, so not every codependent reacts all the time with every person, nor is their reaction always of the same intensity.

If you said only your significant other triggered codependency in you, this would make perfect sense, since those closest create the strongest trigger. Think of the people in the life of a codependent as rings of influence. The first ring is partner and children, second ring is extended family, third ring is friends, fourth ring is acquaintances and coworkers, and the final ring is "people."

CHAPTER 11

Codependents at Work

Unlike the relationships discussed in the previous chapters, work relationships often are unequal by design. Also, work relationships typically do not carry the emotional weight that more intimate connections do. Sometimes there is an overlap with a coworker who is also your friend, but friendships made at work, more often than not, stay at work.

Your Work Family

Psychologists have studied the psychosocial similarities between the work place and the family. If you were to look at the work environment as a family system of sorts, with the boss or bosses as the parent figures and the coworkers as siblings, you might understand why your job can sometimes trigger intense feelings. In certain ways, your office resembles a family system and may trigger feelings of codependency, abandonment, self-esteem, favoritism, and competition. It's not that workplace players are as important to your identity as your family members, it's that they can unknowingly mimic the behavior of your family members and trigger the same feelings you felt as a child.

The Control Freak: Margaret

Margaret is an excellent example of how work relationships can interface on an unconscious level with unresolved childhood issues. Margaret is the departmental executive assistant in the political science department at a large university. She is the direct assistant to the department chairperson, Dr. Rashid. In addition, she supervises an office staff of six.

Margaret knows what her job description entails, and she gets plenty of positive feedback from Dr. Rashid verbally and on her performance reviews. Margaret knows she is an excellent employee who has an exceptional professional relationship with the department chair.

There are over thirty faculty members in the political science department. Margaret is in a "triage" position with the work that comes into her office—the letters, tests, handouts for classes, and other documents that need to be typed and duplicated for faculty. This work she delegates to her staff.

Several times in an academic semester, Margaret assists Dr. Rashid with the class schedule for the department. She is the only staff trained in this work, and it can be quite time consuming. She is also responsible for all of Dr. Rashid's work—preparing class materials, taking department meeting minutes, scheduling his time, and handling his phone calls. She is indispensable.

Five years ago, when Margaret was promoted to executive assistant, she implemented a system for faculty to submit their work, using a form indicating date submitted and date needed along with short written instructions, copies needed, etc. This form streamlines the triage function and nips in the bud favoritism and "pushiness." It is an excellent idea, but some of the faculty members have trouble adjusting to it. They don't like being controlled by "the secretary." For those few, Margaret is ruthless. She is determined to make them conform. One professor in particular complains on a regular basis to Dr. Rashid about Margaret's disrespectful treatment of him and her "unfair practices." When Dr. Rashid talks to Margaret about it, she threatens to leave if this professor doesn't leave her alone. Dr. Rashid comes to Margaret's defense, but even after that, she is more rigid with that faculty member on his work submissions.

FACT

Overfunctioning at work is often a sign of codependency. When this becomes most obvious is when the overdoing employee is whining about how put upon she feels. Overfunctioning is half of a status-quo relationship in which the other person underfunctions to maintain balance.

Margaret rarely takes her breaks and often works through her lunch hour during busy times. Her friends, administrative assistants in other departments, tell her she's doing too much, but Margaret doesn't want to disappoint Dr. Rashid. Unfortunately, her hours at certain times during the academic year are ridiculously long. Margaret's husband is tired of complaining about it and tired of Margaret canceling things because of work. Margaret knows that his requests are reasonable, and that what her friends tell her is true, but she finds herself making excuses and defending her decisions.

Margaret insists on handling any task, however small, for Dr. Rashid. If she sees Dr. Rashid giving his work to another staff member, she takes over even though other staff could easily handle it. Dr. Rashid is not demanding; in fact, he often insists that Margaret take a summer vacation, and constantly reminds her to stop working so hard.

The Psychologist's Opinion

This work situation illustrates how work relationships can replicate a family system. Dr. Rashid is the father; the others, the faculty and staff, are siblings. Margaret is establishing her place in the work family. She accepts that faculty hold a higher place in the family as defined by the academic system. From what Margaret has seen, she figures they have their own turf issues, with instructors, assistant professors, associate professors, and full professors vying for position within that hierarchy.

Margaret is the top dog in the administrative staff and can easily manage her underlings. But when unruly faculty members bully her, she's apt to react with rage. Finally, she's not above using her strong alliance with Father, Dr. Rashid, to keep the upstarts in their place.

FACT

On the surface, codependents can make excellent employees. They abide by the rules, get their work done, and are reluctant to put themselves first by taking time off even when they are sick.

Overdoing to maintain her position in her work family as "father's favorite" defies all logic. Margaret couldn't be a better assistant, but given the fact that she grew up with an abusive, unpredictable father, she doesn't trust her abilities. She overfunctions, to make sure she has all possibilities covered and then some. Despite his easy manner, even-handedness, and professional integrity, Margaret doesn't quite trust Dr. Rashid. She's just waiting for that moment when she displeases him and he becomes dangerous. This isn't a logical thought; it is a codependent thought.

Margaret is still codependent with her husband who has been even-tempered and understanding for fifteen years. Now with her work codependency, Margaret has created a loyalty conflict. She feels torn because she is codependent with two men, both of whom trigger her unresolved issues with her father. This conflict is self-made, given that Dr. Rashid is not making demands on Margaret—she is.

It may seem like a simple case of a woman who is choosing her work over her marriage, but that is not the whole story. Codependency is at the bottom of it, and Margaret just may end up sacrificing her marriage if she doesn't start working on the real issue.

The Gossip: Pete

Pete works as a dozer operator at a family-owned excavating business. Pete used to date the owner's daughter Stacy in high school and that's when he started working for the family. Even though the high school couple broke up in their senior year, they remained friends. Pete was already like a member of the family, so he was asked to stay on as an employee.

Pete is the only employee at Grove Excavating who is not a member of the family. But he's been working there for fifteen years. He's been offered a management position, but he's not interested.

Stacy Grove, his ex-girlfriend, went on to college, but after a few years working in another state, she returned to the family business as the CFO. The summer after she moved back, the family hosted a huge wedding for Stacy at the family home on their private lake. As always, Pete and his girlfriend, Jenn, were included in the family celebration.

FACT

Codependents gossip because they aren't comfortable with direct communication. Gossip also provides a passive type of power. To be "in the know" even if it's through gossip can feel like a powerful position.

As a chosen family member, Pete has been invited out to the lake, included in holiday dinners, and given holiday and birthday gifts since he was a teenager. He's even gone on a couple of family vacations with the Groves. As the company expands, Mr. Grove hires more workers. Along with Pete, now six other employees are "outsiders."

For the first time, Pete feels awkward. He has breaks and lunch with his coworkers, and for quite a while he fails to mention he isn't a "Grove." Actually, Pete's family has a rather checkered history. His dad died when he was five years old from a drug overdose and his mother is barely making it on Social Security Disability.

Once the guys at work find out that Pete is "just like them," Pete senses they are treating him differently. He wants them to know he has been a member of the Grove family for over twenty years. In Pete's mind, not only has he lost his status at work, but his identity seems in jeopardy. He talks to Jenn about it, but she can't understand why he cares what his coworkers think. Pete can't seem to stop himself from revealing inside information about the Grove family to his buddies at work, things only a family member would know.

Pete knows Stacy's marriage is in trouble, so he mentions it at lunch. His buddies seem very interested, wondering how Pete knows. Pete reiterates that the Grove family confides in him because they see him as a member of their family. The guys ask him all kinds of questions, because Stacy is the CFO and they are worried about their jobs. Pete finds himself reassuring them as if he had inside information in that regard. Almost every day, he is saying something to his coworkers about the family's private affairs. When one of the Grove sons gets arrested for drunk driving, Pete is right there at morning break filling the gang in on the details. If any of the workers have any questions about the family, Pete feels compelled to give up the family secrets.

Stacy and her husband end up working out their problems, but unfortunately it comes to light that Pete has been gossiping to their employees about her private life. Mr. Grove calls Pete in and tells him how disappointed he is. Pete is devastated.

In the next year, Pete is told by one of the brothers that Mr. Grove wants to retire and has talked about restructuring the business. The brother asks if Pete would be interested in becoming a part owner. Feeling vindicated, Pete can't resist telling the others. After all, they'll probably be his employees soon. Hearing Pete's gossip, one of the employees goes to the brother to see if he'll still have a job when they make the changes. The Grove son is furious at Pete's lack of sensitivity in this matter. He talks to his dad about it and they agree they will allow Pete to stay, but they won't ask him to be a partner.

The Psychologist's Opinion

It would appear that Pete has no reason to gossip about the family who has taken him under their wing and treated him as one of the family. On the surface, it looks like betrayal, ingratitude, and lack of empathy, maybe a case of "biting the hand that feeds him." But in all fairness to Pete, there is a reason: Pete's codependency. He finds his identity threatened, and feels desperate to strengthen his affiliation with Mr. Grove even if it means gossiping about the family. By gossiping, he presents himself as an "insider." He is using his coworkers' reactions to reassure himself that he truly is special, truly is a family member. He really has no evil intent, but his codependent feelings with Mr. Grove are so strong that he doesn't think clearly. In the process, he jeopardizes the love and respect of Mr. Grove, who is his father figure, and he risks losing his sense of identity and belonging in the Grove family.

The Pleaser: Jessica

Jessica is a registered nurse and works in a hospital in Phoenix. She is relatively new at her position, and, like all new employees, she is finding her place in the "hospital nursing family." Barb, the charge nurse, is Jessica's direct boss. Unfortunately, Jessica got off on the wrong foot with Barb and is having trouble getting back in her good graces. Above her, the nurse supervisor, Karen, seems to like Jessica, but she is relatively inaccessible, spending most of her time in her office with administrative duties.

Office politics refers to that chaotic jumble of triangles formed by indirect communication at work. The best type of communication is straight-line communication, from me to you. It takes way too much energy to unravel the trail of gossip and innuendo in search of the truth.

After a few weeks, Jessica notices that when Karen comes in, she is carrying a Starbucks cup. She sticks her head into Karen's office and chats about Starbucks coffee—the different flavors and the closest shop to the hospital. Jessica doesn't really like coffee, but she begins to stop before work, pick up the brew of the day, and drop it off on Karen's desk, pretending to be a coffee drinker so she can connect with Karen. Before long, it becomes a little tradition she has developed with the nurse supervisor.

It doesn't take long for Jessica to see that the real power lies with the physicians. Just divorced from an abusive marriage, Jessica knows how to please. She is continuously on the lookout to see what she can do for the doctors, especially the men. She bakes cookies and brings them in, offers to serve them coffee, generally turns herself into a "girl Friday." The other nurses are offended by Jessica's behavior. They've worked hard to achieve a professional standing at the hospital, and see Jessica as undermining that with her subservient need to please.

ALERT

When you hear yourself gossiping at work, ask yourself if you are enabling the person you are complaining about to continue to do the wrong thing by not confronting the transgression directly.

Jessica is adept at picking up on a negative vibe. She grew up in a family where there was no overt conflict. All would appear to be fine, then suddenly her parents would flare up in a vicious fight. In order to protect herself, Jessica learned to pick up on subtle clues to impending disaster. She also discovered that sometimes she could circumvent a fight between her parents by attempting to "put them in a good mood." Jessica developed her pleasing behaviors as a defense against violence. After she married her husband, she fine-tuned her pleasing behaviors in order to keep her husband from flying off the handle and physically abusing her.

FACT

Codependents do not do favors out of altruism. They are trying to get attention and approval in order to compensate for poor self-esteem. Often, favors become a sort of self-protective bargaining chip, for example: "If I do this for you, you will be in a good mood and not get mad at me."

The Psychologist's Opinion

At work, Jessica is a very talented nurse. She has excellent people skills, and is keenly attuned to her patients' needs. This is the upside of her childhood experience. The downside is that she continues to manipulate and control the people in her life who she feels hold power over her. By pleasing them, she assures her own well-being and safety. These codependency traits appear to work on one level, but the price Jessica pays is a continued assault to her self-esteem. She is no longer in an abusive situation, but she continues to use codependency patterns. Jessica isn't authentic; she is trying to manipulate for approval from others. In other words, she is trying to control others, and at the same time she is reinforcing that she is what she does.

The Victim: George

George works as a manager with Spreemart. He's been there for three years. George doesn't enjoy his job because he often feels persecuted and demeaned by the associates he manages, the higher-ups, and even the customers.

George tells his wife Val that he wants to quit the job. He constantly complains about the associates disrespecting him and doing whatever they want. He talks about the Spreemart store as if it were a person. "Spreemart just doesn't understand. I'm only one person trying to manage twelve associates who act like two-year-olds." "Why did they give me all the troublemakers?" "Doesn't Spreemart see I'm the best manager they have?"

George comes home almost every day complaining about how no other employee in the store—not one manager besides him—is treated so unfairly. "John gets more vacation than I do and he hasn't even been there two years." "Everybody knows Judy isn't sick, but she's put one over on Spreemart again. I could be half-dead and they'd expect me to show up." "You'd think I'd get a compliment once in a while, but the only thing Spreemart notices is when I'm a few minutes late." George feels like he walks around Spreemart with a big target on his back.

Val has been here before with George. Throughout his work history, George is satisfied for only a short time before he begins to feel like a victim. Val knows this cycle. The more victimized George feels, the angrier he gets; the angrier he gets, the more inappropriate his behavior becomes; the more his inappropriate behavior is pointed out to him, the more victimized he feels . . . .

Val tries to reason with him because she knows George has been known to blow up and walk off the job. Val works a demanding job as well as caring for the kids and maintaining the house. Like many working families, George and Val need two incomes. Val knows that when George feels like a victim, he can become exceedingly unreasonable, thinking of nothing but vindicating himself. By now she knows there will never be a job where George feels valued and treated respectfully, because this is all part of his codependency.

FACT

Sexual abuse leaves a scar at the deepest level. It is a violation of a body boundary. A child can't control much, but he is supposed to have control over his own body. Sexual abuse can shatter identity, resulting in intense codependency patterns.

George was sexually abused by his parish priest when he was an altar boy. Val knows about this because George told her early in their marriage when he wanted to leave the church. But she doesn't have the knowledge necessary to connect George's trauma with his behavior on his jobs.

The Psychologist's Opinion

George thinks he was the only kid abused, singled out from the others, abused and forced to go on like nothing ever happened. George has a huge wound that begins to fester each time he experiences victim feelings. "Spreemart," like "the Church," is the very powerful entity that can't see, that turns a blind eye to a grave injustice imposed on an innocent boy who did nothing wrong. No wonder the rage boils up, and George wants to run away.

Val can't be faulted for not making the connection between the damage inflicted in George's past and his current difficulties. But maybe she's enabled him to repeatedly blow up and walk out on jobs by not holding him accountable for jeopardizing the family's livelihood.

More importantly, it is George who must make the connection. Until he understands why he feels and reacts the way he does, he will continue to find himself in the victim role, reacting badly and trying to justify his behavior when he doesn't understand it himself. As with other males who are codependent, George shows characteristics of narcissism: "negative" specialness, lack of empathy, and the belief that the world turns on his wishes. When he feels powerless and humiliated, he can react quite aggressively.

Letter to the Psychologist

The following letter is taken from Here-to-Listen.com and helps explain the subtle signs of codependency.

Dear Doctor,

I am the president of my union, and my friend and I served together on the collective bargaining team at our company. We negotiated a contract with the administration through the human resources department. We got to know the members of the other side quite well, and I thought there was mutual respect at the table.

Two months ago, an administrative position came open in the human resources department. My friend knew I was applying and even asked me if I minded if she applied for the same position. Quite frankly, I didn't think she had a prayer of getting the job over me, and she is my friend, so I said go ahead. Let me add that I know what constitutes fair hiring practices, having served as the union president for four years. Clearly I am more qualified and better educated, have more work experience and more experience in human resources. We are both women.

Last week she called and told me she got the job. I was shocked and said so. She said she thought I would get the job and also was surprised. I wasn't mad at her or anything, but I felt really bad. When the director called to tell me the job had gone to Portia, I expressed my dissatisfaction, reiterating that

I was more qualified. And do you know what he said? "Well, it's better than a sharp stick in the eye."

Two days ago I learned Portia is having an affair with the director of human resources. I'm so mad, I could spit. What should I do?

Carissa

Dear Carissa,

First of all, don't be so quick to respond with approval when a friend asks if you would mind . . . think it over, consider all the options, and don't hesitate to be honest if you do mind. This knee-jerk approval suggests codependency.

You are in no way responsible for your friend's behavior, and this is quite a betrayal. It doesn't really matter what the sordid details are. Portia kept the affair from you because she knew it was wrong. And I guess she really doesn't care about you the way you care about her. This is a sign of a codependent friendship. Healthy friendships are based on honesty and a balance of mutual needs and strengths.

This is a sticky situation. If you weren't on the bargaining team with Portia, you might leave the whole sordid situation behind, check her off your list of friends, and report the director for unethical behavior. But the membership voted for you and Portia to represent them with management. You both know it is not ethical for Portia to have an affair with somebody on the management side of contract negotiations. Frankly, this director sounds like a slick operator. For him to be so oblivious of wrongdoing and then so contemptuous when he called you about giving Portia the job, he's a predator—he's done this before.

A sexual relationship with a member of the opposing team is never okay, nor is it appropriate with a prospective hire. There's no doubt you can make a solid case against this director. He used his power to snag Portia into this situation. If you file a grievance, he'll likely be fired. You know there will be fallout, so prepare yourself for a fight.

As the union president, see if you can protect the identity of Portia. I can imagine you don't feel much sympathy for her, but if you consider the abuse of power of the director, Portia is a victim too. If you try to seek revenge, or focus on how you can hurt Portia, you will be bringing the codependency full circle. First, you are more invested in her than she is in you. Second, you are reluctant to report the director for fear of getting Portia in trouble, and if you try to punish her, you will have the third codependency strike against you (anger and revenge).

CHAPTER 12

Social Codependency

The term *social codependency* is used in this chapter to describe a perceived sense of disapproval created by codependent thoughts of being judged. The disapproval does not come from a particular person or group of people. Listen to your self-talk and notice if you say something like, "People will think I'm . . . ." Who? Who is thinking this? If you don't have a specific answer, this is your cue that you are projecting your doubts about your self-worth onto the infamous "other people."

Low Self-Esteem

The feeling that people are judging you is a reflection of your diminished self-esteem. Every time you use negative self-talk, it's like ripping the bandage off a wound. Of course the wound won't heal. And if that isn't self-defeating enough, try pouring a little salt on the wound by calling yourself names like "stupid" and "dumb." Try to notice how often you say, "This probably sounds stupid, but . . . ." or "I know this is dumb but . . . ." or "I know I'm stupid for thinking this, but . . . ."

FACT

One of the ways you can damage your self-esteem is to compare your inside to someone else's outside. Usually, the only reason you're comparing is to diminish yourself. As in, "Nobody else in the office seems to have trouble understanding the change." Interpretation: "I'm the only dumb one here." But in reality, how do you know what everybody else is thinking?

Negative self-talk is like an alternate reality, a parallel universe inside your head that you may not be aware of. As you know, self-esteem is the way in which you perceive yourself. Everybody in your world can think you're just swell, and it doesn't quiet that self-doubting demon in your head. That demon can take in positive messages and transform them into something negative, something that eats away at your self-esteem.

Sandy's Damaged Self-Esteem

Sandy is a successful wife and mother. She enjoys keeping the family happy, volunteering for causes she believes in, and working a few hours a week at her children's school.

Sandy is the type of person whom people gravitate toward. She is outgoing, friendly, and even-keeled. To all outside appearances, she is a happy, healthy, young woman with a beautiful life. However, Sandy has a big hole in her self-esteem. When she was growing up, she was constantly criticized by her dad. All through childhood, college, and to the present time, her father has been the demon inside her head, telling her about her shortcomings and creating a feeling of inferiority in Sandy. When Sandy married Jim, her dad began to criticize him, making snide comments about his work, his character, and his faithfulness. He always has something to say about Sandy's kids, finding fault and picking out flaws. He never misses an opportunity to tell Sandy she is wasting her life. He continues to comment on her parenting, her clothes, her weight, money-management, everything!

Through therapy Sandy begins to see how she has been carrying her critical parent around in her head. Everything she experiences in life is filtered through the judgments of her father. She begins to notice how tentative her speech is, not only with her dad, but with her husband and everybody else.

She realizes how often she uses these tentative, codependent phrases like: "Now, don't get mad, but . . . ."; "This may not sound like much to you, but . . . ."; "You probably don't agree, but . . . ."; "This may sound strange to you, but . . . ." She notices how she deflects compliments with phrases like: "Oh, this is old thing . . . ."; "It was nothing . . . ."; "Anybody would have done the same . . . ." She is startled to recognize that she never has just said "Thank you." To Sandy, accepting compliments feels like boasting.

Sandy also notices that she is continuously explaining herself in an attempt to hide her inaccurate perceptions of herself as stupid. She makes excuses about her appearance constantly, focuses obsessively on her weight, and is extremely anxious when meeting new people and speaking in a group.

The Psychologist's Opinion

Language can be a powerful clue to the presence of codependency. When you begin your own work on codependency, notice your words, phrasing, and tone. Notice your self-talk and see if you can hear a parent or other critical voice in your head, a voice you have now adopted as your own.

Sandy doesn't think much of herself, and she projects this self-doubt onto others. She often feels she isn't appreciated, isn't liked, or isn't as accomplished as others. No matter how much her husband reassures her, she doesn't believe him. Even her children find themselves trying to boost mom's self-esteem. And it isn't the job of a child to provide this type of support to a parent.

Sandy may seem content on the outside, but inside she is constantly degrading herself. The voice of her father is now her own self-deprecating voice reinforcing her inferior status. No matter what the outside world is saying to her, Sandy's codependency is short-circuiting the positive. Codependency is interfering with her ability to have healthy, trusting, secure relationships with others. She worries about pleasing everyone, even people she doesn't particularly like. She spends a lot of time processing what people say to her to see if she can uncover proof that they don't think much of her. She filters everything through her damaged self-esteem.

ESSENTIAL

People with high confidence spend time thinking about what they want in a partner ahead of time. People with low confidence wait for somebody to come into their world and then react. Often, if a person likes them, they feel compelled to like that person back.

Jewel's Fear of Judgment

Remember when you were in high school and you showed up to your Algebra class without your homework done? Do you remember how panicked you felt when your teacher called on you to come up to the board with one of those unfinished problems? That's how Jewel feels most of the time.

When Jewel's oldest daughter starts school, Jewel is terrified of the teacher. She is sure that the teacher will blame her for any problems Courtney has. After all, teachers are trained; she will see that Jewel isn't a good mother. When it comes time for the first parent-teacher conference, Jewel asks her husband, Gordy, if he will go. Gordy is happy to go to the conference, but he expects Jewel to go too. Jewel tries to make an excuse, but she knows she should go. After all, she's Courtney's mother.

As soon as the teacher starts the conference, Jewel jumps in with an explanation of what a challenge Courtney has been as a youngster, how concerned she is about Courtney's progress, and that she is a hands-on mother who welcomes input from the teacher. That couldn't be further from the truth, and Gordy is confused, but he keeps his mouth shut. The teacher assures Jewel that their daughter is doing just fine. The teacher has no issues with Courtney's behavior or learning. Jewel leaves the conference feeling relieved. She has received the stamp of approval for her good parenting from a stranger. Something she logically already knows, but doesn't trust.

ALERT

If you assume codependents are meek and amenable all the time, think again. A codependent is worried about how others perceive him, so he may pretend to be compliant and thoughtful while at the same time plotting revenge for perceived insults. It's a very dishonest situation. It's almost impossible to have an authentic relationship with a codependent.

Each day Jewel picks out Courtney's clothes. She is worried that Courtney will wear the wrong thing and the teacher will wonder, "What was her mother thinking?" Jewel likes to send small gifts to school for her daughter's teacher and doesn't consider how all the gift-giving might impact Courtney; she is only thinking about herself and whether or not she is getting an A from the teacher.

The Psychologist's Opinion

It's hard to be the spouse or child of somebody like Jewel whose level of anxiety is always higher than most. The slightest misunderstanding or perceived judgment throws her into a funk, and sometimes into a deep depression. She is trying to be perfect, and because of it, she's her own worst critic. The compassion that she easily gives to others, she feels unworthy of.

Reassurances from Gordy about what a great person she is and how much he loves her fall on deaf ears. Gordy is wearing himself out trying to be the ego mirror for Jewel. He is finding himself increasingly more impatient and irritated with Jewel because she is so needy and wants so much from him, but never really accepts it.

Even the children are affected because their mother asks them constantly if she looks okay, or if the meal is good, or if they are mad at her. Her codependency is becoming a burden for the whole family.

Diane's Fear of Rejection

In high school, Diane had a hard time fitting in. She never was able to find her place with any group of friends. As an adult Diane finally is a part of a group. She is well-liked by her coworkers. Still, Diane feels some of that old dread about being rejected by others. "If they only knew . . . ."

Because of her old fears, Diane is continuously weighing what she talks about with her friends at work. With her husband's income, Diane is able to dine out frequently, go on vacations, and buy things for herself. She knows others at work are not as fortunate, and she doesn't want to appear "snobby" or possibly be rejected because others feel she's acting "too good for them." She makes a conscious effort not to talk about things she feels may put off her coworkers.

ALERT

Mind-reading is a dangerous activity. The closer the relationship, the more dangerous it becomes. To assume you know how your partner feels or what he is thinking and then respond to him based on that guess diminishes him and makes you the pretentious expert on his inner experience.

Remember, this is all in Diane's codependent head. She has no idea whether or not others share her interests or opinions, or whether they are thinking she's a snob. In fact, they haven't given any hint of this. Diane inadvertently is distancing herself from people who might relate to her because she is acting out of her codependency and the fear of being rejected. Diane is not being authentic. She's arbitrarily holding back parts of herself. Ironically, she is pushing away the people she wants to be close to with her dishonesty.

Diane is doing the same thing with the group of friends she meets for lunch every few weeks. She is trying to assimilate into this group just as she does at work. Because this group enjoys literature, Diane wants to be sure that she catches the titles of the books they talk about so she can read them, or read a critique of them, for discussion. If they criticize a book and Diane has read it and thinks it is fabulous, she keeps her mouth shut. Again, even though the criteria is different with her two social groups, Diane is filtering her authentic self to make sure she fits others' expectations, thereby hiding herself in the process. No wonder Diane is distracted. She is busy trying to decide which Diane she needs to be at any given time.

FACT

"Be yourself; everyone else is already taken." —Oscar Wilde

The Psychologist's Opinion

Diane is like a chameleon, changing colors as she walks from situation to situation. She's been doing it for such a long time, she doesn't really know what color she is. The self-doubt that comes from continuously remolding herself to fit the expectations of others has her anxious and distracted a lot of the time. Instead of just letting her guard down and figuring out who she is, she's petrified somebody won't like her. Logically, she knows it's okay if somebody doesn't like her, and it's unreasonable to think everybody would. But Diane isn't always operating from a logical vantage point. Emotionally, she's gripped by something she isn't yet aware of.

Diane's codependency stems from abandonment issues. When Diane was an infant, she was put up for adoption. Her first placement didn't work out, and she was returned to foster care. She was a toddler by the time she found her permanent home, but by that time she had already experienced a deep fear of rejection and abandonment. Diane was too young to have visual memories, but this did not keep her from experiencing this trauma. Later, in therapy, she will discover her irrational codependency thoughts are based on something she did not directly remember from long ago.

Barb's Deferring to Others' Needs and Desires

A codependent can seem so flexible and easygoing on the surface, right up to the moment they explode in a fit of rage. This is the case with Barbara. She and Jim decide to buy a larger house when their second daughter is born. Barb agrees they need a third bedroom and another bath and a finished basement for Jim's man cave and the girls' play area.

Barb has been grappling with codependency her whole life and finds the process of finding a new house excruciating. There are so many decisions to be made, she feels overwhelmed with confusion and anxiety. Finally defeated, she follows her usual pattern; she throws up her hands and turns everything over to Jim. Jim would like Barb's input, but every time he asks her about something, she says she doesn't care.

Jim finds the family a house, and with Barb's blessing the family moves. They realize the house isn't perfect, but it's within their budget, and they are able to get most of what they want. For the extras, Jim has set aside money to finish the basement or hire it to be done. Jim asks Barb several times if less than two baths will work, and she assures him they can add a bath as the girls get older.

ALERT

"Anger . . . it's a paralyzing emotion . . . you can't get anything done. People sort of think it's an interesting, passionate, and igniting feeling— I don't think it's any of that—it's helpless . . . it's absence of control— and I need all of my skills, all of the control, all of my powers . . . and anger doesn't provide any of that—I have no use for it whatsoever." —Toni Morrison (CBS radio, September 15, 1987)

As she often does, Barb did not express her needs during the house hunting process. Every time Jim came to her with a decision about the house, she would say she really didn't care. Now she is complaining about the yard, the bathroom, and the mess of the basement remodel. Jim is in a real Catch-22. He would have loved to have her help in this important decision, but she refused to participate. Now, after they've moved in, Barb feels she is the victim of Jim's selfish choices. In her many complaints, Jim feels she's telling him he's incompetent in not figuring out what is important to her.

This is what it's like to be in a relationship with a codependent. Jim never really knows what Barb is thinking or feeling. He asks and asks and gets the same noncommittal response. He knows there will be repercussions, but what is he to do? He does his best to honor Barb's proclaimed feelings, but he just can't win because Barb isn't being honest. Barb, of course, is prone to seeing herself as a victim, so five years later she's still angry about the bathroom.

The Psychologist's Opinion

Like most codependents, Barb wants to control everything, but she will gratefully shift responsibility onto Jim. If there are any mistakes to be made, he can make them.

She simply refuses to be the equal partner Jim needs. She loves being seen as the understanding, self-sacrificing wife and mother who puts her family's needs first. But there's a dark side. Barb easily shifts into the victim role when her needs aren't met (even though she never makes her needs known), and then explodes in a fit of rage with no warning.

By pretending to be agreeable with no expectations of her own, Barb maintains her perfect status. But look how selfish her husband is and how disrespectful her children are? How could they treat her so badly when she's such a good person? Being in a relationship with Barb is like living with an alien: Everything is going great and all of a sudden the monster pops out.

Brook's Fear of the Spotlight

Codependents know at some level they are not perfect. But they lack the ego strength to accept their imperfections and still be okay. The overwhelming need to believe they are a good person, and the lack of an internal thermostat to gauge their worth, leaves the codependent with a fear of being seen too closely or too critically by others. Brook is one of these people.

Brook often has an inflated sense of how much attention others are giving her. The feeling of being watched, or evaluated, or judged by others also comes into play on special occasions like showers, receptions, receiving a gift, or being part of a group where she is expected to speak. This fear has kept Brook from participating in social events and group activities like biking or yoga where she feels everyone is looking at her. Since Brook's self-esteem is low, she automatically believes others are making negative judgments about her merely by glancing her way.

Brook would love to earn a degree in computer science, but she is afraid of the classes, afraid to be tested and evaluated, afraid her peers will be smarter, afraid she won't be good at it. She's so terrified of being called upon in class and panicky about being wrong or sounding dumb, or sweating, or misspeaking, she has yet to register for a single class. Brook is paralyzed by her codependency.

The Psychologist's Opinion

Brook's irrational fear of being scrutinized by others, sure that she will come up short, keeps her stuck in a life full of anxiety and fear. This is one of those areas where codependency overlaps with the *DSM* diagnosis of social anxiety or social phobia. This phenomenon, sometimes referred to as "spotlight" phobia, also creates high anxiety and worry about what people might think. Even simple questions like "How's your summer going," or "Did you watch the game yesterday?" can seem intrusive.

The codependent who fears attention will feel anxiety at an off-handed comment or question because it seems as if the person asking is invading the personal private space inside the codependent's head. Many times the codependent *is* having private thoughts in his head. Usually ruminating and judging himself to make sure he's acceptable. With a parallel universe of negative thoughts going on, and the pretense of being cool and collected, it is no wonder the codependent is wary of being put on the spot.

Brook doesn't have many friends, and probably won't advance in her career because she can't speak at meetings or give a critical opinion. As Brook works on her codependency, it would be helpful for her to include behavioral techniques. For example, she could make a list of things she's afraid of, things that actually affect her ability to have the life she wants. She would start with the least threatening and check off each situation as she conquers her fear. The trick is to stay in the stressful situation through the anxiety instead of shying away never to conquer the fear.

Candy's Lost Self

This continuous battle between the codependent person inside your head and the person you wish to project to the outside world results in a kind of disconnect that prevents you from finding your true identity. When the identity is congruous—that is, it matches all the way through the layers of your psyche—you feel confident in who you are. There is very little internal struggle, and not much conflict going on in your head. You can settle in comfortably with yourself.

FACT

"The soul, fortunately, has an interpreter—often an unconscious, but still a faithful interpreter—in the eye."—Charlotte Bronte, *Jane Eyre*

Candy is never at peace. She has often described her brain as a plate full of spaghetti with a lot of loose ends. Candy doesn't really know who she is. She worries constantly that someone will ask her opinion or expect her to discuss something. It's obvious from Candy's self-talk that she hasn't reached the integration needed for a solid identity. Over the years, she has adapted to this continuous mismatch between her inner thoughts and what is happening on her outside.

In Candy's mind, it's just how she is. Candy's sense of humor helps her deal with her insecurity. She admits she has identity confusion and once said of exploring her mind, "Don't make me go in there alone." If you are able to see any humor in your codependency, you are closer to acknowledging imperfections.

If we did go inside Candy's mind it would sound something like this. *I wonder if she meant I should have called? I don't think so, I never call if I'm planning to go, she knows that, but this was a special occasion. What is the expectation in this case, what would the normal thing be to do, should I ask her if she's offended? Well, if I do that, she's going to think there's a reason she should be offended. I don't think it's necessary to talk to her about it, why make a big deal out of nothing. But if she is offended, how am I going to know? She had a strange look on her face when I came in. Kinda like she was mad at me. Why would she be mad at me? I better say something. I can't stand it if she's mad and doesn't tell me. . . .*

The Psychologist's Opinion

Codependents can be so programmed to this type of ruminative thinking that they come to except it as normal. They often have long dialogues in their head where they play the role of all those involved. Candy has many long conversations about difficult issues with her partner where she plays both herself and her partner. She thinks she knows how he will respond, but she's really mind reading. When she's done with this "in her head" conversation, she's done, and she may even make a decision based on the conversation, but she's never actually said a word to her partner. If a codependent stays in the safety of her own mind and doesn't actually engage in a real conversation, she never risks rejection or judgment or uncomfortable questions.

If Candy is not battling with herself about how a good mother acts, how a good employee behaves, what decisions a good wife makes, she is left only with her authentic self. Now, who is she?

How does Candy really feel about politics, religion, world events, the neighbor's divorce, or the conflict at work? If Candy isn't reacting from social codependency, how does she find her authentic self? Perhaps this is what is meant by a "midlife crisis," that confusing time in your life where you begin a journey inward. Or maybe you continue to search for your identity out there, in other people, or in how you are perceived, by buying an expensive sports car, getting a facelift, or divorcing your spouse.

Letter to the Psychologist

The following letter is taken from Here-to-Listen.com and helps explain the duplicity of codependents.

Dear Doctor,

I've been married for thirty-two years. I just realized my wife is a codependent. All our friends think my wife is easygoing and flexible. Man, do they have it wrong! My wife always feels like she is a victim. It's raining because she has the day off. All the people at church are hypocrites. She's the only one who does anything around the house. If I cared about her, I'd know she had a headache and offer to help out. It's too hot, it's too cold, and so on.

Anyway, here's the reason I think I have to divorce her. She can't let anything go, and she always rewrites history so that I'm terrible and she's the poor victim. I could give you a million examples, but this is the pattern. We have a decision to make, or a conflict to resolve, and she never says how she really feels. She says yes to things or volunteers to do something, and I think everything is fine, and then later she's pissed that I've taken advantage of her.

Here's the straw that broke the camel's back. A few days ago, we were talking about money and she says she gave me all her inheritance money from her father to pay off some bills. (I never have had bills that needed paying off that weren't joint.) For thirty years, she's been feeling like I've victimized her by taking her money. When I questioned her, she couldn't remember what the bills were. I remember using some of her inheritance to help build a garage on our home. She willingly volunteered to contribute to that. She got all "her" money back when we sold the house and bought another one because, of course, she shares fifty/fifty in the equity in our home.

I'm really feeling despair at this point. To be unable to resolve any conflicts in over thirty years? Some years ago I gave up trying to explain to her what I saw happening. She can't respond with anything but blame and defensiveness. The way I've dealt with this is I tell myself she's got a problem, I didn't do anything wrong, and I let it go. I'm sick of her inability to communicate and resolve a conflict. And I'm sick of always being the bad guy.

Pat

Dear Pat,

It does look like you and your wife are in a codependency pattern of long standing. After thirty-two years of unresolved conflict, my guess is that you no longer have an intimate relationship. I don't mean sex, I mean trust that the other has your best interests at heart, and is interested and capable of doing whatever it takes to have a healthy relationship.

Neither one of you knows how to fix this, so I also assume you do the same dance every time with the same bow at the end, but no resolution. Educate yourself and get to couples' therapy.

CHAPTER 13

Eliminating Codependent Communication

If you make a recording of you and your spouse trying to resolve a conflict, you will find that codependency is likely to reveal itself in your communication. In this section you will develop communication skills and a vocabulary to move from codependency to interdependency. It's like learning a new language. You weren't taught these skills in school, and it's unlikely that you learned them in your family or with your friends. As you take responsibility for how you communicate, you are building a bridge from your authentic self in the pursuit of a real connection with someone else.

Focus on the "I"

An essential component of good communication is the "I" message. This important tool was part of communication training for U.S. diplomats formulated over fifty years ago by the U.S. government. The "I" message is currently outlined in some detail at the U.S. Department of State website. Today the "I" message is a fundamental skill learned in couples' therapy, and it is within this context that you will learn about this transformational tool.

The Internal Shift

Using an "I" message actually restructures your thinking and compels you to do some self-reflection before you speak. Since language shapes reality, every time you say "I" instead of "you" in conflict resolution, you actually shift your internal reality. You are forced to process and identify how you feel and how you perceive things before you even open your mouth to discuss an issue. Think about how easy and automatic it is to start a discussion with "You do this, you do that . . . ." What is reflected in this type of language? You see yourself as a victim, and you want someone else to atone.

The External Shift

In couples' therapy, the therapist begins communication skills training with the introduction of the "I" message. The focus is on the external—that is, what is an "I" message, and how do you use it in intimate communication and conflict resolution? This is a behavioral intervention. Many times, it is more effective to start with the behavior change and work toward the cognitive and emotional shifts that follow.

ALERT

When you attend couples' therapy, it is for you to change, not your partner. Your partner is responsible for his own changes. Most couples come to their first session armed and ready to fire at their partner. To prepare for your first session, spend time thinking about how you contribute to the problems in your relationship.

How many times have you started a discussion with "You always . . . ." or "You should have . . . "? Using "you" statements means that you are blaming the other person for your experience. You are presenting yourself as a victim, and are paving the way for your partner to defend or explain herself. It's hard to believe that beginning a discussion with an "I" statement can have such a profound influence on how the conversation proceeds. But it can. It's as simple and as challenging as that. Substitute "I" as the first word of a lead-in sentence and experience the change.

The "I" Message Formula

The "I" message has three components: your feelings, a description of what created your feelings, and a reason why you feel this way. It looks like this: "I feel _____ (a feeling, not a thought) when you _____ (a nonjudgmental description of behavior) because _____ (reason why you feel the way you do). It looks like this when you fill in the blanks: "I feel angry when you yell at me to turn off the radio because the music really relaxes me."

Here are some examples of the "I" message that can be used in conflict resolution:

- I feel sad when you won't talk to me because when I was little, my mom gave me the silent treatment and I felt so alone.
- I feel angry when you say I'm lazy because I'm not lazy; I just do things at my own pace.
- I feel rejected when you laugh at me because my dad made fun of me all the time and it hurt.
- I feel hopeless when you promise to stop drinking and I find empty liquor bottles because I'm afraid you're an alcoholic and if you won't admit it, you'll never get better.
- I feel frustrated when you answer me with defensiveness because I think we're growing apart and that we just can't talk.

The examples here show that giving an "I" message requires you to own your own feelings and the reasons for them and to share this with your partner in a nonblaming way. Look at the following example in comparison to the one listed preivously and see if you can identify why it is not an accurate "I" statement. Notice that the statement is corrected step by step until it fits the formula.

1. "I feel you are not listening to me because you have your eyes on that stupid football game because you're a selfish jerk and that's all you really care about."
2. "I feel unimportant* because you have your eyes on that stupid football game because you're a selfish jerk and that's all you really care about."
3. "I feel unimportant* because you aren't looking at me when I talk* because you're a selfish jerk and that game is all you really care about."
4. "I feel unimportant because you aren't looking at me when I talk because I need that direct eye contact to feel listened to." ***

In conflict resolution, the pronoun "I" denotes a sharing of yourself. The pronoun "you" denotes blame. If communication were represented by arrows, an arrow would originate inside the speaker with the "I" message. Conversely, the arrow would originate on the outside of the speaker with a "you" statement. "You" statement arrows may be immediately deflected by the recipient, and hope for resolution of a conflict may end right there, in the first few words.

Conflict Resolution—Whose Problem Is It?

Many couples get along well until it's time to resolve their differences. It is unreasonable to expect that each spouse will see an issue exactly the same. Conflict is not the enemy as many believe. Conflict is a normal part of any relationship. When a couple avoids conflict or simply argues until they can't argue anymore, the conflict becomes the monster in the shadows, ready to pop out at the next opportunity.

The beauty of healthy communication is that each person values and respects the other's opinion (no matter how different it is), accepts the other's right to think and feel as he or she does, and then begins working toward a compromise.

John hates it when Mary leaves makeup and beauty products on the bathroom counter. He has asked her to put her stuff away, and each time she explains in great detail why she didn't: she was in a hurry, she forgot, etc. Mary promises to be more aware, but her products are still left out most of the time.

Every time John finds her bottles and tubes on the bathroom counter, he seethes inside. He has given up trying to get his wife to change, but whenever they have a disagreement about anything, John ends up telling her how inconsiderate she is because she refuses to put her stuff away when she knows how much it bothers him.

Whose problem is it? Maybe most people would say it is Mary's problem because she leaves her stuff out. But what if Mary had a husband who didn't care if she left her products on the counter? There wouldn't be a problem, would there?

ALERT

Where in your life is it possible for you to always get what you expect, want, and need? Nowhere. And yet many people still believe this is possible in a marriage. It is wiser to accept that you might get what you want most of the time, and the rest must be negotiated for. Develop the art of negotiation; learn to compromise.

When a couple comes to therapy, the first thing each of them says is how the other is the problem. It just makes sense that if a husband brings up a problem, he's the one with the problem. The therapist knows this, but she has to teach this to her clients. If you asked John, he'd say the problem is Mary. And Mary could very well agree with him, especially since she's codependent.

If you don't even know where (or with whom) to start, how can you resolve a conflict? It's like trying to play a football game when you can't figure out which team is kicking off. Once you determine who is kicking off, it is possible to proceed down the field. John kicks off with his problem about the bathroom counter.

Taking Responsibility for Your Feelings

In his book, *Getting the Love You Want*, Harville Hendrix describes a way of communicating that encourages couples to take responsibility for their own feelings of dissatisfaction as a start toward better conflict resolution.

The transcript of John and Mary's therapy session begins with John establishing he has a problem (taking responsibility for the problem and his feelings about the problem). Then he will use an "I" message to impart his feelings to Mary (using the "I" message). Once she has received his message accurately, John will propose to Mary three different options for things she could do to help him with his problem (presenting options to resolve the conflict). Then Mary will agree willingly to one, two, or all three options, or she will not agree.

The communication session with the therapist removes the main obstacles that typically occur when couples try to resolve a conflict: The therapist intentionally asks the couple to provide a simple, yet real, conflict so they can begin slowly and quickly *feel* what a successful conflict resolution is like. These communication tools work on even the most complicated conflicts, and they work every time. Over time, they will work effortlessly for Mary and John, melting away all the animosity accumulated from years of frustration. Conflicts come up often in a relationship, so smoothly moving through them is continuously re-enforcing the new behavior. The couple is invested in communicating well because there is such an immediate pay off for both of them.

Therapist: "John, you have a problem with the bathroom counter; would you like to start off with an 'I' message?"

John (turning toward Mary and with the therapist's guidance): "I feel dismissed and hurt when you leave stuff on the counter because I can be a neat freak and it just sets off my anxiety when I have to deal with clutter first thing in the morning."

Therapist: "Mary, don't defend or explain yourself. Simply mirror back to John what you heard him say."

Mary (turning to John and with the therapist's guidance): "You feel hurt when I leave my stuff out because it makes you anxious."

Therapist: "Is that accurate, John?"

John: "Pretty much, but I also feel dismissed, like I'm not important. And I guess I also want Mary to acknowledge that I admitted I can be a bit obsessive."

Therapist: "Mary?"

Mary (looking at John): "You feel hurt and you feel unimportant when I leave my stuff out. I did notice you said you can be a neat freak. I appreciate that."

ALERT

When you misbehaved as a kid, your parent might have responded with, "Why did you do that?" Did your parent want to know the reason for your action, or was she really saying "Don't do that"? The word *why* in conflict resolution can be a powerful negative trigger from childhood and almost always throws up a defense. Use phrases like "Help me understand," "I'm confused about that," "I'm not sure what you mean."

Therapist: "Message received, John?"

John: "Yes."

Therapist: "Now John, since this is your problem, would you like to ask Mary for some help with it?"

John (smiling): "Yes."

Therapist: "I've explained that couples aren't obligated to give their partners anything, right? But if you want to have a healthy relationship, each of you must be willing to give to the other. Otherwise, you won't feel loved.

A, B, or C

Therapist: "John, you're responsible for solving your own problem, but let's say you have a loving partner who is willing to help you with it. I would like you to ask Mary if she might consider giving you, as a gift, any of the three requests you are now going to make. Please make each request in this form: 'A, Would you be willing to . . . ?' (and give your first request); 'B, Would you be willing to . . . ?' (and give your next request); and 'C, Would you be willing to . . . ?' (and give your third request)."

John: "I don't have to ask for three things. If she'd just put her stuff away, that would solve the problem."

Therapist: "Well, Mary might agree to do that, and that could be one of your requests. But it helps push you off your one-dimensional position and moves you toward compromise if you could think outside the box here and figure out what other options might work."

John: "Okay. (Smiling, turns toward Mary.) Would you be willing to put your stuff away?"

Therapist: "Okay, that's request A. Now, B?"

John: "B, would you be willing . . . to . . . use the other bathroom just on the mornings I have an early schedule?"

Therapist: "C?"

John: "C, would you be willing to . . . (turning toward therapist) I can't think of a C."

Therapist: "Take your time. Think outside the box."

John (pauses, thinks): "Okay, I've got one. C, we have that big drawer across the whole front of the vanity where we keep bathroom stuff. If we empty out the top drawer of the vanity, would you just open the drawer and sweep all your stuff in there when you're done in the bathroom?"

Therapist: "Okay, good. Mary, please repeat the requests back to John so he is sure you received his requests accurately. A?"

Mary: "A, will I put my stuff away after I use it; B, will I use the other bathroom sometimes; C, we clean out the stuff from the big vanity drawer, and will I just sweep my stuff into it when I'm done."

Therapist: "Is that accurate, John?"

John: "Pretty much. I guess it's not very reasonable to expect her to use the other bathroom."

Therapist: "You have a right to ask for whatever you think will help. It's up to Mary to agree or not agree. Now, Mary, you can agree to none of the requests, one, two, or all three. Go ahead."

Mary: "Well, I really don't want to move my stuff around to another bathroom. That's my least favorite request. I can't agree to B. I thought I was willing to do A, but I've agreed in the past, and I haven't done it. But I'm thinking if that drawer were empty, I could just make one sweep. I wouldn't have to take the time to put everything in its place. I could do that. I can do C. (Turns to John.) Are you sure you want to move that stuff? Where would you put it?"

Therapist: "John is the one who suggested it, Mary. Why would you try to talk him out of it when you two have just reached a resolution? It could be your codependency coming out. You're not used to directly saying no to John, are you feeling guilty?"

Mary (shrugging her shoulders): "Probably. I don't want to put him out. Okay. I'll do C."

Therapist: "John, anything you want to say to Mary?"

John: "Not really."

Therapist: "She did just give you a gift."

John: "Oh. Thanks."

Therapist: "Very good job, both of you. We've used a cognitive/behavioral approach this morning in resolving John's problem about the bathroom counter. You two have used new communication skills, which probably seem very wooden right now. With practice, you'll incorporate this into your own style of talking and eventually it will be second nature."

Mary: "Are we supposed to remember all of this?"

Therapist: "Well, that would be a tall order. No. I'll give you a handout to take with you and you'll practice the "I" message and this conflict resolution exercise every day for half an hour. It'll get easier."

Therapist: "We've started at a behavioral level and I'm considering this issue solved. To summarize, John, you agreed to clean your stuff from the top drawer of the vanity. Can you get the drawer cleaned out by this evening?"

John: "Yes."

Therapist: "Great. Mary, starting tomorrow morning you've agreed to sweep your cosmetics and other stuff off the counter before you leave the bathroom, correct?"

Mary: "Yes."

Therapist: "Each time you two have a conflict resolution, I'd like you to summarize your agreement as I just did. Your goal is to be absolutely clear with one another. Now tomorrow morning you'll have an opportunity to test your plan. Then we can talk about how it went in our next session. Again, good job."

Processing the Conflict Resolution Model

This model looks pretty straightforward on paper. That's because it is a behavioral intervention. Communication training, assertiveness training, empathy training—all of these skill-building formulas focus on behavior.

ESSENTIAL

If you make a graph of the recorded voices of a couple in therapy and Line A shows activity of 80 percent and Line B shows 20 percent activity, this recording identifies another communication problem, usually of long standing. One partner talks too much and the other talks too little. Line A gets frustrated and talks more, and Line B gets frustrated and stops listening.

When a relationship therapist begins with a new couple, he asks them to identify their issues. Communication is typically number one on the list. If you can't talk to one another, you cannot solve problems in your relationship. An important role for the therapist is to determine the layers of dysfunction. It is rare indeed if a couple knows how to talk to one another when they come in for therapy. Because of this, communication skills training is layer one. To prioritize therapy in any other way is like pushing a couple off a boat into the ocean without life jackets or swimming lessons.

Once the couple can successfully manage conflict resolution, their new skills become an umbrella under which all other issues huddle. Is relationship therapy as simple as the exercise presented in this chapter? Absolutely not! Relationship counseling is extremely complex. If it were easy, we'd all have it figured out. Couples come to therapy because they want to fix things, but they just don't know how. Another role of the therapist is that of teacher.

Recognizing the Power Struggle

Many couples make the mistake of entering into a battle with one another when there is a problem. A "contestant" in the match steps onto a platform from which she will defend her truth. Her opponent also steps up on his platform to defend his truth. From each position, an opponent will try weapon after weapon to defeat his enemy, knock her off her platform, at the same time remaining steadfast in his own truth. Last man standing is "right" and therefore has won the match.

WEAPONS IN THE MATCH TO BE RIGHT

- **"That's not what I said, did, felt, and that's not what you said or did."** This is the rewriting-history weapon used to prove that your opponent's recollections are false. He doesn't even know what really happened and is therefore wrong.

- **"You do that same thing."** *or* **"I've seen you do that all the time."** This is the bounce-back weapon, used to divert to your opponent his expressed concern with you. It both deflects and deflates your opponent's concerns by blaming him and thereby discounting his right to have that particular concern. So, he's wrong.

- **"That's totally unfair. I would never get upset with you over something like that."** This is the self-righteous, shame-on-you weapon. It is intended to stop the opponent in his tracks by implying he's somehow less than reasonable for having his concern. He's wrong for even feeling as he does.

- **"That's ridiculous (or silly, or mean, or crazy, or overreactive). You're upset about that?"** This is the what's-the-matter-with-you weapon. You are turning his concern back on him and at the same time discounting the possibility that your opponent might have a legitimate issue with you because he's flawed in some way. So, of course, he's wrong.

- **"How could you even say that?"** (accompanied with either tears or anger) This is the shut-up-I-can't-handle-this weapon. You are attacking your opponent for being insensitive or for some other negative fault and emphasizing that he's wrong for even trying to resolve his issue. The goal here is to make him feel bad and go away.
- **"Now, that really pisses me off."** This is the shut-up-or-I'll-show-you-what-anger-really-is weapon. This weapon is designed to wound the opponent if he doesn't back off.

Do you see yourself in any of these power struggle arguments? Most people can identify with them because the battle to be right happens so frequently.

These examples are especially typical of a codependent partner who does not have the capacity to listen, take in a loved one's concern, and remain centered in her own self-esteem. It's almost impossible for her not to feel attacked over each small concern and defend herself. Remember, the codependent has no identity other than that reflected in the mirror of her partner's opinion of her. Her only hope is to change the thinking and feelings of her partner, overpower him, punish him, prove him wrong, attack him, or tire him out until he gives up.

Go back over the list of battle weapons; speculate how the skills you've already been exposed to would circumvent the use of these weapons with your partner. These skills are: accepting responsibility for your own dissatisfaction, using an "I" message, and the three-option ABC compromise skill. Really spend some time thinking how using these skills could prevent a war.

Affirmation

This simple skill sets the tone for compromise and resolution. When your partner presents a concern, the first thing you do is affirm. (Most of the time, people defend). You are affirming in a nondefensive way that you have heard the concern. And you do this by repeating back to your partner what he said in your own words. Partner: "Why didn't you finish that plowing?" You: "You thought I'd have the plowing done by this time." From here the tone of understanding is established. "I've heard you, now let's discuss it." You have pretty much let the wind out of the anger sails and are coming across as someone able to hear the concern and move forward.

Affirmation is not something you use only at the front of a discussion; you use it all the way through to gain more information from your partner and to let him know you're in there to resolve the problem. For example: Partner: "You were home all day, why couldn't you finish the plowing? Now it's too cold." You: "You wanted it done today, before it froze too hard to plow it."

This first time you use affirmation with your partner, he might look at you like you're crazy. Most people are waiting for a defense before they get the complaint out of their mouth. Often, they're already planning what they're going to say when you get angry and defensive.

Validation

Affirmation and validation are almost interchangeable. Both create a spirit of cooperation and they are often used together. Validation is used to accept your partner's feelings. So if you add validation after affirmation, it sounds like this: You: "You thought I'd have the plowing done by now. Well, I can certainly understand why you'd feel that way. It's really dark and cold now." The second sentence was the validation sentence. Adding validation to the next exchange: Partner: "You were home all day, why couldn't you finish the plowing? Now it's too cold." You: "You're thinking it's too cold to plow now. I know exactly what you mean and I agree." As important as this is, when couples communicate, especially around a conflict, they use very little, if any, validation or affirmation.

ESSENTIAL

A feeling is never wrong. An idea or a thought can be misguided or inaccurate and may need to be clarified. Don't confuse thoughts with feelings by saying things like, "I feel you are just testing me." That is a speculative thought. When you use the word *feel*, give a real feeling, like mad, sad, frustrated, irked, annoyed, devastated, hurt, confused, furious, happy, elated, calm, bored, tired, etc.

First, you will need to become aware of your listening skills. Do you listen all the way through without beginning a defense in your head? The first step is internal. Really focus on what your partner is saying instead of preparing your comeback. If you don't understand what he's saying, try to get clarification before you get defensive. You will see the problem in the following scenario where there is no validation or affirmation.

Calvin: "Honey, is there something wrong? You seem distant."

Felicia: "That's ridiculous. Why would you think that?"

Calvin: "I don't know."

Felicia: "Why do you always think something is wrong? For God's sake, Cal."

Calvin: "I just miss talking to you. You're always doing something else."

Felicia: "Like what? What are you talking about?"

Calvin: "You were staring out the window."

Felicia: "Really? So arrest me. I'm in a no-stare zone."

Calvin: "Just forget it. Stare all you want, I'm going upstairs."

You can see the difference in the same situation where affirmation and validation is used.

Calvin: "Honey, is there something wrong? You seem distant."

Felicia: "You think I'm distant?" (affirmation)

Calvin: "I notice you just staring out the window."

Felicia: "I guess I was. If I were you, I'd probably think the same thing. (validation) But nothing is really wrong. I'm just enjoying the beautiful snow and thinking about when my parents used to take us tobogganing when I was a kid."

Calvin (squeezing her hand): "I love it too. Mind if I sit with you?"

Affirmation and validation can take practice. Focus on your partner, listen fully, and affirm by acknowledging what you heard him say. "You think I should finish the dishes now." Ask questions if you need to in order to clarify your understanding. "What is it that bothers you? Is it the dishes sitting there?" Don't rush into a response. Validate. It is not necessary for you to agree with your partner, but validate his right to feel the way he does. "It doesn't matter to me if they sit there until after we walk the dog. But I know clutter bothers you and you seem frustrated. Is that it?"

FACT

"When we are listened to, it creates us, makes us unfold and expand. Ideas actually begin to grow within us and come to life." —Brenda Ueland

These simple communication skills pack a wallop. When a therapist introduces these skills to couples, at first they may discount them, feel awkward, or resist following through.

In the case of codependent relationships, there is a lot going on beneath the communication level. It's hard for some to admit they don't know how to talk to their partner, and when the couple comes in for therapy, they are usually on guard against their partner's disapproval. It can be incredibly uncomfortable for a codependent to show his perceived weaknesses in couples' therapy. And it also is hard for him to honestly ask for what he wants. It is the responsibility of the therapist to walk the line between teaching and therapy, between reassuring and holding a client responsible, especially with the codependent client.

Letter to the Psychologist

The following letter is taken from Here-to-Listen.com and helps explain you only have control over yourself.

Dear Doctor,

I finally got my husband to come to therapy with me. We have a lot of problems, and I'm giving this a try as a last resort. The thing is, he is showing up, but he's a pain in the butt. The therapist is teaching us communication skills, and I can see how this will really help us. But my husband feels he's being treated as a child. He's a big shot in the business world, and he just doesn't want to be told what to do.

He actually has made fun of her exercises. She's been upfront with him about his resistance, but he just rolls his eyes and acts like a spoiled little boy or he puffs up and says how he talks with people all the time in his profession. His behavior isn't surprising to me, but I'm really disgusted at this point.

Dear Joyce,

There is an adage about taking risks that says, "Just show up." People who are afraid of a challenge, something they fear they may not do well, usually blame some external cause. It sounds like your husband made excuses not to come to therapy. But now he's showing up. Your therapist knows all about resistance, and she is trained to handle it in therapy.

Stop focusing on your husband's antics; in fact, stop focusing on your husband altogether. Become aware of what you are doing or what you are learning in therapy. Learn all you can and apply it to your relationship. If one person changes, the other must also change.

CHAPTER 14

Codependency Quizzes

Use this opportunity to practice what you have learned so far. It will be interesting to see how you do in evaluating the short scenarios presented in this chapter. Test your ability to identify codependency. The situations give just enough detail for you to consider them carefully. Perhaps you may need to fill in some blanks for yourself before you make your decision. It is a forced-choice quiz, which means you aren't given a scale or allowed to address the gray areas in your answer.

Codependency Quiz Number 1

In the case of these short vignettes, you are not privy to all the details. Just like real life, there may not be a definitive answer. Just give your opinion with a yes or no. These scenarios might also spark a good discussion with your significant other, family members, or friends. Consider the following situations.

1. Jenny's son, who is twenty-seven and has a police record, is in jail awaiting a hearing. Jenny is convinced that he is innocent. She will have to get a loan for his bail. Should she do it?

   - Yes
   - No

2. Rachel's boyfriend says he's not available to go shopping with her on Saturday. When she's downtown with a friend, she spots him in the coffee shop and breaks in on his lunch, yelling at him for lying to her. Is she justified?

   - Yes
   - No

3. Betty has been looking forward to gardening this afternoon. As she gathers her tools from the garage, her daughter pulls up with her three kids and asks if she can leave them with Grandma for the afternoon. Should Betty do it?

   - Yes
   - No

4. John doesn't want his wife to go out for a birthday dinner at an upscale bar and grill with her girlfriends. He says it's not appropriate for a married woman to be in a bar. Should she go?

   - Yes
   - No

5. Bev's son is marrying his partner, Jeremy. The wedding is out of town and would require a drive and a night's stay in a hotel. Bev's only sister, Joanne, calls and says they just can't afford the extra money to attend. Later Bev finds out they are going on an elaborate cruise. Should Bev say something to her sister?

- Yes
- No

6. Irene's parents are very strict Catholics who sacrificed to send Irene to parochial school. After graduation, Irene stopped going to church, but she hid this from her parents, who think she still is a practicing Catholic. Now Irene is getting married and her parents are lining up the priest to say Mass. Should Irene go along with it?

- Yes
- No

7. Shirley and Bart have always gone to her parents, who live nearby, to celebrate Christmas with Shirley's family. Bart has been asking for the last three years to travel to visit his family for the holidays, but it's never happened. This year he's insisting, but Shirley says her parents aren't well, and missing Christmas would break their hearts. Should they visit Bart's family for the holiday?

- Yes
- No

8. Lori and Steve have two children. They have agreed to a budget for the kids' school clothes. Lori is the one who shops for the kids, so she just spends more if she needs to. After all, Steve is busy with work. He also has no idea how expensive children's clothes are and doesn't want to shop. Is she right?

- Yes
- No

Reflections on Assessing Codependency

After you have considered the situations and made your decisions, feel free to check the answers at the end of the chapter.

More importantly, think about any conflicts you may have experienced. Of course, the major source of conflict might be between what you intellectually know is the correct answer and what you would honestly do yourself in the situation. This is exactly how change takes place. The first step is awareness, where you know something on an intellectual level; then the change must be absorbed through the layers of your psyche. The end result will be a match between your inside and outside. That is, there is congruency in what you believe to be true, your feelings about that truth, and the resulting behavior.

It was once believed that personality traits could not be changed. Codependency is not officially a personality type, but it fits the criteria. The personality is formed in adolescence and is typically consistent over time and is predictable in most situations. The personality is deeply seated, but not entirely unchangeable.

Often when an individual reads a self-help book or is in psychotherapy, he imagines his progress will be like climbing a mountain. He believes that once he has an insight, there will be a steady upward movement until he reaches his goal. This notion can actually impede progress, because if the client senses a lack of upward or forward movement, he may feel he's doing something wrong, that he's back-sliding or failing in some way.

There are many theories about the process of change. One idea is that a person reaches rock bottom in her life and is forced to change in order to survive. This theory is popular with AA. Another theory is that a person changes out of pain. When the personal pain outweighs happiness, it compels a person to seek relief.

Try to imagine personal change as a Slinky, the toy that is a long, flat steel wire bent into a continuous series of circles. The Slinky can be compressed or stretched, like a squeeze box. So if you take an end in each hand, and stretch your arms apart, and then raise one of your arms, this is an accurate image of psychological progress. The whole thing moves forward and up, but each circle creates a back tension. In therapy, these points of back tension create momentum for continued movement forward. It's definitely not failure, and it's not even a back slide because this tension is necessary for continued progress.

ALERT

If the values you hold are not reflected in your behavior and you wish to change that, you have two choices: Re-evaluate your beliefs, or change your behavior. Healthy guilt may be a sign of this conflict.

As you review your answers to the quiz, some of your answers may not match the choices you would actually make in the situation. You are to be commended on your self-awareness and honesty. Your response illustrates the process of change. You understand what the answer is supposed to be, but your awareness has not yet been fully realized in your feelings and behavior. If you want your feelings and behavior to match your thoughts, this is your therapeutic goal. When your thoughts, feelings, and behavior all match, then you've reached your goal.

The Beauty of Compromise

After you've checked your quiz results, it's time to put on a different pair of glasses. These are your compromise glasses, through which you will look at each scenario for possible compromise.

Compromise is sometimes seen as an ugly no man's land where each person is disappointed. There's the story of the couple on their first date who show up at the movie theater to watch a much-anticipated film. Gus is far-sighted and is most comfortable near the back of the theater. Grace is near-sighted and refuses to wear glasses, so she always sits in the front. The couple compromise and sit in the middle of the theater, and neither one of them enjoys the movie!

Compromise sometimes means dividing the difference, but certainly two people are not going to agree to something if it ruins things for both of them. Nobody wants a lose-lose outcome. Nor does compromise mean somebody gives in and then resents it later. Compromise must be a win-win decision or at least result in an okay-okay outcome.

ESSENTIAL

In your primary relationship, you should feel supported and accepted for who you are. While compromise is extremely helpful in negotiating your relationship needs, don't give up everything important to you. Everyone should have nonnegotiable values that are part of who they are. Make sure you have "bottom-line" expectations—such as fidelity, for example—for your relationship.

The trick to reaching compromise is the willingness to get there, honesty about your own needs, and an openness to hear the needs of your partner. Trying to convince your partner that her needs should be changed because they don't make sense to you is off limits.

Try this technique in reaching compromise: Roberta comes into the therapy session complaining that Marsha is too involved in building their new home, and the summer is passing with no fun times. "All she wants to do is look at plans, shop for house stuff, and talk about the house. She spends every weekend on a house project. She's so exhausted, she doesn't even have the energy for me."

Marsha is the one who suggested they come to therapy because she thought Roberta wanted the house as much as she does. The house is to be their family home. But now Roberta is just sitting around complaining while Marsha does all the work.

The first thing the therapist does is validate that both women are "right." There is absolutely nothing wrong with each of their priorities. Having fun, especially in a new relationship, is important. And nesting behavior like building a home for the two of them also is important.

When Marsha and Roberta came into therapy, they were ready to break up. They tried to talk, but they just couldn't resolve the issue. Marsha tried her best to argue Roberta into backing down from her position. After all, the house is for both of them, so how dare she complain? Marsha feels like a victim, slaving away and resenting every minute of it. Roberta also feels like a victim. She had no idea how involved Marsha would get in this house project. She sees the relationship she enjoyed with Marsha slipping away. She feels the house is all Marsha cares about. They are barely talking at this point.

ALERT

> When you do something and you believe that particular behavior is bad, you may feel embarrassment. When you do something and you believe YOU are bad, you feel shame.

Because each of them is stuck in an adversarial position, each discussion is another battle designed to prove one of them right and the other wrong. The simple affirmation from their therapist that each of them is right begins a shift that will lead to compromise.

Therapist: "Would each of you state your needs without judging or disparaging the other?"

Roberta: "I want to spend time with Marsha having fun, being intimate, and nurturing our relationship, but . . ."

Therapist: "No 'buts'."

Marsha: "I want to spend the rest of my life with Roberta. I want us to have a warm, cozy home to share our life in."

Therapist: "Would it be accurate to say you both love one another, and you have the success of your relationship at heart?"

Both: "Yes."

Therapist: "Same goal, different ideas about how to get there?"

Both: "Yes, I guess so."

Therapist: "I wish to repeat that you are both right. Roberta, you are seeing the importance of daily connection, sharing fun times, and making love as a way to have a good relationship?"

Roberta: "Absolutely."

Therapist: "Marsha, you're seeing building a home, building permanency, making a long-term commitment as a way to have a good relationship?"

Marsha. "Uh-huh."

Therapist: "Roberta, do you agree with Marsha?"

Roberta. "I do."

Therapist: "Marsha, do you agree with Roberta?"

Marsha: "Yes."

Therapist: "To summarize, you both agree that having a good intimate relationship, relaxing, enjoying fun times and working toward a future together, nesting, making a commitment are all important in your relationship."

Both: "Yes."

Therapist: "We're ready to solve this problem. Would you like me to lead, or can I invite you each to make a suggestion?"

Roberta (smiling for the first time): "No, you go ahead."

Therapist: "Okay. I'll lead. What would you each think about this compromise? Sunday night sit down with no distractions and share how you would each like to spend the upcoming week. Given what you've already said, Marsha, you talk about some goals regarding the house. Roberta, you talk about goals regarding leisure time. Now these goals are for the two of you together. You will both participate together in the house, and the same goes for leisure. The end game is to accommodate each other's needs. Don't question or argue about the other's desires; validate and compromise, and move forward, making sure each of you feels good about your goals for the week. Try it, and report back next week."

Roberta: "Jeez, it's that easy?"

Therapist: "It could be, yes."

Marsha: "I'm ready. Roberta?"

Roberta: "Let's try it."

Very few clients are capable of learning a skill right away, understanding how that skill can help, and implementing it on the spot. Roberta and Marsha grasp the concept and are confident they can follow the directions given by their therapist. Their enthusiasm will go a long way. However, there is no guarantee that their new awareness will translate into a behavior change. Communication patterns are deeply engrained and usually take a lot of patience and practice before they change. Many find these concepts so foreign that they need to read about them or follow written instructions, need to hear how they sound by having the therapist demonstrate frequently, and need to experience the good feelings that come from resolving conflict over and over again.

Codependency Quiz Number 2

Codependent thoughts can stand alone in your head and not necessarily lead to feelings or action. There are five scenarios in this quiz. Each scenario has four choices. The scenarios focus on thoughts, feelings, and behaviors. For each scenario, choose the responses you believe are codependent.

1. Your husband is always home from work around five. Dinner is at six. It is now six-thirty and he hasn't called, and you can't reach him on his cell phone. What are your thoughts at this point? Choose the thought choices you feel are codependent.

   - Something may have happened to him and he's unable to call me. I'll just go ahead and eat and see if he shows up.
   - There's no reason not to call me. It's just selfish when he knows how hard I work to fix a nice dinner.
   - It's not like him to do this. Did he already tell me he would be late tonight, and I just forgot?
   - That's the last time I'm fixing dinner if that's all the appreciation I get. Now everything is cold.

2. Your fourteen-year-old daughter gets home from school and immediately goes up to her room. You call up to her to see if everything is okay. She hollers down that she's fine, just tired.

   - It's really strange that she didn't say anything to me. I'd better check and see if she's mad at me.
   - She's in one of her moods.
   - Why would she be so tired? That can't be it. Maybe Chad broke up with her.
   - I'll just let her sleep if that's what she needs. We can talk later.

3. You're not feeling well and have dozed off on the sofa in the living room when the kids get off the bus. They are noisy, screaming "Mom" several times before you can answer.

- Damn it, I could just strangle those kids. Can't I even be sick without them hassling me?
- Oh no! I must've fallen asleep. They're scared I'm not here. "Kids! Kids!"
- "Hold it down, kids. I'm in the living room on the couch. I'm not feeling well."
- "Will you kids shut up? Did you ever think I might be sick in here?"

4. You are all dressed up and ready to go out for the evening with your girl-friend. You've made reservations at a wonderful restaurant to celebrate her birthday. When you pick her up, she's in shorts and says she wants to go to the beach.

- "Oh, are you sure? I wanted to take the birthday girl out to *Horner's*."
- "What? We can go to the beach anytime. Can't you see I had big plans for your birthday?"
- "Well, isn't this just like you. It's always about you. Did you ever think I might have made plans?"
- "You really want to go to the beach? I'll have to stop by my apartment and get my shorts. Can we stop on the way for food? I'm starving."

5. Your wife promised to help you with the yard work by weeding the roses today so you can mow. You get home from work and she hasn't done it.

- You storm into the house. "I am so sick of this. If you're not going to weed, just say so. Don't lie about it." You say to yourself, "Wait until she asks me for a favor."
- You calmly enter the house and greet your wife as usual with "Hi, honey." You're glad that you said nothing about the yard when she hurries in, gives you a long hug, and tells you, "I'm afraid I have some bad news. Bernie died today."
- As you get out of the car, you see she didn't weed. You get back into your car without a word and go to a fast-food restaurant even though you know she's made dinner.
- Your wife is on the front porch with a glass of lemonade for you. You greet each other and sit down and share your day. When it's

appropriate, you say, "I'm feeling disappointed that the rose bed isn't done because now I can't do the mowing."

Answers to Codependency Quiz Number 1

The primary function of this quiz is to assess how the folks in the vignettes are codependent. Briefly, and without further development of the stories, these are the results and the reasons.

1. No. Jenny's son is an adult and has been in jail before. He needs to solve his own problems and come up with his own bail or stay in jail until the hearing. If Jenny bails him out, she's codependent.
2. No. Rachel's boyfriend did not lie. He said he wasn't available to go shopping with her. He is having lunch with a friend, and Rachel's tantrum is codependent behavior.
3. No. Betty has a right to her own needs. At the point where her daughter shows up unexpectedly with the grandchildren is when Betty might have felt pressure to ignore her own needs for her daughter's. If she does that, she is codependent.
4. Yes. John is trying to control his wife going out with friends because of his own insecurities. He is codependent. His wife should go out with her friends if that's what she wants to do.
5. Yes. Bev knows her sister made an excuse not to attend her son's wedding because she's homophobic, not because she's poor. If Bev keeps her mouth shut, it seems she's more worried about her sister feeling uncomfortable than she is in defending her son's right to marry. This would suggest codependency.
6. No. Irene fears her parents' disapproval, so she lies to them about leaving the church. She's an adult and needs to assert her own needs for her wedding. To perpetuate the lie is to carry on a codependent relationship.
7. Yes. It's time for Bart to have a say in the holiday plans. He's way overdue to visit his parents, and that's what they should do. Otherwise, he has his own codependent self to blame.
8. No. Lori is lying to her husband. Even after agreeing to a budget, she's spending what she wants. She is codependent because she's dishonest, manipulating to get what she wants.

Answers to Codependency Quiz Number 2

When you took the second quiz, you were given possible reactions in particular situations and asked to identify which of four responses showed codependency. Here are the results from that quiz.

1. Husband is late for dinner: responses 2 and 4 show codependency.
2. Teenage daughter goes straight to room, says she's tired: responses 1, 2, and 3 show codependency.
3. Sick mom on couch when kids get off bus: responses 1, 2, and 4 show codependency.
4. Boyfriend has big plans for girlfriend's birthday: responses 2 and 3 show codependency.
5. Wife doesn't weed the roses: responses 1 and 3 show codependency.

This quiz and the results may inspire some good conversation about codependency as it shows up in your friends, family, and coworkers.

ESSENTIAL

The only person you have control over is you. No matter what happens in your world, you have a choice about how you respond to it.

Letters to the Psychologist

The following letters are taken from Here-to-Listen.com and help explain the mixed messages of codependency.

Dear Doctor,

I'm in a relationship with a control freak. My wife never listens to my needs and she treats me like a little kid. She says things like, "Don't even think about a fishing boat, it's not going to happen" or "If you come home with another bike, I swear to God I'm going to run over it with the car." She's not kidding. If she tells me I can't have something, and I insist on it, she flies into a rage like you wouldn't believe.

I don't try to micromanage what she buys for herself. How do I get what I want without being punished?

Stan

Dear Stan,

You need to sit down with your wife when there is no debate on the table about a purchase you wish to make. Try to initiate a discussion about how you two want to handle situations when one or the other wants to buy something. See if you can agree to a process beforehand.

Look at your own behavior first and start with that. For example, are you spending beyond your means? Do you have a history of buying things when you two have agreed not to? Are you meeting your obligations to the family before you think of yourself?

It's a chicken-egg situation, but no matter how this began, you and your wife are now in a parent-child relationship regarding this issue. She forbids you to buy something, like your mother would. But you might also be responding like the rebellious kid and doing it anyway. Try to use good communication skills, don't get in a power struggle, and work out a way you can each be an adult on this issue.

Dear Doctor,

I'm an adult daughter. I'm at a loss to understand my mom. She can be so giving at times, and at other times if I ask for a favor, she goes on and on about how ungrateful I am, how I should be able to handle my own life, etc.

I rarely ask her for anything, but she shows up with presents for me and for my kids, and asks if she can treat us to lunch, stuff like that. She just offered me her old car now that she bought a new one. I swear, I don't know whether to accept her offer or not. I could use the car, but then I'm sure I'll hear how I never appreciate anything. I always feel like the axe is about to fall.

Sandy

Dear Sandy,

What you describe is a codependent pattern. It looks as if your mother helps out and then expects something back, something that affirms she is okay. When she doesn't get it, she is angry and resentful. The clearest answer for you would be to stop accepting her help if it has strings attached.

I realize you may need help from your mother and it may not be easy to just do without it. Here's a suggestion. Sit down with her and discuss this ahead of time. Tell your mother how much you appreciate her help (which I'm sure you do). Ask her what you can do or say to show how much you appreciate it. Insist that she give you some specific words or actions to thank her. The next time, use those words.

I'm predicting there may not be a way for you to thank her because she's doing things she doesn't really want to do and then resents you for it. Codependency can be a double-edged sword, and you've experienced both edges.

CHAPTER 15

Tracing the Codependency Within

When you were a child, your world was your family. Parents impart certain "truisms" that teach their children about life. For example, *Don't trust strangers; Keep family matters private; Share with others; If somebody hits you, hit them back; Give adults a kiss; Be careful; Don't be a sissy; Don't sass back.* A young child does not have the ability to pick and choose what he accepts as true. He believes everything he's told. If his mother says she'll take him to an orphanage if he's bad, he believes it.

Family Rules from Childhood

A child is a sponge, absorbing everything in her environment in an attempt to make sense of her world. It's not just what parents overtly teach a child, it's also how parents behave and how they react emotionally that convey certain "rules to live by."

ALERT

Any time "family" is used, it describes all family constellations: foster families, adoptive families, single-parent families, stepfamilies. It is a unit composed of one or more adults with or without one or more children.

Parents—and also siblings, grandparents, and other extended family members—contribute to a child's view of the world. Certainly, other points of view are introduced as a child attends school, matures cognitively, and questions authority. But the deeply rooted messages of childhood, reinforced daily within the family, are powerful and sometimes unshakable. It is important to explore and question these messages to see if they contribute to codependency in your current life:

- Strive to be perfect; making a mistake is not okay.
- Don't question authority.
- If you don't stand up, you're a sissy.
- It's not okay to say no.
- Nobody likes a loud-mouthed girl.
- Always put others first.
- Don't be selfish or conceited.
- Be careful; the world is a dangerous place.
- Don't get angry.

As you think about the family you grew up in, try to identify some of the messages conveyed to you when you were a child. Many of them are unspoken, so be on the lookout for messages taught by behavior. Consider obvious contradictions; e.g., your mother tells you it is never okay to lie, but she's on the phone making an excuse to your dad's boss that he's sick and can't come in to work.

You will be controlled by these unconscious messages until you make them conscious. Once you have awareness, you can decide whether these messages are working for you in your current life.

Walking on Eggshells

Deena's mom is moody and sullen most of the time. She is passive with her husband, but often explodes in anger when her children act up. She is obviously unhappy, but she feels powerless to change things. She works part-time at a retail store, hates her job, and is constantly complaining about how badly she is treated by others.

ALERT

If you are dishonest and indirect, or you have trouble saying no, it can lead to a manipulative and sometimes abusive behavior called *passive-aggressiveness*. If you don't want to do something, you have a right to say no. But say it directly. Don't agree and then "forget" or make up some excuse why you didn't. That's *passive-aggressive* behavior.

Deena's dad is quiet and withdrawn when he comes home from a twelve-hour day at an automotive repair shop. He's tired and wants to relax and enjoy TV. He is easily angered by his wife or kids asking for his time or attention when he's home. Deena never really knows what might set her dad or mom off. On the weekends, Deena's parents are more relaxed. The family likes to camp on the weekends in their camper and spend summer vacations at their grandparents' cottage on the lake. When they are together like this, Deena enjoys being around her parents.

Deena is now an adult married to an even-tempered guy, but she is still following old "rules" from her family. There is no reason in her current marriage why she should feel like she's walking on eggshells, but she does. Even when her husband says he's not angry, she doesn't believe him. If she notices that her husband is more low-key, or has a sour look on his face, she thinks it's something she's done. Even when he reassures her that it's not, she keeps checking to make sure he's not angry. Her husband can't understand why Deena reacts so strongly when he expresses even mild anger. He, too, feels like he's walking on eggshells.

Perfectionism

Bill's dad wears his perfectionism like a badge of honor. He constantly talks at the dinner table about how well he does at work, how many sales he has made, how his success gives Bill the extra things in life, like vacations and a go-cart. Bill's mother is a teacher and is successful in her own right, but she usually comes home from school, makes dinner, and focuses on making her husband comfortable.

Bill is a smart kid who enjoys taking things apart and exploring how they work. Bill's dad is constantly on him about ruining things and leaving things undone. Whenever Bill tries something new, his dad ends up berating him for not doing it perfectly.

Now Bill is married to his high school sweetheart. Bill's wife is frustrated with him because he keeps switching jobs. Bill keeps promising her he'll stick with it, but he doesn't like to follow the rules, and he ends up quitting. He thinks his wife is unreasonable and critical, yet he doesn't speak up and he doesn't change anything. He's stuck in a codependency pattern, but he doesn't know it. He'll need to explore his childhood to see how old feelings and beliefs are keeping him stuck.

Role Models

By virtue of their important influence in a child's life, parents are always role models. The important thing to remember is that when an adult takes a critical look at his childhood, including his parents and siblings, he is not seeking to cast blame; he is trying to understand himself.

An interesting twist is that family loyalty tends to increase as family function decreases. Adult children of abuse, neglect, and addiction not only fear reliving their childhood pain, they also feel a tremendous burden to keep family secrets and pretend everything was fine. Even if past family dynamics are more subtle, less abusive, there is sometimes a reluctance for adult children to examine them. It's as if childhood is a sacred place where you dare not venture without your rose-colored glasses.

FACT

The term *family of origin* comes from family systems theory. It simply means the family or families you were a part of from birth to adulthood.

The potential for self-understanding is so great that the journey back to your original family is well worth it. Some clients argue that the past is over, done with. Some even say, "There's nothing you can do about the past." But keep in mind that the past is never over as long as it is alive in your current life. Everyone has a past. Some have "baggage" that they carry with them. Since codependency traits are formed in childhood and are pretty well established by adolescence, it would be short-sighted not to explore your family of origin for clues about your personality. Besides, there is no single "past," only your personal map of it. If you look at it that way, with new insight and awareness, you actually *can* change the past.

Your Value Is in What You Do

Joe's mother has many friends and enjoys joining organizations and clubs, where she spends a lot of her time. When anyone asks her to join something, donate to something, or help somebody, Joe's mom is always there to do whatever she can.

Joe's mom also works hard. She has her main job at an office supply company and then delivers newspapers on the weekends. When Joe is old enough, he rides along with his mom on her route. However, he still feels lonely a lot of the time and wants his mother to spend more time with him. His mom is funny and interesting, and Joe is proud whenever anyone says what a great person she is.

In high school, Joe plays sports, but his mom misses most of his games because of her other obligations. Joe begins to feel cheated because all the other boys have their parents cheering from the sidelines. When Joe talks to his dad about it, Dad makes excuses for Joe's mom, reminding Joe how hard his mom works and what a compassionate person she is. Joe's mom modeled behavior embedded with the following harmful messages:

- Your value is in doing, not just being.
- Relationships are not as important as work.
- Never say no to somebody who needs something.
- Success is measured by supporting your family financially.
- It's more important to have many acquaintances who admire you than it is to develop meaningful relationships with your family.
- It's okay to put your family last. Outside recognition is what counts.
- Never stop doing; self-understanding and time to look inward is not important.

It's Okay to Be a Victim

While Joe's mom is out making a splash in the community, Joe's dad is working at the saw mill. After a long day of physical labor, Dad comes home and does everything else. He's pretty much raising the kids alone. He often feels taken advantage of, but he tells himself it's not fair for him to feel this way. He knows his wife is a hard worker and helps others who are needy. He's been lonely since Joe was born, and now that he has three children, his life is pretty much tied to home. Even though the kids are older now, it's been too long since Joe went out anywhere. He wants to do things with his wife, but she's always too busy.

Dad feels responsible for difficulties the kids experience because he's the one who is raising them. He's frustrated trying to be both parents. In the few times he's shared his feelings with his wife, she gets angry and says he doesn't appreciate all the things she does. Joe's dad doesn't want to leave his children, but he is not happy in his marriage. He longs to be close to his wife emotionally and physically. But he is stuck in a relationship with a woman who is unavailable and apparently not interested in a close relationship with him and with their children. What potentially unhealthy messages has Joe learned from watching his dad? Joe's dad modeled behavior embedded with these messages:

- It's okay to be a victim.
- Somebody else's needs are more important than yours.
- Don't talk. Don't feel.
- Don't be direct and honest and ask for what you need.
- It's okay to be powerless; just make the best of it.
- Keep busy; don't get in touch with your loneliness.
- It's okay to stay stuck and miserable.

ESSENTIAL

The work of Harville Hendrix, *Getting the Love You Want,* is incredibly important in understanding unconscious choices. He points out that a person is unconsciously drawn to his or her partner for the purpose of mastering unmet needs in childhood. Unless the unconscious is revealed, a person will make the same mistakes over and over again.

You can see that both of Joe's parents have conveyed messages that influence Joe in his life, messages about character, value, self-esteem, and dependency. When it comes time for Joe to fall in love, unconsciously he may be drawn to a partner who will join him in re-creating the marriage that was modeled in his family. Each child in Joe's family may develop codependency traits and patterns because of the learning they received from their two most important role models, Mom and Dad.

ALERT

It's not as simple as saying you chose someone who is like your father or mother. That could be true, but it also may be true that you misinterpret your partner's appropriate behavior by filtering through your own childhood fears and responding accordingly. For example, a slightly raised voice is heard as rage, and you're scared.

When you are attracted to a potential partner, of course you are drawn to her good qualities, the qualities you consciously desire in a partner. Nobody wants to fall in love with someone who elicits the same shameful feelings he had with his alcoholic father. But on an unconscious level, he is drawn to this person so he can master, or conquer, his childhood pain. It's as if the unconscious is saying, "Mary is controlling and has anger problems just like your dad. If you can love her and get her to love you, at last you will get the love you need." Sounds strange, but it is true. How many people do you know who have left a bad marriage only to find themselves in a similar situation the next time around?

Codependency Patterns

Another way to follow the thread of codependency in your life is to take a close look at your past significant relationships. The closer the relationship, the more noticeable the codependency may be. See if you can identify the ways in which you created or escalated problems. Apply what you already know about codependency and see if you fit.

It's tempting to focus on your past partner as the problem, but try to remember the feelings you experienced in the relationship and also some of your own negative behaviors and responses. Sometimes a person may believe one past relationship is the reason for his codependent behavior, that his partner was so ornery or controlling that he had to respond in a codependent way. But this is rarely the case. If you accept the premise that you choose your partner in part based on some unconscious motivation, then you have to accept that codependency first develops in childhood.

Remember that each developmental stage requires mastery of the previous stage. The first stage, Trust vs. Mistrust, begins when an infant is born and should be mastered by the time the child is eighteen months old. Think how basic this task is. Trust. An infant cannot survive without someone to take care of him. It is a matter of life and death that he trust his caregivers. So this first building block must be firmly in place to keep the subsequent developmental building blocks solid. As a child matures, if needs go unmet, negative influences may come into play and healthy development can go awry. Think of development as a tower. Cracks in the top few blocks are not nearly as serious as a crack in the foundation blocks. Cracks in the foundation lead to disordered personality traits like narcissism, paranoia, obsession, dependency, aggression, and codependency. The earlier the wounds, the more extensive the scars.

It makes sense to start your exploration chronologically. Once you become aware of codependency messages and role-modeling in your family of origin, see how those codependency patterns played out in your first serious relationship, second, and so on. Once you do this, you will have a good idea of your own codependency patterns and will be ready to work on them.

An Example of Codependency Patterns

Amy's parents are Mark and Cindy. Mark owns a small landscaping business and is the designer and manager. He is outgoing and friendly, and does well with the customers. Cindy does the bookkeeping and marketing. Cindy has a tendency toward mood swings, and any small upset can throw her into a rage. Mark works long hours, and when he's home he reads professional journals and surfs the Net for landscaping ideas. Both Mark and Cindy work very hard and seldom take time to relax.

Amy has never observed a good conflict resolution model from her parents. Cindy is easily set off about something, and then starts yelling, pointing her finger, and dancing around with agitation. Mark immediately closes down and refuses to talk. He's learned over the years that responding simply adds fuel to Cindy's fire. On a couple of occasions, Mark has left the house to get away from Cindy's rage. Amy is left to fend for herself in a home environment that is charged and unpredictable. She usually retreats to her bedroom, hoping her mother will calm down and the blowup will be over.

Over the years, Mark and Cindy have grown apart because of the unresolved conflicts and resentment over things said and done out of rage. Amy seldom sees her parents enjoying each other, laughing, chatting, or showing affection.

Amy has been exposed to a distorted communication pattern. If there's a conflict, Amy has learned that she has two choices: rage like her mother or withdraw like her father. When she was a child, Amy chose to withdraw because she was powerless to go up against her out-of-control mother. She went to her room, cowering, and waited.

Amy came into her first relationship with the model her parents gave her. When she was in high school, she was very passive with her first boyfriend. Anything he wanted, she went along with. She was terrified of a conflict, because for her it meant chaos and danger. Amy had practically no tolerance for anger; to her, anger meant rage.

ALERT

Often complicated family systems are reduced to "You're just like my mother (father, brother, sister)." This statement is a blaming accusation aimed at your partner. Not only is the connection oversimplified, it is misguided. Your job is to find out how you processed the dynamics in your family and how *you* can change in ways that will heal those old wounds.

In college, Amy began a relationship with a boyfriend who was very social but not available emotionally. You might say she chose someone like her dad. When she couldn't get the love she wanted, she became very angry and sometimes she raged like her mother. The more she raged, the more detached her boyfriend became.

Amy then married her husband, who is even-tempered and kind, but he is not professionally ambitious. He enjoys staying home and loves to make pottery and care for the children. Amy often criticizes him with sarcasm for not supporting the family. She frequently works overtime to make up for the second income she feels she deserves, but she feels put upon and victimized by her husband's choices. Her resentment results in a pattern where she either gives him a cold shoulder or she explodes in a rage, threatening to divorce him.

What does Amy need to do so that she will not be stuck in a codependency pattern? First, she needs to understand that she learned these patterns in her family of origin. On a deep emotional level, she doesn't really know any other way to handle conflict. She can either withdraw completely or rage as taught to her by her parents. She keeps bouncing back and forth between her parents' patterns, trying to make them work. She has married a passive person because growing up with her mother's rages was painful. But now she's raging just like her mother did. She's tried punishing her husband with silence, or ridiculing him—or trying to be his mother, showing him jobs in the paper. But on an unconscious level, Amy resorts to rage when nothing else works, because that's all she knows.

ALERT

The deep insight that would be most helpful to people like Amy is very hard for an individual to achieve on her own. It is usually most helpful to work on this unconscious material with a therapist.

The ideal insight Amy could have is this: "I either rage or I withdraw from my partner. When I grew up, my mother raged and my dad withdrew. I keep bouncing back and forth between two patterns I consciously know do not work and I also know cause pain for everybody involved. I hate feeling powerless like I did when I was a kid and my parents fought. So, I'm unconsciously opting for the more powerful response, rage. I don't know what my healthy options are."

Once Amy gains insight into why she behaves as she does, she is ready to make changes in the previously unconscious codependency patterns that have caused her so much pain.

Letter to the Psychologist

The following letter is taken from Here-to-Listen.com and helps explain why self-awareness is key in breaking a codependent relationship pattern.

Dear Doctor,

I'm single now after two failed marriages. I'm working with my therapist to figure out why I ended up married to two emotionally abusive men. Now that I'm single, I feel pretty good, but I do want another relationship, and I don't want to make another mistake.

How can I work on relationship issues if I'm not currently married?

Brenda

Dear Brenda,

Actually, you are in a good place in your life to work on relationship issues. Work with your therapist on family-of-origin patterns. Try to get a full picture of what you learned in your environment growing up that made you think emotional abuse was normal or okay. Then, see if you can reconstruct the early stages of your marriages. When did you first see signs of abuse?

Unconscious material can come through as an immediate attraction to somebody who is not good for you. If that material becomes conscious in your therapy, you will understand yourself in a way you didn't before. The more you know about yourself, the better choices you will make.

When you first meet a potential partner, use insight. Try to lead with your head. As soon as you become aware that this new person does not match the criteria you have already established for a healthy partner, you must recon-sider the relationship immediately. It is better to follow your new awareness before you become emotionally involved. From the first interaction with this person, start gathering data to identify whether or not he is controlling. Your therapist will help you with this.

CHAPTER 16

Seeking Professional Help

Most people with codependency issues can be greatly helped by seeing a psychotherapist. The availability, cost, and confidentiality of treatment are all factors to weigh when considering this option. But your own opinions and beliefs about the value of psychotherapy will carry the most weight. It can be daunting for someone with codependency issues to seek therapy. What will people think? Misinformed notions about psychotherapy and fears about the judgments of others can be hurdles to getting professional help.

Codependency Within the Medical Model

Since codependency is not an official diagnosis as defined by the *DSM-5*, you will not be given a diagnosis of codependency or codependent personality disorder. It will be the role of the clinician to give you the official diagnosis that describes your symptoms.

Medical Insurance for Therapy

Because health care is costly, most people need or want to use their insurance coverage. Insurance companies require an official *DSM-5* diagnosis from a clinician who holds the appropriate credentials, usually degree and license, in order to reimburse for mental health services. If you decide to call an individual practitioner, either call your insurance company ahead of time to see if her services will be covered or ask the therapist when you call for an appointment if she accepts your insurance. If you call a private clinic or community mental health, they will usually ask you about your insurance coverage and handle it for you.

Codependency and Diagnosis

The symptoms (behaviors, thoughts, and feelings) identified in this book as codependency are also part of other diagnoses. Don't be surprised if your therapist makes a clinical decision for some type of anxiety disorder, adjustment disorder, mood disorder, personality disorder, or addiction-related disorder. All of these diagnoses may contain the symptoms you now associate with codependency.

Creating a Diagnosis

It might be helpful to think outside the box a bit here. Visualize a diagnosis as a meal. That meal consists of various ingredients. The chef (therapist) is at the food prep area when a patron (client) comes in carrying a large bag. The patron empties the bag of ingredients and places them on the counter. Among these ingredients are self-blame, tearfulness, episodes of rage, resentment, difficulty sleeping, poor insight, loss of interest in hobbies, fear of abandonment, unstable self-image, overly dramatic behavior, lack of empathy, tendency to exaggerate, excessive worry, irritability, food binges, chronic tenseness, need to control, racing thoughts, sense of victimhood, fear of being alone, and indecisiveness.

ESSENTIAL

A mental health diagnosis is the same as a diagnosis for a physical condition. The clinician evaluates your symptoms and determines what illness is causing the symptoms. Any claims made to your insurance will be made under this diagnosis. The insurance company matches the diagnosis with any number of approved treatments and reimburses for the service claimed.

In this greatly simplified example, the chef makes a preliminary assessment of the ingredients given. She discovers she has ingredients for either anxiety disorder, codependency, or narcissistic personality disorder.

- **Anxiety disorder:** Difficulty sleeping, excessive worry, need to control, chronic tenseness, racing thoughts, indecisiveness, self-blame, fear of abandonment.
- **Codependency:** Excessive worry, indecisiveness, irritability, sense of victimhood, episodes of rage, need to control, unstable self-image, and poor insight.
- **Narcissistic personality disorder:** Tendency to exaggerate, lack of empathy, overly dramatic behavior, need to control, poor insight, unstable self-image, episodes of rage, irritability.

In this example, some of the same ingredients are needed in the recipes for anxiety disorder, codependency, and narcissistic personality disorder. But other ingredients are unique to each of the three recipes, and a few of the ingredients are not used in any of the recipes. This is the process of making a diagnosis. It is both an art and a science and requires the skill of a professional.

The point is, codependency has some of the same features as other clinical disorders. It is possible for a symptom to show up as part of the diagnostic criteria for more than one diagnosis. For example, you can have codependency traits and meet criteria for an anxiety disorder at the same time.

Does Medication Help Codependency?

If you continue to follow the ingredient analogy, it may help you understand why medication might be appropriate for codependency. Medication can have a positive impact on the ingredients within the codependency syndrome. For example, antidepressants have shown effectiveness in treating rage, excessive worry, irritability, and depression.

ESSENTIAL

Medications treat symptoms. They effect a physiological change that may mask symptoms, reduce symptoms, or eliminate symptoms. Psychotropic medications make changes in brain chemistry.

Teasing out one symptom, episodes of rage, illustrates the point. If Mary is prone to raging, she reinforces the negative view of herself as bad every time she rages. On top of that, her husband or children reflect her badness by their hurt feelings or fears during the rage. Because she is codependent, Mary cannot hear that her behavior is bad without believing she is bad, so she gets defensive or withdraws. You can see by this example that rage is a kingpin feature in her codependency cycle. If the rage component of the cycle went away (in this case through medication), the pattern would be broken while Mary works on her codependency in therapy. In this case, a combination of therapy and medication would likely be an effective intervention.

Finding a Therapist

Finding a psychotherapist can be a daunting task. "How do I find the right therapist for me?" One option is to ask around for a recommendation from family members, friends, and coworkers. Unfortunately, some people don't feel comfortable asking people they know; there is still a stigma about being in therapy. You might not want others to know that you need help, or might be afraid of making other people uncomfortable if you ask them.

Word of Mouth

Despite holdover stigma about the weakness of "needing help," word of mouth is still a good suggestion. Ask around among those you feel comfortable asking. Fortunately, the tendency for people to be misinformed and judgmental continues to lessen. True, it's hard for a codependent not to worry about what people think, but your own life is the only one you are responsible for, so you might as well get help if you need it.

Advertising

Print advertising and websites are very helpful. Yellow pages advertising usually requires that professionals be licensed to list under certain categories. While going to a licensed professional does not guarantee a good therapeutic fit, you can make certain assumptions. Licensed professionals:

- Have the education and training needed to pass licensure requirements in the state.
- Have ethical standards they must maintain, and if they do not, you have recourse for disciplinary action.
- May be required to have continuing education in the field to maintain a license.
- Must follow certain professional guidelines in providing treatment for patients.

When you look for a therapist, yellow pages and web search categories include psychotherapists, psychologists, psychiatrists, marriage and family therapists, social workers, and counselors. Setting categories are mental health, social service organizations, crisis intervention centers, domestic violence and women's shelters, alcohol and drug treatment centers, and human service organizations. These may vary somewhat within your local phone listings, but you get the idea.

You might get a referral or recommendation from your primary care physician or check the local phone book as a first step. Then do a web search on the provider and see if he has a website or is listed in some of the online directories.

As a point of clarification, psychologists have a PhD and do psychotherapy and psychological testing. Psychiatrists are medical doctors (MD or DO) who have a specialty in psychiatry, so they can also be found under physicians with a specialty in psychiatry in your directory. Psychiatrists can prescribe and manage psychotropic medications, but most do not do psychotherapy. For codependency issues, you typically would not start with a psychiatrist.

ALERT

Do a web search of codependency groups in your state. Pick one close enough for regular meetings. Also search CODA groups (Co-Dependents Anonymous) for support groups you can attend at no cost.

Referrals from Other Professionals

Professionals who deal with people in distress, such as psychotherapists, medical doctors, chiropractors, massage therapists, attorneys, human resource offices at businesses, teachers and school psychologists and counselors, and police and the courts, all may be sources for referrals. Some communities also have a referral system. You could dial Information for your area and see if there is a physician referral, which is a call-in service.

Finding the Right Therapist

Sometimes a client believes that he cannot be understood by a therapist unless the therapist has had the same critical experiences he has. For example, "I can't go to a therapist who has never been married," or "She can't understand, she's never had children," or "He's advising me, and he's divorced," or "He's never lost anyone, how could he know how I feel?"

There is a reason why therapists do not talk about their personal lives. Psychologists go through extensive training to become professionals in their field. Part of that training often involves therapists becoming patients so that they can work through their own personal issues before they help others. Just as the medical doctor has not had all illnesses, therapists cannot possibly have experienced every life situation. They learn through training and clinical experience.

FACT

> Therapists must decide how much they wish to share about themselves. Most standards advise against therapists talking about their own lives. In any case, clinicians must be judicious and aware of the therapeutic purpose of their personal disclosure.

Here are some things to think about as you search for a therapist to work with you:

- Would you feel more comfortable with a man or a woman?
- Do you think you can connect better with a younger or older therapist?
- Do you need to have a professional who accepts your insurance?
- Do you need a therapist with evening or weekend hours?
- Are you aware that you work better with a certain treatment approach or style?
- Do you want a therapist who will be supportive for your lifestyle? For example, a therapist who is gay/lesbian/bisexual/transgender affirming or a therapist who understands your culture or religious beliefs?

Unless a therapist lists a particular specialty in his advertising, most therapists are general practitioners and can handle most problems. But it would be helpful if you would ask the therapist on the phone if he works with codependency issues. If he appears too rigid or fails to understand what you mean, it might be better to move on. It is not your job to educate your therapist on issues he should already be aware of.

If most of your misery is stemming from your relationship and your partner is willing, start with couples' therapy. Often couples' therapy specialists have had additional training and experience that qualify them specifically for the marriage and family therapist licensure. Again, this doesn't guarantee that one of them will be a good fit for you, but it does mean they have met certain skill requirements in the field.

The Personality Factor

There really is no way to assess your comfort level with a therapist until you meet with him. Since the first session is usually history-taking, give the new therapist two or three sessions to see if your personalities are compatible for entering into this most important trusting relationship, a relationship that will promote healing and personal growth.

The length of time that patients spend with a therapist can vary. When talking about codependency patterns, much depends on the client's response to therapy and her life situation, and the resources available to her. In an attempt to pin down the length of treatment, it would be safe to say that very short-term therapy is considered to be eight to twelve weekly sessions, short-term therapy is three to nine months of weekly sessions, and weekly therapy for two to three years or more is considered long-term therapy.

Modes of Therapy

A description of who shows up for a therapy session is formally called the "treatment modality." In addition to the therapist, if one person is there, it's individual therapy; if two people are there, it's couples' therapy (or conjoint therapy); if more than two members of a family show up, it's family therapy; and if three or more people participate who are not a family, it's group therapy. Other configurations are possible, but not common.

Individual Therapy

The most common treatment modality is still individual therapy. Historically, mental illness has been treated by one psychiatrist seeing one patient in either the hospital or the doctor's office. It wasn't until the introduction of family systems theory in the late 1950s that other configurations of therapy were considered. From that point, the treatment landscape changed to include other modalities, like family, couples', and group therapy.

Individual therapy can be done inpatient (during the time a patient is admitted to a hospital or treatment facility) or outpatient (in a setting other than a hospital or treatment facility, like a therapist's office). If a person is seeing a therapist at the therapist's office, that is individual outpatient therapy.

Insurance companies reimburse for therapy services in fifteen-minute increments. And the fifty to sixty minute session is the standard. It is worth mentioning that sessions can be longer or shorter, but when you make an appointment with a therapist, it is very likely that your session will be fifty minutes. Cost of individual therapy varies widely throughout the United States, although it is usually higher in metropolitan areas and lower in rural communities, higher in the East and West and lower in the South and Midwest.

ESSENTIAL

The disciplines of psychiatry, psychology, social work, marriage and family therapy, and counseling are governed by professional ethics, standards, and procedures. Guidelines such as length of sessions, relationship boundaries, and payment are there for a reason. A therapist must answer to his profession about the standards he maintains.

The fee for a visit with a psychiatrist, who is a physician, averages $150 to $250 per visit and can go much higher. The PhD psychologist fees average $120 to $150, and social workers, marriage and family therapists, and counselors may charge less, but not necessarily. Fees depend heavily on what the insurance companies deem to be reasonable and customary for a service. And it is the insurance company that uses a hierarchy of professional credentials to determine their reimbursement scales. Some professionals opt out of insurance reimbursement altogether and charge whatever their ethics will allow.

Community mental health is another option. Services are provided to those who qualify on a no-fee or reduced-fee basis. Most nonprofit clinics offer a sliding fee scale, and private clinics frequently offer reduced fees for those who cannot afford the full fee. Clinicians in private practice sometimes do a certain percentage of their caseload pro bono or at a reduced fee. Note that professionals are governed by rules of ethics and must work within the parameters of insurance regulations in order to implement an equitable fee schedule for their clients.

Children have the option of school psychologists and counselors, and college students also have free services through college counseling centers.

Businesses sometimes offer employees limited short-term therapy through employee assistance programs.

Conjoint Therapy

Often codependency shows up in intimate relationships like marriages and domestic partnerships. If this is the case, you might want to seek out couples' counseling. It is not essential, but it is probably the most expedient way to deal with codependency issues in your intimate relationship. Especially as it pertains to communication, conflict resolution, and sharing intimate feelings, there really is no better modality than conjoint therapy.

Typically, a couple will experience difficulties and each partner will immediately think the other is the problem. Seldom will a codependent partner initiate a discussion about getting help by saying "I think the problem is my codependency." It's just not the nature of the beast. If a couple already understood the dynamics of their relationship, they wouldn't need help. So, it doesn't matter what they think the problem is when they come in; all they have to do is show up, which can be no small feat. Once they are sitting in front of the therapist, what matters is the rapport with and the expertise of that therapist.

ALERT

Conjoint therapy has a set of guidelines about confidentiality, sidebar discussions, phone calls, scheduling, and termination of therapy that is necessary when two or more people are in therapy together. The therapist must be in tune with these issues to avoid damaging the therapeutic relationship.

Codependency can be addressed through all of the treatment modalities. However, it's not unusual for a codependent person to seek individual therapy because she is usually anxious, depressed, angry, and resentful. In conjoint therapy the codependent initially sees her partner as the problem, but through the process she gains the same insights about herself as she would in individual therapy. And in conjoint therapy her partner also learns to understand his role, so the therapy may be more intense, but the duration may be shorter.

Sessions of conjoint therapy usually last fifty minutes or more. It's entirely up to the therapist how long the sessions will last and how frequently they will occur. The cost is usually slightly higher for a conjoint session; e.g., one might pay $135 for a fifty-minute conjoint session as opposed to $120 for an individual session.

When you make an appointment for couples' therapy, be sure to ask the therapist if he does this type of work. Not everyone enjoys working with couples because it is hard work—for all involved. If a therapist does not have additional licensure, certification, training, or at least experience in marriage and family therapy, you may not be getting the best service. Couples' counseling is different than individual counseling; the therapist may be more active or more directive, and may give homework or insist that the couple practice things in the session. Generally, couples' therapy is more focused on cognitive-behavioral change.

Family Therapy

Codependency would not usually be the presenting problem when a family seeks family therapy. When one member of a family is experiencing difficulties, it's not unusual for the entire family to be referred, perhaps by the school psychologist, the court system, or the therapist or treatment facility of one of the family members. Examples of this might be a daughter with an eating disorder, a son who is suicidal, a daughter who is in trouble with the law, a son who is aggressive at school, a dad who has a gambling problem, or a mom who is an alcoholic.

The cost of family therapy is usually slightly higher than individual therapy. Once the family therapy begins, if the emphasis of the therapy is not exclusively on the identified patient (family member with the perceived problem), codependency is very likely to be a part of the clinical picture. Through family therapy, the family system can move away from dysfunction. As the family system gets healthier, codependency patterns can be expected to lessen.

Group Therapy

Group therapy can be very effective for issues like addiction, codependency, incest and sexual abuse survivors, childhood abuse survivors, battered spouses, anxiety, depression, eating disorders, and post-traumatic stress disorder (PTSD). These groups consist of individuals with commonalities based on their current life situation or past life experiences. The power of the group in healing is in a sense of acceptance, belonging, and validation. Groups teach through sharing experiences, and they provide an environment of caring and hope as group members model recovery.

FACT

Therapist-led groups help protect privacy and confidentiality of group members. The therapist can also control the process and the structure of the group experience, giving guidance about equal sharing time, abusive behavior, and conflict resolution within the group.

Facilitated groups have a designated facilitator, usually a professional or paraprofessional who can offer information, respond appropriately, answer questions, and invite participation. The facilitator is trained in group dynamics and understands the intricacies of the identified problem around which the group members are gathered.

Ideally, the group would consist of four to six individuals, perhaps in different stages of healing. The group could meet once a week for two to three hours in a private place like a therapist's office. The format would be fairly structured, with time for open sharing. An example would be a six-week group, meeting for three hours on Wednesdays in the therapist's office. There are certainly other possible patterns, like an ongoing, open-membership group with rotating facilitators. Only groups facilitated by an appropriate professional may be reimbursed by insurance. The cost is usually half or less the cost of individual therapy.

Self-Help Groups

Alcoholics Anonymous leads the way in providing support in recovery from alcoholism and drug abuse, gambling, and the like. With groups like Alcoholics Anonymous (AA), Narcotics Anonymous (NA), Gamblers Anonymous (GA), Al-Anon and Nar-Anon for families, Adult Children of Alcoholics (ACoA), and Co-Dependents Anonymous (CODA), there are choices for support groups at no cost. Look in your local newspaper for appropriate groups. Keep in mind that the codependency groups may be focused more on addiction systems, but you may be able to tease out what applies to you and gain support in the process.

Look in your local community for church- and agency-sponsored free support groups for codependency. Call your community mental health department and see if they are interested in offering a codependency support group.

Letter to the Psychologist

The following letter is taken from Here-to-Listen.com and helps explain how to get professional help for codependency.

Dear Doctor,

I really need help. I've known for some time that I have some codependency tendencies, but I still can't change them. I used to fear going to a therapist, but now I really want to. I'm afraid if I don't get professional help, my girlfriend is going to leave me.

Where do I start? I work for a small company in rural Ohio. I think we have some kind of Employee Help Program, but I'm not comfortable having them know about me and my relationship. But, I'm not sure I can afford to pay for therapy.

Brandon

Dear Brandon,

Employee Assistance Programs are a good place to start, but I'm not sure you have all the information you need. Call your EAP office. You don't have to give your name, just inquire about psychotherapy. Ask if they have an in-house therapist with an office on site or if they do an intake and then refer you to participating therapists in the community. Is there a limit to how many sessions you can get, and will you have to pay anything?

Most people will agree to an intake and then may want to be referred off-site to a participating therapist at no cost or a low copay to them. You do need to see how many sessions your company will pay for because you don't want to start and then have to quit for financial reasons. Let's say your company pays for twenty-five sessions. Work with your therapist to determine a weekly or every-other-week treatment schedule. With twenty-five sessions, you can go to therapy every other week for a year or once a week for six months.

CHAPTER 17

How Psychotherapy Works

If you were asked what type of psychotherapy works best for you, chances are you wouldn't know, especially if you've never been in therapy. This chapter cannot reduce complex theoretical ideas to a few pages; the goal is to give you a surface understanding, and to let you know that there *are* different approaches to psychotherapy. Reading about the types of therapy appropriate for codependency, even in a greatly abbreviated way, will give you some ideas about what might feel right for you.

A Therapeutic Approach

Every clinician learns about psychological theories and how these theories form the underpinnings for therapeutic methods. There are scores of therapeutic approaches based on the various psychological theories of human behavior. The theory underlies the approach; the approach informs therapy techniques, goals, and outcomes.

Several approaches are effective in treating codependency. The two most popular therapies are psychodynamic therapy and cognitive-behavioral therapy. A third approach, eclectic (also called *blended* or *integrated*) therapy, is probably the most widely used. The eclectic therapist tends to operate primarily from one approach, and adds techniques and ideas from other approaches to meet the individual needs of her clients. In other words, she uses what her education and experience tells her works.

Some licenses require continuing education for renewal. But even if this is not required, many clinicians seek out workshops, seminars, and further training as a way of staying current and learning new skills.

Because of the importance of couples' therapy in treating codependent relationships, family systems therapy focusing exclusively on the couple will also be included in this chapter.

You will explore these four therapeutic approaches as if you were the client, Jory Mathews, who is forty-three years old, is married to Chuck, and has two children. Jory is seeking therapy to change codependency traits she has identified in herself.

Psychodynamic Therapy

Psychodynamic therapy is the offspring of the Freudian analysis of the 1800s. Over the course of a hundred years or so, psychodynamic therapy retains the importance of early childhood in the understanding of current behavior, identifies unconscious motivation, and understands unconscious and conscious conflict to be the source of problematic behavior and psychological symptoms.

ESSENTIAL

Lying on a couch and streaming out thoughts and feelings without interruption is not what modern psychotherapy is like. You will sit upright, and your therapist will play an active role, guiding you with his input in a two-way discussion of your problems.

Jory, Intake Session

In Jory's first session with the psychodynamic therapist, she likely will be asked to explain what brings her to therapy, what her problems and concerns are, and what symptoms she is experiencing. From there the therapist takes an extensive history, focusing on Jory's childhood. The therapist's goal is to begin to understand what it was like for Jory growing up in her family of origin. From here, he will already begin formulating a roadmap for Jory's therapy based on psychodynamic theory.

ALERT

What if you know right away that a therapist is not right for you? Don't make another appointment—trust your instincts. But don't give up. Call another therapist for an appointment. That next therapist just might be a perfect fit for you.

Therapist: "I believe your rage and depression may be tied to issues in your childhood that you are not yet aware of, unhealthy patterns you learned, and pain you don't want to feel. For example, when you talked about how angry you get with your husband, I suspect this conflict triggers unresolved issues from long ago."

Jory: "You mean when he won't talk to me?"

Therapist: "Yes. That's a good example. Do you remember feeling cut off like that as a child?"

Jory: "I'm not sure."

Therapist: "Anybody ignore you or give you the silent treatment?"

Jory: "My mom. But I didn't feel angry like I do with Chuck."

Therapist: "Do you remember how you felt?"

Jory: "I was scared she'd never talk to me again."

Therapist: "Is there any fear under that anger toward Chuck?"

Jory (after long pause): "I'll have to think about that."

Jory, Much Later Session (Excerpt)

Therapist: "You weren't able to control your anger."

Jory: "I'm so stupid. I knew what to do, but he just made me so mad!"

Therapist: "Did you try to take a time-out when it got heated?"

Jory: "No. I didn't want to. I wanted to yell and scream at him because he was so mean."

Therapist: "Chuck was mean? How?"

Jory: "He just walked away from me."

Therapist: "Now close your eyes and try to remember when he walked away. What did you feel?"

Jory: "I remember thinking, Here we go again. This is never going to get better."

FACT

When emotions are deeply felt and words used to describe them are extreme, this can signal a repressed memory or unconscious trigger.

Therapist: "Feeling?"

Jory: "Crushed. Just crushed." (Sniffles.)

Therapist: "Can you talk more about 'crushed'?"

Jory: "What do you mean?"

Therapist: "Can you put an age on that feeling? How old did you feel when you felt crushed?"

Jory: "About five."

Therapist: "Do you think you felt crushed for any reason when you were five?"

Jory: "My dad left. I thought it was the end of the world."

Therapist: "Can you tell me about it?"

Jory: "Nobody said anything to me. I saw my dad packing up some boxes. Then he came over to me . . . (weeping). He kissed me on the forehead . . . . That was it."

Therapist: "He left for good?"

Jory: "Yes."

Therapist: "Go ahead and feel your feelings, Jory. You were only five."

Jory (weeping into her hands): "I need a tissue."

Therapist: "Do you see why you panicked, got so angry, when Chuck walked away?"

Jory: "It crushed me like when I was a little girl."

Therapist: "Yes. And the little girl in you needs to cry."

Jory: "Okay."

Therapist: "But the adult Jory has options other than feeling crushed or lashing out. Doesn't she?"

Jory (wiping her eyes): "Uh-huh."

Therapist: "Chuck is not your dad. He has a right to walk away from your anger. But you're also not a child. You have all the options available to you as an adult."

Jory, Summary

Right from the start, Jory's psychodynamic therapist is interested in her childhood. He believes that if she understands where her intense feelings are coming from, she can give herself permission to deal with them now. This would take the air out of an unconscious balloon full of rage from her past. Once this happens, Jory will not be overwhelmed with rage she cannot control, and can begin to make conscious decisions about how she responds.

Family Systems Therapy

Family systems therapy is based on the notion that the family is a system and every person affects every other person in the family. In family therapy, each individual in the system is helped, but one family member is not singled out. Systems therapy focuses on alliances and triangles, family rules, and the like. The marriage relationship can be the entire family, or it can be part of a larger family.

Jory and Chuck, Couples' Therapy Intake

Since Jory has been in individual therapy for several months, her therapist knows her quite well. Chuck will be "the new kid on the block" for couples' therapy, so the therapist meets with him individually prior to the first couples' therapy session. The therapist will collect the information he needs about Chuck's childhood to see what kind of triggers Chuck may be bringing into the mix. Usually, after one individual session with the spouse, the couple will begin conjoint therapy.

ESSENTIAL

Some people are afraid that they will cry in their sessions. Unfortunately, men are still taught that it's a sign of weakness to cry. Therapists do not become uncomfortable with high levels of emotion, although they may need to set boundaries with anger. Therapy is a place where you can express all your thoughts and feelings freely. Doing so is actually a sign of strength.

Therapist: "What do you two want to talk about today?"

Chuck: "I want to talk about Jory's bad moods."

Therapist: "What would you like to say about that, Chuck?"

Jory: "He's here to beat up on me."

Therapist: "Just a sec. Chuck, go ahead."

Chuck: "It's not just me, the kids are afraid of her."

Jory: "Who said that? They just don't like my rules."

Therapist: "Is this how you two talk to each other? Now it makes sense to me why you can't resolve things."

Chuck: "What?"

Therapist: "Well, you blamed Jory. Then she got angry and defensive. And there you have it. You're derailed."

Jory: "I told you that, Doc."

Therapist: "Each of you sit back and take a few deep breaths. First of all, I need each of you to start couples' therapy today. Jory, anything you and I have talked about before today Chuck wasn't here for, so he won't know what you are talking about. We will need to start each discussion as if it were the first time you and I have talked about it. At the start, I'd like to introduce you two to a conflict resolution model. It will really help you talk to one another respectfully, and you will have the skills to resolve a conflict, not just give up in frustration. It will take some time for you to get used to your new communication skills, so I'll guide you in session. You will also practice during the week at home."

Jory and Chuck, Much Later Session (Excerpt)

Chuck. "We've had a better week."

Therapist: "Good. Jory?"

Jory: "Yeah. It's going good."

Therapist: "What is your agenda for today's meeting?"

Jory: "I think we've agreed to finish a discussion that failed."

Chuck: "What's that?"

Jory: "The sleepover?"

Chuck: "Oh, yeah. Should I start? (Jory nods.) Well, we disagree on Abbie spending every weekend with Jory's mom."

Therapist: "Okay. Go ahead with your 'I' message, Chuck."

Chuck: "I feel worried when Abbie is at your mom's overnight because she has a boyfriend, and I don't like our daughter seeing that."

Jory: "You're afraid she'll see them doing something inappropriate."

Chuck: "Yes. And it bothers me a lot."

Jory: "I can definitely see how you would feel that way. Actually, I'm a little worried too."

Chuck: "You don't seem worried."

Therapist: "Chuck, Jory just said she is worried."

Chuck: "Okay, okay. What about?"

Jory: "Well, I totally trust my mom, but it's not like John is my dad. I don't trust him as much, I guess. But my mom loves having Abbie over. She'll be hurt if we stop her."

Therapist: "Jory, am I hearing codependency?"

Jory: "I know. I'm putting Mom's needs before ours."

Chuck: "I understand where you're coming from. Abbie loves her Grandma."

Jory: "I don't know what the middle ground is. My mom is pretty careful about her behavior with John. It's not like they're all over each other or anything."

Chuck: "That's true. I've been thinking about this, and there's something else going on for me. My mom had boyfriends over after the divorce and I hated it."

ALERT

If a decision seems reasonable to you when you think about it, but you just can't seem to do it, try to identify what might be creating the disconnect between your mind and your gut.

Jory: "I didn't know that, honey."

Therapist: "Chuck, that sounds like an important trigger. Would you be willing to talk to Jory about what that was like for you as a kid?"

Chuck: "It sucked. I could hear them from my bedroom. I got up to use the bathroom one night, and a naked guy was coming out."

Jory: "That must've been awful."

Chuck. "It was."

Therapist: "This discussion about Abbie has brought up some strong emotions from your own childhood, Chuck. I imagine it influences the way you see your daughter's situation."

Chuck: "Yeah. I think so."

Therapist: "How so?"

Chuck: "I think I may be overreacting to the possible danger for Abbie."

Jory and Chuck, Summary

The issue brought up about Abbie visiting her grandmother impacts the entire family. As the therapy moves forward, the details of how this family system works will emerge from the dialogue between Chuck and Jory, but the emphasis will remain on the marriage.

ESSENTIAL

If troubled couples knew how to communicate, most could solve their problems without professional help.

One thing we can see very clearly is that, through therapy, the couple now knows how to talk to one another with barely any coaching from the therapist. They have learned to share on a deeper level, are not entrenched in an adversarial dialogue, and genuinely seem interested in resolving the conflicts.

Cognitive-Behavioral Therapy

Cognitive-behavioral therapy is a combination of behavioral therapy and cognitive therapy. Behavioral therapy uses rewards and consequences to address a particular problem behavior. Cognitive therapy focuses on changing thoughts that create negative feelings and behaviors. Challenging these thoughts by taking them apart and analyzing faulty connections and irrational conclusions has been an effective treatment for depression, anxiety, and relationship dysfunction.

Jory, Intake Session

The cognitive-behavioral therapist takes a history, but she's not focusing particularly on Jory's childhood, how her family system operated, or what unresolved issues she may have. She's focusing on Jory's current problem with the intention of collecting details. The therapist wants to know how Jory perceives the problem, what her feelings are regarding the problem, and what she is thinking just before a conflict arises.

Therapist: "What is the problem you are dealing with, Jory?"

Jory: "I'm not happy in my marriage. There are too many arguments, and my husband is threatening to divorce me if I don't get a handle on my anger."

Therapist: "Can you tell me about the last time you two fought?"

Jory: "It was this morning. I got up early and made cookies for my youngest to take to school. I was busy in the kitchen when Chuck got up. The first thing he said to me was how loud the children were."

Therapist: "How did you feel about what he said?"

Jory: "It really irked me. Here I was working my butt off and he has the nerve to complain about the kids?"

Therapist: "So, when he complained about the kids, what did you think?"

Jory: "That he was selfish, only thinking about himself."

Therapist: "And how did that make you feel?"

Jory: "Like a slave."

Therapist: "Your husband commenting on the children being loud made you feel like a slave."

Jory: "Well . . . yes."

Therapist: "What did you do?"

Jory: "I dumped the rest of the dough in the sink, and told him he could make the damn cookies."

Therapist: "And?"

Jory: "He gave me a disgusted look, left the kitchen, and in a few minutes I heard him leave. He never even said goodbye to me. I was so mad I could hardly breathe."

Therapist: "What were you thinking when you got so angry you could hardly breathe?"

Jory: "I was thinking, How many times have I tried to make things nice for him? Make a nice home and raise the kids, and he treats me like dirt."

Therapist: "I'm listening to you fire up quite an anger, Jory. Do you realize you are making all this up in your head?"

Jory: "Huh?"

Therapist: "The only behavior of your husband's I heard you describe was that he commented on the kids being so loud. The rest is of your own making; your rage is coming from your own thinking. You've added all this on, the ingratitude, the disgust, the contempt."

Jory: "No, I don't think so."

Therapist: "Did your husband do anything besides say the kids were so loud?"

Jory: "Yes. He left the house without saying goodbye to me."

Therapist: "Yes, I understand that was upsetting to you. Why do you think he did that?"

Jory: "I was screaming at him."

Therapist: "Let's look at the situation before you got mad."

Jory: "Okay."

Therapist: "You're baking cookies. Your husband says the kids are so loud. Is that correct?"

Jory: "Yes."

Therapist: "These are two separate things, baking cookies and loud kids. Am I right? The two are not connected."

Jory: "Well . . . I thought he was being inconsiderate."

Therapist: "Why would you want to think that?"

Jory: "What do you mean?"

Therapist: "I mean these two things are not connected, cookie baking and loud kids, so why would you want to connect them in a way that makes you angry?"

Jory: "But . . . ."

Jory, Much Later Session (Excerpt)

Jory: "Okay, I know I'm responsible for my own anger. I'm getting much better; even Chuck thinks so. But I'm hung up on this feeling that he's not in love with me. I think he's just putting up with me because of the kids."

Therapist: "Okay. What is the feeling, Jory?"

Jory: "Why would he love me?"

Therapist: "A feeling."

Jory (tearful): "I'm afraid he'll leave me."

Therapist: "You're afraid."

Jory: "Yes."

Therapist: "Tell me your thoughts on this."

Jory: "Well, I'm not that . . . I've been . . . I'm not that easy to live with."

Therapist: "Yes. Nobody is warm and loving all the time. And you have an anger problem you're working on."

Jory: "My mother always said I was worthless. She never really loved me either."

Therapist: "You were just a little girl."

Jory: "Yeah."

Therapist: "So it's not true you were worthless. No little girl is worthless, is she?"

Jory: "No."

Therapist: "So what if you chose to see yourself as worthy, worthy of being loved and all the good that comes with that?"

Jory: "Well, that's a different idea."

Therapist: "I believe it to be true."

Jory: "Hmmmm."

Therapist: "It's time for you to stop being your own rejecting parent, Jory."

Jory, Summary

The cognitive-behavioral therapist realizes that certain thoughts and behaviors have been learned in childhood, but she doesn't explore this to the degree the psychodynamic or systems therapist would. She focuses primarily on the here-and-now thoughts, feelings, and behaviors of her client. She helps Jory see that her negative feelings are indeed created by her thoughts. As a result, Jory has come to accept that she's responsible for these feelings and has stopped blaming others for her misery.

The good news is that Jory now knows she can think differently about an experience and have positive or neutral feelings. She has learned to calm her own anger by telling herself that Chuck is his own person with his own perceptions, needs, and opinions. She doesn't need to take his beliefs as an attack on her. This change in thinking moves her away from her codependent thoughts where everything Chuck did and said was about her. Now she is moving toward interdependent thoughts. She's substituting positive self-talk to counter all the negative self-talk she is now aware of.

Eclectic Therapy

From the name, it is clear that the eclectic (or blended) approach does not adhere to one theoretical framework. It blends or integrates any number of theories in developing a therapeutic approach. Typically, a newly minted professional leaves graduate school with a substantial set of therapeutic tools in his back pocket. Throughout his practicum, his internship, and his years of experience, through ongoing education, he continues to collect tools that he can use to tailor his treatment to each individual he sees.

Jory, Intake Session

Jory's eclectic therapist sends her an eight-page history form to fill out and bring in. The therapist briefly reviews the form and asks clarifying questions. He asks Jory about her parents' divorce, her relationships with all her caregivers, about any traumas Jory hasn't mentioned, her relationship history, her current life situation, and anything else that wasn't clear from the form.

ALERT

Perhaps the reason eclectic therapy is so widely used is because so many therapists believe that no single answer fits everybody. Part of the expertise of a therapist is going outside the box, or at least opening many boxes to find what works best for each individual patient.

Therapist: "Jory, of the things you mentioned are troubling you, which is the most painful right now?"

Jory: "My marriage."

Therapist: "Is there a reason Chuck isn't here today?"

Jory: "I didn't ask him to come."

Therapist: "But your marriage is causing you a lot of pain?"

Jory: "I think the problem is me."

Therapist: "How so?"

Jory: "I'm codependent."

Therapist: "What does that mean to you?"

Jory: "It means I always feel bad. I can't seem to feel happy. Mostly I just hate my husband for how he treats me, and I'm always blowing up and making things worse."

Therapist: "Okay. Would you be willing to have a pretend conversation with him right now so I can help you figure this out?"

Jory: "What?"

Therapist: "It's a Gestalt technique called the empty chair. (Gets up and pulls a chair in front of Jory.) Pretend you're having a discussion with your husband. He's sitting right here in this empty chair. Start with a statement about how you feel when he treats you badly."

Jory reluctantly begins the discussion, stating how mad she is at her husband. On the therapist's cue, Jory alternates between the two chairs, simulating a discussion with her husband, for about five minutes until the discussion has escalated to a loud fight.

Therapist: "Your discussion quickly escalated, Jory. Is this typical?"

Jory: "Yes."

Therapist: "You blamed your husband for ignoring you and then wanting sex."

Jory: "Yes, yes I did! (Starts crying.) He doesn't care anything about me, he just wants sex."

Therapist: "How do you know he doesn't care about you?"

Jory: "It just seems that way."

Therapist: "You know, just because you two have a difference in needs, it doesn't mean he cares less about you."

Jory: "I hate him."

Therapist: "You quickly reached a point of rage during the empty chair exercise. What's going on?"

Jory: "I don't know."

Therapist: "You said there was no sexual abuse in your early life, is that correct?"

Jory: "Not in my family, no."

Therapist: "Anything that could be thought of as sexual abuse in your family or otherwise?"

Jory: "My brother's friend had sex with me."

Therapist: "How old were you?"

Jory: "Nine."

Therapist: "Oh no. You were raped when you were nine, Jory?"

Jory (lowers voice, gets teary-eyed): "Yes."

Therapist: "You must be in a lot of pain over this assault. And I think it is still affecting you today, in your marriage."

Jory: "Yeah, I guess . . . ."

Jory, Much Later Session (Excerpt)

Jory: "Chuck is being really sweet to me."

Therapist: "You deserve it, Jory. You've worked really hard."

Jory: "I'm not so angry anymore."

Therapist: "You've worked through a lot of your anger and you've reconnected with the sweet you. We've done the rapid eye movement sessions. We've met with Chuck a few times to talk about your sexual relationship. We'll continue to work with how the sexual assault affected your identity and self-esteem. How it has made you feel and act codependent with Chuck and with others."

Jory: "I still find myself expecting Chuck to know what I need and want."

Therapist: "What happens when he doesn't?"

Jory: "Well, I don't fly into a stupid rage anymore, but I do find myself getting angry and talking to myself about how insensitive Chuck is."

Therapist: "You know, you're creating your own anger with this thinking. Any guesses why you're still doing it?"

Jory: "I think so. I get all up in my head and talk myself into feeling like a victim. I know I was a victim, but it was a long time ago, when I was a kid. Then I think I can get Chuck to feel sorry for me . . . something like that."

Therapist: "That seems like a long way around to get what you want. What is it you want from Chuck?"

Jory: "I want him to put his arms around me, tell me he loves me, and that I'm just perfect the way I am."

Therapist: "What would happen if you just asked him for what you need?"

Jory: "Whew. That feels like a big risk."

Therapist (squeezing Jory's arm): "You're ready."

Jory, Summary

Jory's eclectic therapist is well equipped to deal with Jory's codependency. He recognizes that Jory's childhood trauma changed her identity from one of an innocent child to someone who felt she was damaged and unlovable. Because she had a fractured identity and a dismally low self-esteem, Jory looked to her husband to tell her she was okay. When they had conflicting needs, Jory was devastated and retaliated by raging at Chuck.

Jory's therapist is licensed in marriage and family therapy as well as in psychology, so he involved Chuck early on in the therapy. The sexual relationship, in particular, was a source of shame and pain for Jory. What was a normal desire on Chuck's part became an assault in Jory's mind. She felt used and devalued, and the rage roared to the surface. Jory was unable to see Chuck's desire as a good thing, a way for them to be close and to share. The therapist had training in sex therapy and was comfortable and skilled in dealing with that part of the relationship.

In addition to codependency traits, Jory suffered from PTSD because of the sexual abuse. Her therapist also had taken postgraduate training in the Eye Movement Desensitization and Reprocessing (EMDR) techniques that helped Jory get through her PTSD more quickly. After time in individual therapy, conjoint therapy, and more individual therapy, Jory was referred into a codependency support group by her therapist. The varied tools used by Jory's therapist worked well in helping Jory move through major obstacles to a more balanced life.

Letter to the Psychologist

The following letter is taken from Here-to-Listen.com and helps explain the screening process in choosing a therapist for codependency issues.

Dear Doctor,

I called a licensed marriage and family therapist to make an appointment. During the call, I told him my partner and I were gay, and we didn't want to work with anybody who might be homophobic. He got very defensive and said my question was silly. He said he was qualified to work with couples "of any kind." He quickly asked if I wanted to schedule an appointment with him or not.

I did schedule, but when I told my partner about the conversation, he said this therapist is definitely not for him. He said we are gay and he wants to go to somebody who is gay-affirming. He said the therapist should have offered something like what kind of training or education he had in the special issues and needs of gay clients.

Van

Dear Van,

Your partner has a point. When people say things like "Gay couples are just like straight couples" or "We don't see color, we accept everybody," they are speaking from an arrogant point of view, as if they have the power to approve of or withhold approval from a minority. It is imperative that a professional educate himself on how racism, ageism, sexism, and homophobia might rear its ugly head in therapy. To say there are no differences is to diminish the minority client. Yes, there are differences, differences that should be valued and addressed.

You would be happier with a therapist who "got it" and could respectfully respond to your concerns. It is shocking that a professional would tell you that your concerns are "silly." Make an appointment with someone else.

CHAPTER 18

Making Your Own Internal Changes

Not everyone will choose to make that call to a therapist to get help with his or her codependency issues. This book certainly does not advocate a one-size-fits-all approach. If you decide to tackle your codependency work alone or with a significant other or friend, these next three chapters will give you tools to help with that. They are also helpful tools to use in conjunction with therapy or self-help groups.

Your Journal

You probably had a diary as a child, a small bound book with a fancy cover that could be locked with its own little key. By the time you were a teenager, you may have kept a journal where you wrote your most profound thoughts, kept tabs on your friends, and spilled out your heartbreak and angst.

FACT

In a controlled study reported on the website of *Psychosomatic Medicine*, women who participated in expressive writing exercises healed faster from physical wounds. In the current Professional Training offerings at Duke Integrative Medicine, the course, Leading Patients in Writing for Health, includes "reviewing more than thirty years of studies that demonstrate the efficacy of this healing modality."

Now, as you begin this important self-exploration of codependency, it is extremely helpful to keep a journal. It can be in any form that fits your needs. Buy yourself an expensive leather-bound book, grab a spiral notebook, or use your computer. It's up to you.

Put It in the Vault

Your journal can serve as a vault where your codependency work is kept. It can be a "home base" you return to when you need to express yourself, remember how you used to think and feel about something, or pat yourself on the back for how far you've come. Journals are often a part of therapy and self-help groups because they work. With a journal, you never have to wait for an appointment or try to reach a friend; nor do you need to work around the needs of your family. You can just find a quiet spot, get out your journal, and record those important thoughts and feelings as they occur.

Some people are afraid to write down their thoughts and feelings. They are worried that somebody will discover their journal and read it. Adults who were abused as children may have a general feeling of anxiety about privacy, secrets, and being found out. Everyone should have a private place to keep her personal things. Even if you have to keep your journal in the trunk of your car, it is still worth starting. Maybe as you work through old issues, you will feel more confident about your privacy.

As you consider how you wish to use a journal—whether you want to write in an unstructured, free-flow style or a more planned, organized way— you may want to explore some of the ideas presented here.

Mindfulness

The term *mindfulness* has become more mainstream in recent years. It is a term that describes a practice of focusing on your experience in the here-and-now without judgment. According to the Mindfulness Research Guide website there is substantial evidence-based support of mindfulness as an effective tool in preventing and managing physical illness and addiction relapse; reducing stress, anxiety, and depression; and improving the quality of life. Mindfulness is akin to meditation, yoga, and other practices rooted in Buddhism and other Eastern religions. The positive effects of these practices is firmly established by years of clinical research. To illustrate the acceptance of the benefits of mindfulness in our culture, some schools have introduced mindfulness as part of the daily routine of the classroom.

The state of mindfulness is important in your work with codependency. It can remove you from the daily distractions of life. It facilitates your ability to know yourself intimately, accept yourself, and get rid of the negative talk in your head. It is a practice that can improve general happiness, and may create a state where your creativity can flourish and new insights can emerge. In conjunction with your journal, mindfulness can bring you into yourself to observe how you are in the present. It can also help with your codependency work by directing you away from self-blame and old judgments. You may want to begin each journaling session with a mindfulness exercise.

Meditation and Mindfulness

Mindfulness doesn't need to be formalized, nor does it need to take up much time. Mindfulness techniques like sitting quietly, attending to your breathing, and allowing thoughts to come in without evaluating them as bad or good can be done in a few minutes. Once you are familiar with how mindfulness works, you can go to this state whenever you need to for as long or as short a time as you wish.

What follows is a simplified instruction for meditation: Sit on the floor on a pillow or folded blanket. Cross your legs in front of you as a child would, in a way that is comfortable for you. Make sure your hips are higher than your knees. Place your hands on your thighs and turn up your palms. The most basic finger position is to join your thumb and index finger. Your posture should be erect but not stiff. Use the natural curve of your spine, with shoulders slightly back and your chin forward. Your eyes should be open and focused on the floor about five or six feet in front of you. Some people like to hang a prism or use another focal point. If you do this, use the same distance, five or six feet.

ALERT

In the article, "Overcoming the Barriers to Self-Knowledge: Mindfulness as a Path to Seeing Yourself as You Really Are," March 2013; vol. 8, 2: pp. 173-186. in the journal *Perspectives on Psychological Science*, psychologist Erika Carlson concluded that paying attention and observing without judgment is a way of knowing oneself. She points out that mindfulness reduces emotional reactivity in the form of low self-esteem and feelings of inadequacy, allowing a person to know himself more accurately.

Breathe easily and begin to notice your breathing. Don't be too focused on it. Just breathe and let it happen. The next segment of your attention will be on your body and your environment. Just notice. Unlike some types of meditation, the goal is not to clear your mind. Your thoughts are an important part of mindfulness. Just notice your thoughts coming across your mind like a ticker tape—notice them, but don't make any judgments about them. If you should become too involved in your thoughts and begin to lose awareness that you are sitting in a room, gently bring yourself back to your breathing. If your breathing has become faster, notice that, and let it return to a relaxed pace. Remember, the goal is to be mindful of whatever happens. There is no right or wrong.

You may want to practice this meditation for ten minutes, increasing to thirty or maybe even longer over time. However much time you wish to devote to your mindfulness meditation, it will not be wasted. Once the process comes easily, you can use it almost anywhere as you need it.

Anger: Quieting the Storm Within

Healthy anger is a small gray cloud quickly moving over the sun. What turns anger into a storm is you. It's sort of like a mental cloud seeding. Once you add your instigating self-talk to a little cloud of anger, you can stir up quite a storm. You are like Dorothy in *The Wizard of Oz*, swept up, swirling out of control, uncertain where you'll land. You can unwind if you change the thoughts that create anger. You can also calm yourself if you feel anger stirring. One way is through journaling and mindfulness.

Codependency and Anger

There is such a thing as healthy anger. For one thing, anger is a signal of a boundary violation. If someone walks up to you and kicks you in the shin, it's reasonable for you to raise your voice and say, "Hey!" It's also expected that you would insist that this kicker stop kicking you. It's the unreasonable anger that interferes with your enjoyment of life and destroys relationships.

ALERT

Since codependents are typically out of touch with their inner feelings and thoughts, they can be confused about anger. They get angry over things they shouldn't, and don't get angry over things they should. The journal will help with this confusion.

A codependent person very often has rage, resentment, or anger problems because of those antennae searching for signs of disapproval. She is honed in on her significant other, who becomes her ego mirror. She is bracing for rejection, on edge to see if she is still okay. If confronted with a less than perfect image of herself in her ego mirror, she may use anger to bully that person into silence or get him to change his mind. Sometimes anger fuels hurtful comments aimed to punish the ego mirror for his unfair impressions.

Once you have accepted that your anger is created by you, you are on your way to recovery. Whether anger is expressed or simmers inside you as resentment, it affects your sense of peacefulness and keeps you at a distance from the people you care about. Rage is so destructive to you and to anyone you engage that mastering it is essential in your codependency work. As with any other feeling, anger is on a continuum of intensity, from mild irritation or frustration to a full-blown rage. Codependents are generally angry people because they are continuously trying to control others, something that cannot be achieved.

Be Mindful of the Gathering Clouds

One way you can use the mind-body connection in reducing anger is the ongoing regular practice of repetitive exercise like swimming, walking, and running. These physical activities can help you identify your "zone" of well-being. Making this feeling of physical balance a part of your daily life resets your trigger point for anger.

It's like you've been walking on sharp stones and your body is tense and tentative and bracing for an injury. It takes little to set you off in this state. Once the endorphins kick in, and your mind is relaxed, it's as if you've come upon cool soft grass where you are relaxed, trusting, and comfortable as you walk. The occasional prick of dry grass is taken in stride.

Another way to achieve inner calmness is through Zen practices like meditation, relaxation techniques, breath work, yoga, tai chi, guided imagery, massage, and mindfulness. If you can include one of these practices in your day, you can affect your anger threshold. You may want to record Zen experiences in your journal.

Mindfulness is helpful on the front lines as well. Body sensations provide the first clues to rising anger. The heartbeat increases, breathing becomes shallow, the jaw clenches, eyes narrow or widen, tendons in the neck stand out, voice rises, and muscles tighten. Record your particular body signals of anger. At the slightest warning, it is time to take a break and practice mindfulness until you have calmed yourself.

It can be helpful to elicit assistance from your partner in your anger work. For one thing, your partner has learned to notice changes in you and can often see your anger coming before you do. More importantly, your partner will shift his position from adversary to helpmate. Meet at a time when there is no anger looming. Agree to an intervention where he will let you know if he sees your anger rising. You have asked him to do this, so there is no need to get defensive or deny what he sees. Agree to stop immediately, no questions asked; take a break and do your mindfulness meditation. Return later when you are calm and use your communication skills to resolve the conflict.

Don't Seed the Clouds

This is where your journal will be helpful. Start your anger work by listing all the things you are angry about right now. Now go through the list and see if you are trying to control somebody or something you have no control over. Cross them off the list. Look at the remaining items. Are there items you have some control over but cannot change for the positive by any action you might take? Cross them off. Of the items remaining, which items could you take action on but are choosing not to? Cross them off.

ESSENTIAL

"The weak can never forgive. Forgiveness is the attribute of the strong." —Gandhi

Of those remaining, stop and ask yourself what your motivation is for acting. Will your action resolve an issue? Will it bring you closer to the person involved? In other words, is your heart in the right place, or are you trying to get the upper hand? If your intentions are pure, plan and act as soon as possible. This should completely eliminate the list you had. If the item is gone, let it go. There is nothing to be done about it. Remember, you are the one who suffers from carrying the anger. Forgiveness is a letting go that benefits you. You know that gaining mastery over anger is not as simple as crossing items off a list. How you deal with anger likely has been a developing process over the course of your lifetime. You may have accepted your anger as something that is appropriate even when it is not. You may even justify your inappropriate behavior by thinking if you're angry, of course you behaved badly, but that is not healthy. Because codependents often perceive themselves as victims, they feel quite self-righteous about expressing anger and rage.

Each day as you notice angry feelings inside, or you get angry at someone or something, don't seed the clouds. Do the exercise outlined in this section. Make your list and empower yourself to resolve issues without anger. This will be an ongoing process until you have mastered anger management.

Talking Yourself Into Anger

Another essential exercise is this one. Record your instigating self-talk in your journal. These entries will testify in black and white how you create your own anger. In a sentence or two write down the incident that caused you to become angry. Now draw a line down the middle of the page. Use the left side to list all the anger-fueling self-talk. When you are done, write a counter statement on the right side that would help reduce anger.

John is angry with his wife because she's overdrawn the checking account. This is an ongoing conflict in John and Judy's relationship. In the past, he's become extremely angry, accusatory, and self-righteous when confronted with the overdrawn account. Here is an example of how John might begin to work on this issue. He makes two columns in his journal. The first column would reflect his knee-jerk, anger-inciting self-talk; in the second column John would think of an anger-reducing self-talk:

She never listens to me.	She's busy.
She doesn't care what I think.	She probably needs help.
She does this on purpose.	Something's wrong with our method.
She's so selfish.	We're in this together; what can I do?
I work hard; she just spends.	She works hard, and I spend too.

This exercise alone will give you much needed information about yourself. There are still people out there who believe somebody else "makes them angry." Do you see how this fits in with codependency? Blame is externally motivated. To change codependency patterns, you must be internally motivated. You must know why you do what you do, know how you feel and why, know what you want, and then take that information and act on the world. Not the other way around, where you react to the world.

Melting the Stone Heart

The same mind-body techniques can help you become the loving person you were before hurt, anger, and resentment turned your heart to stone. Notice yourself as you move through your life doing your thing. Is your face tight with tension, brow furrowed, mouth turned down? Look in the mirror. Do you look mean or discontented?

FACT

One of the best definitions of love is: kindnesses given consistently over time. —Unknown

Remember when you were cranky as a kid and your mother told you that if you didn't stop looking so grumpy, your face would stick that way? Well, that's not exactly true, but the body does hold memory. When you're sitting outside on a sunny day, walking on the beach, listening to music, gazing at the water, if your face at rest looks crabby, you probably have had the look way too often in your life. Codependency traits of self-doubt, trying to please, disappointment in what others do and say, high standards, inflexibility, overfunctioning, and being all things all the time are not only exhausting and frustrating, they affect your physical well-being.

Again, use your journal. Write down the times in your life where you felt the best, most loving, tender, excited, peaceful, content, warm, loved, secure, and safe. You will remind yourself of your capacity for love. Now use these times of joy in this exercise. Do this often.

Choose a quiet private space where you won't be interrupted. Pick one of the joyful moments from your journal, close your eyes, and re-create the setting. Let's say the moment is when you first held your newborn baby. Think about the color of the baby's blanket, who was near, how the infant's face looked, his tiny hands. Allow yourself to feel that joy; notice how it changes your face, your breathing, and your muscles.

If you feel hardened toward your spouse, think about a time you felt very close to her, very loving toward her. Let go of all the bad feelings, let your heart lead and your resentments fall away. Allow yourself to get into the experience. Following this particular exercise, write all the things you love about your partner in your journal. Any time you feel distant from her, or angry with her, try this short meditation before you talk about it.

ALERT

If you need the structure of a guided meditation, there are many choices on YouTube. Try one that focuses on love, specifically for reconnecting with the love you have for your partner.

If you want to feel better, inside and out, make these practices a part of your life. As you know, one of the most debilitating features of codependency is a disconnection with the self. Anything you can do to reconnect and stay connected will change the way you see yourself and, in turn, will empower you in your life.

Letter to the Psychologist

The following letter is taken from Here-to-Listen.com and helps explain the overfunctioning of a codependent.

Dear Doctor,

I'm so busy, I feel like I'm losing my mind. I have a million thoughts going on in my head all the time. I'm responsible for my kids and worry about them constantly. My husband has been down in the dumps, and I can't figure out what's wrong with him. I keep trying to get him to go get help, but he won't go.

My parents just retired and they are moving to my town to be closer to the grandkids. I really like the idea, but my mom is very controlling and will try to run my life. I know she will. But I can't tell her not to move here. I'm lucky my husband loves my parents, but he just doesn't understand what I'm going through. I can't sleep.

Bobbie

Dear Bobbie,

You need to get help. If that's not possible (and please don't say you're too busy), try to do some self-help reading, focusing on codependency and anxiety disorders. You are heading for a meltdown. You are doing too much, worrying too much, and trying to control everything and everybody around you.

Think about your mother and how controlling she is. Get in touch with how you feel around her. This is how you are coming across to your family. Now this revelation should scare you a bit. Find something, anything, that gets you out of the house, on your own, that will relax you and help you relieve this stress. Take a yoga class, join a gym, sign up for a spinning class, swim, join a book club, go to the library, or get a massage.

But the most important advice I can give you is to call and make an appointment with a therapist.

CHAPTER 19

Ending Codependency with Significant Others

If you draw a bull's-eye chart with a person at the center, on each consecutive ring from center to edge are the people who influence her. The first ring around the center represents the people with the strongest influence, her partner and children. They are her significant others; she cares how they feel, what they think, and how they behave. Someone with codependency relies too heavily on the influence of her significant others. She not only cares what they think, feel, and do; she needs them to define who she is. Her partner becomes her ego mirror, that person she counts on to reflect her value and self-esteem. Unfortunately, the mirror has no gray areas; it reflects either totally black or it reflects pure white, either damaged or perfect.

The Ego Mirror

The term *ego mirror* is used to describe that one person or few people who are used by the codependent as a substitute for her stunted identity. Those who have a well-formed, intact identity do not need an ego mirror. They know themselves from the inside, not as they are reflected by someone from the outside. They listen to people they care about and consider their opinions, but someone else cannot rock the foundation of their identity by disagreeing with them, judging them, or having conflicting needs.

In the fairy tale "Snow White," the queen is compelled to go to the mirror often to make sure she is still "the fairest of them all." The partner of the codependent is that ego mirror. And, like the queen, the codependent needs reassurance that she is okay. She can't tolerate the truth; all she needs is the mirror to tell her she's the fairest. When the queen is told that she's no longer the fairest, she flies into a rage and seeks to destroy the source of her misery. She smashes the mirror.

The identity of a codependent is sometimes quite brittle, easily shattered. This is why codependents are desperate to change their loved one's negative reflection at all costs. They don't know how to change from the inside, so they must change the outside. In the worst scenario, if it takes smashing the mirror, they will do it. But until then, a codependent will use all the manipulative weapons at her disposal to force her significant other to let go of any concerns that might imply she is less than perfect

FACT

According to the *Merriam Webster Dictionary*, the term *ego* refers to the opinion you have about yourself; a part of the mind that senses and adapts to the real world; self-esteem; the self, especially as contrasted with another self or the world.

The codependent does not have the freedom to let others be who they are. He cannot bear to see a significant other angry with him, or disappointed, or thinking badly of him. He is forever tied to a reflection. It is a painful place to be because the only option for a codependent to feel okay is to make sure his ego mirror reflects well of him.

How do you respond to these questions?

- Can you tolerate your partner being mad at you? Must you try to change her feelings?
- After expressing opposing opinions, can you just agree to disagree with your partner?
- When you feel criticized by your partner, can you hear it and not explain yourself, sometimes in several different ways?
- If your partner gives you advice, can you consider it and not get defensive?
- Do you become panicky when you suspect your partner is upset with you and you don't know why?
- Do you defer to your partner's needs and then become resentful?
- Do you feel uncomfortable when your partner asks your opinion without sharing his first?
- Are you pretty much aware of your partner's mood at all times?
- Do you feel anxious when your partner ends a discussion and the conflict isn't resolved?
- In a potentially difficult discussion do you always need to know how your partner feels before you share how you feel?
- Do you feel desperate to get your point across to your partner?

If you answered yes to any of these questions, get your journal out and write about the question. Remind yourself of instances where you did react this way to your partner. See if you can figure out why you need your partner's approval, or why you feel compelled to convince him of your position, or talk him out of his feelings. If you are expecting your partner to approve of every thought, feeling, and action of yours, you may be using him as an ego mirror.

Guilt, Codependency, and the Ego Mirror

At the core, the narcissist and the codependent lack the same thing. They lack a healthy identity. Underneath the bravado of the narcissist is a person who needs somebody else to validate his inflated ego. His ego mirror must reflect his puffed-up, better-than-you, world-revolves-around-me sense of self. If the ego mirror reflects faults, imperfections, or inadequacies, there is something wrong with the mirror.

Narcissists rarely experience guilt because they typically don't have an identity conflict. Their idealized self is perfectly fine with them. All they need is an ego mirror to shine white all of the time. If the mirror fails to provide this, the narcissist looks for a new one. The reflection of a narcissist's identity would look like a perfectly formed diamond; unfortunately, it's made of glass.

In contrast, the codependent has an identity more like a gem that is flawed; it has blemishes, and cracks, and the color may be off a bit. This doesn't make it undesirable; it's just not perfect. The diamond is as sparkly as most other diamonds, but the codependent knows it's flawed. She has a conflict because she knows the flaws are there, but she just can't accept them. She needs an ego mirror that reflects only the brilliance and does not show the flaws.

FACT

"People are like stained-glass windows. They sparkle and shine when the sun is out, but when the darkness sets in their true beauty is revealed only if there is light from within." —Elisabeth Kübler-Ross

A person who has a healthy ego, a positive self-esteem, accepts her imperfections and the imperfections of others. But not the codependent. She cannot accept her flaws and works very hard to deny them. She wants to see herself only as sparkly, as possessing every good quality at all times. She strives to be the most selfless, helpful, considerate, loving, and thoughtful human being. When she knows she's not, she feels guilty. If the ego mirror confirms her flaws, she can't accept it, even though she knows it's true. Instead of looking within, she attacks the mirror.

Misdirected Guilt

When you consider that the codependent has an unrealistic, perfectionistic sense of self, her actual behavior may not always match this distorted self-image. When this happens, the codependent blames the ego mirror.

Andrea and Felicia have been together for twenty-two years. Felicia is turning fifty and has been diagnosed with chronic fatigue syndrome. The doctor meets with Felicia and Andrea and discusses the changes expected with the disease. He spends a lot of time with the couple, educating them and discussing the ways in which the illness may change their lives.

Felicia has always been a very hard worker and now will need to limit her activities to keep herself as healthy as possible. The doctor specifically asks Andrea to make sure Felicia doesn't overdo it. He encourages the couple to sit down and redistribute their household duties to accommodate Felicia's illness. Andrea assures the doctor she understands and supports Felicia unconditionally, and would be happy to take on more of the load.

A week later, they sit down to talk, and Andrea agrees to do all the housework, and Felicia switches to the more sedentary jobs like paying the bills, dealing with phone calls and other business, and cooking. Whenever the couple is asked by friends and family how Felicia is doing, Andrea always includes the fact that she is taking good care of her and making sure she isn't overdoing it.

In reality, Andrea stops doing the housework after a couple of weeks. After that, she does things only as Felicia requests, and not very happily. Felicia is having a difficult time accepting her limitations and finds it difficult to ask for Andrea's help. After several months, Felicia can't stand the dirty house, and talks to her partner about the housework.

Felicia: "Hon, I feel really unnerved by the condition of the house."

Andrea: "What do you mean?"

Felicia: "It's dirty."

Andrea: "Oh, for God's sake, Felicia, it's fine."

Felicia: "No, it isn't. The toilets are getting permanently stained, the stove has burned-on grease I can't get off, the refrigerator stinks, it's awful. There's dust and cobwebs everywhere."

Andrea: "You're such a neat freak. You can ask any of our friends—you're OCD. Nobody expects a house as clean as you want it."

Felicia: "You think my standards are unreasonable?"

Andrea: "Yup."

Felicia: "I understood you to say you'd keep the house up as before."

Andrea: "Don't you think that's ridiculous?"

Felicia: "No. That's the way we've lived for over twenty years. Our house has been clean and tidy."

Andrea: "And you don't think it's that way now?"

Felicia: "Not really."

Andrea: "Nobody can please you, Felicia. You're too fussy."

Felicia: "It really bothers me to see the house so dirty and you're telling me not to do anything, but then you don't follow through on our agreement."

Andrea: "Why do you always have to be so nasty? You should hear yourself. I wish I had a recording of how you talk to me."

Felicia: "Okay. Never mind."

Andrea: "That's right. Just clam up. Why do you get to end the discussion? You're just mean. I'm going upstairs."

Andrea's idealized identity, one in which she is Johnny-on-the-spot to meet Felicia's every need, is not realistic. But Andrea doesn't want to admit she's imperfect. Instead, she makes agreements based on her idealized self, she tells everybody she is this superwoman, and part of her really believes it. When her ego mirror, Felicia, dares to reflect her as less than perfect, she attacks her. This has been going on for twenty-two years, but Felicia has learned to compensate to avoid conflict. If she does everything, never shares an honest complaint, there will be no problems, and Andrea can go on believing she's the perfect partner.

But assume Andrea is journaling and trying to overcome her codependency. When she leaves the room she uses the time to do a mindfulness exercise. From that she is able to see her behavior and not make harsh judgments about it. With her self-esteem no longer at stake, she asks herself what she could do differently. How can she stop being so defensive and let Felicia have her feelings? And then, how can she respond as a partner who has self-esteem and is in an interdependent relationship? She knows she dropped the ball on the housework, and she feels guilty about it. Now Felicia is verifying that she screwed up. Instead of acting like a partner who cares, she gets angry at Felicia (her ego mirror), attacks her, and walks out. Is this the partner she wants to be? She journals about it and goes back downstairs to the kitchen.

Andrea: "Honey, I'm sorry about the house. You're right. I know I keep saying there's nothing I wouldn't do for you, but now I've dropped the ball on the housework. I know you well enough to know it's upsetting for you."

Felicia (starting to cry): "I should have told you sooner, before things got so bad. I just have such a hard time being weak, expecting too much."

Andrea: "I want you to know you are not expecting too much, but I may not be able to keep my commitment to this in the way that makes you totally happy. How about if I pay somebody to come in once a week? I can do the picking-up and the laundry, but I just can't seem to find the time for all the other stuff."

Felicia: "That would be wonderful. Maybe we would even have some time to go to the beach or just hang out together?"

Andrea: "I'd love that."

Turn Away from the Mirror

This is a journaling exercise that will help you gracefully turn away from your ego mirror. The goal is to let your ego mirror resign her job. Let her be herself, with her own feelings, reactions, and beliefs. It is painful for your partner to do time as a prisoner of your codependency. She can't be honest. She is walking on eggshells waiting for your next meltdown or blowup. There is no way, as long as she's with you, that she can be real. And because of that, you two do not have a real relationship based on interdependency.

Use your journal daily to record your feelings and thoughts. Make a line down the center of your page. Record your codependent self-talk. Then counter with interdependent self-talk. You need to know that this is the deepest core issue you have to fix. You're dealing with your identity; it's worth the work.

Make a daily account of your codependent feelings and thoughts. Counter with interdependent thoughts. For example:

Codependent	Interdependent
Jeez, why is he so mad? I forgot to mail his tax return. I didn't do it on purpose. He's so rigid. What a jerk.	I said I'd mail the return, and I didn't. I forgot. I'm not perfect, and I need to apologize and figure out how I can be more responsible. I want him to be able to count on me. Maybe I need to write these things down.
She's overreacting. Why does she get so upset over little things?	She seems really upset. I could have offered to help her with the dishes. What's the big deal? I need to step up and stop being so oblivious.
How could he be so mean? I work all day on dinner, and he doesn't say a word. He can eat beans for all I care.	He's enjoying dinner I can tell, but I need to hear it. I'll ask him how he likes the chicken.
She's never satisfied. I load the dishwasher and it's not right. I give the kids a bath and that's not right. I've just about had it with her criticism.	I know she's a perfectionist, but that's her problem. I'm good with how I'm doing things. Being a good partner and a good dad is up to me, and I'm proud of myself.

Working on this aspect of codependency is fundamental. The goal is to know yourself and stop depending on others to define you. Use your emotions to trigger self-exploration. So what if your partner is angry because you didn't do what she thought you should? That doesn't mean you are wrong. And even if you are wrong, it doesn't mean you are bad. Let you partner feel however she needs to feel. Acknowledge her feelings, and move forward. You're still okay.

Setting Boundaries with Significant Others

As you already know, there is a disconnect between how codependents think they *should* be and who they really are, flaws and all. Because of this, a person with codependency issues is not always honest. He may make unrealistic promises to others because he feels he *should*, not because he wants to. He doesn't really think it's okay for him to say no.

ESSENTIAL

When something is bothering you about your partner, first ask yourself whether sharing it will be a choice for closeness or distance. This question will guide you in disclosing feelings. A choice for closeness: "I'm really sorry about last night." A choice for distance: "Well, are you over last night yet?"

Sometimes this deeply felt codependency becomes self-perpetuating. *If I were a good husband, I would agree to spend every weekend on a project. If I were a good dad, I would take out a loan to pay my son's tuition. If I were a good son, I would ask my mother to live with me. If I were a good neighbor, I would help.*

It is impossible to be all things to all people all of the time. And as a result, the codependent lets people down and makes others angry. To his horror, he is then reflected in a bad light, reinforcing his poor self-esteem.

Assertiveness

One of the ways you can prepare yourself·to set boundaries is to practice assertiveness, first in your journal and then with others. Right now you could sit down and write about whether or not you feel assertive when you deal with your significant others. For the purpose here, *assertiveness* is a word that describes a method of setting boundaries or saying no that is not aggressive or argumentative. Nor is it tentative and vague. It is a delivery that is kind, firm, and direct.

QUESTION

Should I share my journal with my significant other?
Look at your journal as the "raw data." You can record all your anger, frustration, pain, and any other uncensored thoughts and emotions you may have. This allows you to express yourself untethered from another's reaction. From that data, filter out the rawness and decide what to verbally share with your partner that will help make your relationship better.

Do you hold to any of these mistaken beliefs?

- If somebody needs something, I have to give it to them.
- Other people's needs are more important than mine.
- I would be selfish if I didn't help.
- I'm unreasonable if I don't allow this or don't want to do this.
- People won't like me if I'm not generous all the time.
- I can't bear to hurt anyone's feelings.
- If I let my spouse down, he'll leave me.

As you work on assertiveness, use your journal to record instances where you know you agreed to something you didn't want to do and then resented it. Write about what you were thinking when you agreed. Try to dispel any *shoulds* that controlled your decision. See what self-talk creates guilt or fear or the need to please. See what you are doing, feeling, and thinking that sets you up to agree and then regret it.

For each incident you can recall, try to think of an assertive way you could have set a boundary. Write down as many possible assertive responses as you can think of for each situation. There are times you may be caught off guard by a request. Make sure you have several "go-to" assertive statements you can easily draw out and use.

ESSENTIAL

Because you are in a committed relationship, you may believe you are entitled to receive from your partner whatever you ask for. For example, if you ask your partner to help, he ought to do it. If he doesn't want to help, he is selfish or inconsiderate. Your partner gets to say no, too. It's reasonable to expect to get much of what you ask for from your significant other, but not everything.

Use these samples to start your own list.

Son: "Can you bring my notebook to school? I forgot it."

Mother: "Oh, darn. I hope you can do without it today, I can't bring it; I'm totally swamped." (No need to get angry, blame him, or whine about how inconvenient it would be.)

Husband: "Mom called, and I invited her to dinner tonight."

Wife: "I'd love to have Mom over for dinner, but not tonight. I just don't feel up to it."

Wife: "Can you stop after work and get some wine for dinner?"

Husband: "Not tonight, honey. I'm exhausted."

Daughter: "I need to use the car for school tomorrow."

Dad: "Oh, oh, bad timing. It's my turn in carpool."

Now think about some intimate situations with your significant others that might be difficult for you to set boundaries with.

Wife: "I've been thinking about you all day. The kids are going to a movie. We're alone."

Husband (giving her a hug and a kiss): "That is such a turn-on, baby. Can I get a rain check? I'm beat tonight."

Wife: "Do you think I talk too much?"

Husband: "Sometimes you do, but I love you anyway." (Smiles and hugs her.)

Girl: "Would you come over and meet my folks this weekend?"

Boy: "I'm not ready, maybe soon."

These examples seem easy, but they're not! The people closest to you have learned to expect you to say yes. They are not going to understand your new behavior, and they're going to be unpleasantly surprised. With your significant other, and perhaps older children, you may want to let them know what you are working on. Then, when they experience it, they will know what it's about.

ALERT

Setting boundaries and saying no to your children has an additional component. As the parent, you are modeling the behavior you want them to emulate—assertiveness. Secondly, by not bailing them out, you are giving them the opportunity to problem-solve.

As you work on saying no when you want to, remember the deciding factor is whether or not you are feeling or will feel resentful. If so, to say yes would be dishonest and will eventually have a negative impact on your relationships.

You will begin to know your authentic self as you work through codependency. The more honest you are with yourself, the more honest your immediate responses will be. In the meantime, if you find yourself saying yes and then realize you don't want to do what you agreed to, it is okay to go back for a "redo." You can use the examples already given in this section and imagine you originally said yes, but now want to change your mind. Here are a few more examples.

Wife: "Can you run to the store for apples?"

Husband: "Sure, what kind?"

Husband (ten minutes later): "Honey, I know I said I'd get apples, but I want to finish watching the game first."

Daughter: "My hair needs trimming today."

Mother: "Okay. I have some things to do first."

Mother (an hour later): "Becky, I know I said I'd cut your hair today, but I just can't fit it in. How about tomorrow morning?"

Responding to No

There is always the other side of the coin with codependency. Codependents have difficulty setting boundaries, but they can easily feel hurt or angry when someone sets a boundary with them. They are critical of themselves, but they are also critical of others. They expect a lot from themselves and they may expect a lot from others. Because they lack a solid identity, codependents are extremely reactive to perceived judgment; they can feel let down or disappointed, seeing themselves victims of others' "mistreatment." Especially with their ego mirror, it is difficult for a codependent to see another as separate from him, entitled to her own feelings, thoughts, and behaviors. Codependents have a strong tendency to make everything about them, and then react strongly to perceived criticism.

ESSENTIAL

Include in your journal a list of positive affirmations to read aloud to yourself each morning and night. Cross off or delete the affirmations as you accept them as true, and add to the list as needed. In addition to your own affirmations, you might wish to buy yourself a daily affirmation book with quotes from others for your nightstand.

All of the codependency traits you now have identified in yourself and in your interactions with your ego mirror can be changed through your own efforts, using some of the strategies given in this and the previous chapter. Seeing a professional is another important choice.

Letter to the Psychologist

The following letter is taken from Here-to-Listen.com and helps explain the enabling behavior of codependents.

Dear Doctor,

I can't set boundaries with my daughter. She's twenty-three and insisted on getting her own apartment. She works at a fast-food restaurant and she just isn't making enough money to support herself. She has had several roommates, but she just can't seem to make it work. I'm paying half her rent now, but I can't afford it. Now she insists that in order for her to get a better job, she needs a car. Every time I talk to her, it ends up in an argument. She won't give up on the car, and it's wearing me down. I just want to have a good relationship with her. If I buy her a car, I think she'll be grateful and stop bugging me for more. It's worth it to me. Is this codependency?

Dear Fran,

Yes it is. The fact that you are having ongoing arguments where your daughter is badgering you for something and you don't want to give it to her indicates a problem with boundary-setting on your part.

You say you can't afford to supplement her rent, and yet you are doing it. She can't make it work with roommates because she doesn't have to. If she's short on the rent because another roommate moved out, you'll rescue her. It sounds like her arguing with you about getting her a car is the status quo in your relationship right now. Frankly, it sounds miserable, and I understand you are weary of the fight. But if you agree to this, you will add fuel to the codependency fire burning up your relationship with your daughter. For her sake and yours, you must use your resentment and anger to steel yourself into setting an appropriate boundary now. Stop getting angry with her. Validate her feelings, and proceed in a kind and firm manner in saying no.

It might sound something like this. "Honey, I know you're struggling. It's not easy trying to be on your own. I'm really sorry I can't buy you a car, but I just can't afford it. I'd be happy to sit down with you and talk about your options. I can offer for you to move back home, but that's all I can do right now."

CHAPTER 20

Ending Codependency in Your Life

Facing codependency within yourself and in your closest relationships is the most difficult and fundamental responsibility you will take on. It is a giant leap of faith to make yourself vulnerable in the hopes of becoming a more confident person in the long run. To finish your transformation, you must learn to move through your world with confidence and grace, handle problems with assertiveness, interact with others in a kind and direct manner, and set boundaries that are right for you.

Becoming a Better Family Member

When you traced your codependency patterns back to your family, you may have turned up a few skeletons in the family closet. If you have been in denial about the shortcomings or maybe even abuse in your family of origin, this can be a painful revelation. But, as you know, exploring your family dynamics is necessary to understand your own codependency. Just as you are not perfect, neither is your family—nor any family, for that matter.

Your Family of Origin

Use your journal to reflect on your family. See if you can record any patterns or behavior that may have contributed to your codependency traits. Make a heading for each family member and answer these questions:

- From what you now know, is this family member codependent?
- From what you now know, is this family member narcissistic?
- Was this person chronically physically or mentally ill?
- Did this person break the law or engage in reckless or dangerous activities?
- Was this person an addict: drugs, alcohol, gambling, smoking, anger, spending, etc.?
- How did this person handle conflict and deal with anger?
- Was this family member physically, emotionally, or sexually abusive?
- What codependent behaviors did this person model for you?
- What mistaken beliefs did this person impart to you?
- Did this person yell or blow up when angry?
- Was this person able to express feelings openly?
- Was this person available to you?
- What are the feelings you felt most often when you were around this person?
- Did you feel loved by this person?

Once you have written about each family member, using these questions as a guide, see if you can discover or affirm what you already know about your family of origin and how they may have planted the seeds for your codependency.

ESSENTIAL

"Don't let a day go by without asking who you are . . . each time you let a new ingredient to enter your awareness." —Deepak Chopra, *The Book of Secrets: Unlocking the Hidden Dimensions of Your Life*

Now look back at the work you've done here and see if there are any unresolved issues from your family. It's not helpful to dig up pain and hurt and then just leave it.

Decide if these are issues you can resolve within yourself, or if it is necessary to address these issues with a family member. You goal is to get out of the victim role. What would work for you in stopping these ghosts from the past from victimizing you now?

There are two ways to evaluate the information you reclaimed from your family of origin. One way is to see how these wounds affect your current relationships with your significant others, and how you can change your behavior now, with them. The other way is to see if you need to confront old issues with the original family member. Would this help you let go and diminish the power he or she still has over you?

Some people choose to do the work only in their current family, with their partner and children. Some feel the need to talk to their original family members. You can do both, or neither. It's up to you. Here's an example of how Evelyn handled her family-of-origin issues.

Evelyn Finds a Skeleton

Through reading, mindfulness, and journal writing, Evelyn remembered how she was abused as a child by her older sister. Her sister would jump out at her and scare her, turn out the lights and lock her in the bedroom, beat her up and smother or choke her, break her toys, and steal her things. Evelyn always told herself and others that she had the perfect childhood except for a little "sibling rivalry."

When Evelyn takes a critical look at her childhood, it is as if she were experiencing the pain all over again. Not only does she find it necessary to re-evaluate her relationship with her sister; she also begins to wonder about her parents. Where were they? Why didn't they protect her? Why didn't *she* stop the abuse, tell her parents, do something? Evelyn chooses to see a therapist to help with the depression and anxiety triggered by these memories.

Through therapy, Evelyn realizes that she doesn't trust many people. Her lack of trust toward her husband makes her controlling and suspicious, and leads to explosive arguments and unfounded accusations. She also discovers that she feels like a victim most of the time, bracing for somebody to hurt her. Evelyn decides to share this with her husband and asks him to help her with the triggers from her childhood abuse. With her husband's support, Evelyn works on her trust issues. Their relationship improves.

"Family quarrels are bitter things. They don't go by any rules. They're not like aches or wounds; they're more like splits in the skin that won't heal because there's not enough material." —F. Scott Fitzgerald

Evelyn has not had contact with her sister for many years, and expects never to see her again. She doesn't feel the need to confront her about the abuse. Instead, she writes a letter to her sister in her journal, but doesn't plan to send it. While she is still in therapy, her sister becomes ill and wants to come home for a visit. This throws Evelyn into a panic. She explores her thoughts and feelings with her therapist.

Positive affirmations are messages you give yourself as if you already believe them to be true. For example, "I'm great just the way I am"; "I'm not perfect, but that's okay"; "I am a strong person"; "I am a survivor, I can do this." The purpose of these affirmations, said out loud, is to practice them until you believe them.

Evelyn decides to sit down with her parents and share with them her experience growing up. She talks with them about being afraid every day as a child, and she asks them why they didn't stop the abuse. Her parents seem genuinely shocked at this news; they apologize profusely and ask Evelyn what they can do to help her now. Evelyn forgives them. For Evelyn, this alliance with her parents makes it easier to face her sister when she visits. Instead of feeling like a victim of all three of them, Evelyn feels affirmed by her parents' understanding and is able to be cordial with her sister.

In this case, Evelyn chooses to deal with family-of-origin issues in her current relationship with her husband, where she feels the most acute pain. She devotes a good portion of her therapy to working through her childhood abuse, which leads her to talk to her parents. She feels resolved with her parents and decides not to confront her sister directly.

There is never a right or wrong in the decisions you make about family-of-origin wounds. If your family members are still doing the abusive behaviors, your decision may be to insist they stop. Or you may choose to spend limited time with them with firm boundaries. Or you may choose to deal with each of them as the unwanted behaviors come up. It's up to you.

Becoming a Better Friend

Once you begin to change and move toward a life free of codependency, you will undoubtedly attract new friends. These new friendships should be more mutual and interdependent. So, as you work toward becoming a more equal friend, you have two aspects of friendship to journal about.

Journaling Your Friends

Write the names of each of your current friends (not acquaintances) at the top of the page. If you have a couple of close friends, that's pretty typical. You may want to include your second-tier friendships also, perhaps several more. Now you are going to decide if these old friends still fit the new you. If the friendships are codependent, you can choose to move on, or you can work to move the friendships to a better place.

Use these questions to guide you:

- Does your friend always seem to need your advice?
- Does your friend call you often and expect you to drop everything to counsel her?
- Does your friend take up more than 50 percent of the conversation on average?

- Does your friend get angry when you're not available?
- Does your friend seem disinterested in you and oblivious to your struggles?
- Does your friend fail to show up or cancel at the last minute?
- Is being around your friend like walking on eggshells?
- Does your friend seem unstable or fragile?
- Does your friend demand too much of you?

As you've probably discovered, some of your friendships are not life-enhancing. Only you would know if they are hopeless and you need to move on. If you decide to work on them, these relationships can be very beneficial in providing you with opportunities to continue to work on your codependency issues. Read the following example of what Jack did with his friends.

Jack Examines His Friendships

Jack has three close friends. Ben is his running partner; they see each other almost every day, but they do not discuss deeply personal problems. The time they spend together and their level of involvement is based on their shared interest in running. Jack considers his friendship with Ben and decides it's interdependent. No work needed.

Another close friend of Jack's is his colleague at school. Susan teaches the same grade as Jack, and they are very compatible. They have team-taught for several years with excellent results. They often have coffee and sometimes have lunch together. They usually talk about their spouses, kids, families, and almost anything. Susan is more of a talker than Jack, and she enjoys getting the male opinion from him on relationships and family matters. If Jack were a more withdrawn person, he might end up as the listener and find himself in the therapist role, but he enjoys talking about his wife and kids, too. This is a fairly equal relationship.

According to the journal questions in this section, Jack's third friend is a problem. Also a teacher, Lisa is needy and relies on Jack to do small projects for her at school. Lately, she's been asking for favors outside of school. She's single, and Jack is drawn in by the fact that she needs him to help her out. At first, he is pleased that she would ask him, and enjoys her gratitude and reliance on him. Helping her makes him feel like a good guy. After working on his codependency, Jack now realizes that this friendship is not healthy for him. He has set some boundaries by simply telling her upfront that he will help her at school if he has time, but he won't be able to help her outside of school.

ALERT

In an article published in *Oprah* magazine on the health benefits of friendship, it was pointed out that "Harvard research has shown that breast cancer patients with no friendship network are four times more likely to die from the disease than those with ten or more close friends."

Resolving Existing Issues with Friends

Do some writing in your journal about your current friends. Do you have any unresolved issues you've been afraid to discuss with them? Make a list for each friend and go through the process where you eliminate issues you have no control over or you choose not to address. If unresolved issues remain, go ahead and try a kind and direct approach. If you begin to be more honest and forthright and your friend takes offense, you have new data to help you make a decision about this friendship.

Before you talk to your friend, ask yourself what you hope to achieve. What is your motivation? If your motivation is to resolve something and strengthen the friendship through honesty, go for it. If you now feel brave enough to tell your friend what a jerk he is, save your breath and move on.

Assessing New Friends

As you change, new people who come into your life will experience you as a more assertive, well-adjusted, compassionate person who is honest about her feelings and is direct about her expectations and boundaries. Maybe that's not what they're looking for. Maybe they are looking to fulfill some of their own codependency needs in a friendship, or maybe they're looking for a codependent friend to take care of them.

You know enough about codependency to notice red or yellow flags in romantic relationships and also in friendships. Deal with your concerns right away. Know that at any time, you can put your own needs first and discontinue a friendship that is not healthy for you. For example, if your new friend cancels frequently at the start, this could mean a lack of interest in you, a sign that she believes her needs are more important than yours. If a new friend starts asking for favors, that could be a sign of neediness. If your new friend talks on and on about herself, that's not good. If your new friend is easily offended, often misunderstands you, seems moody, and gossips about her other friends, these are all red flags.

There is a saying that partners come and go but friends are forever. Friends are certainly important to emotional well-being and good health, and some friendships do span a lifetime. Choose your friends wisely.

Enhancing Your Freedom from Codependency

Each and every person you meet in the course of your life and every situation you face provides an opportunity to practice and fine-tune your freedom from codependency. How does change happen, and what can you do to facilitate it? Each year, neuropsychological research unearths new discoveries about human behavior. Not too long ago, psychiatrists believed that personality disorders could not be changed. Now the widely held belief is that they can. Beliefs about what exactly influences human behavior have swung back and forth like a pendulum. First it was exclusively a brain thing, then it was a brain/environment thing, now because of advances in neurotechnology, researchers have a renewed excitement about the brain. There is reason to believe that this fascinating world of neuropsychology will continue to evolve.

FACT

It's a myth that brain cells can't regenerate, that if you kill a brain cell, it is never replaced. This myth was believed and taught by the science community for a very long time. But in 1998, scientists at the Salk Institute in La Jolla, California, discovered that brain cells in mature humans *can* regenerate.

The changes you are reaching for are entirely possible to achieve. Your goal is to cultivate your identity. You already have an identity; you just need to remold it. You know that codependency traits are on a continuum. You may be less codependent or more codependent, show one codependency trait or fifty.

You now have new insights and awareness and tools to help you fix your sense of self, increase self-esteem, and become confident in your identity. You will continue to work on your transformation by noticing your feelings, thoughts, and behaviors, and making adjustments as you go. Be present in your relationships, find your honest voice, and value and love yourself, flaws and all. You just may discover that you have the power to expand your capacity for happiness.

APPENDIX A

Resources

Websites

ALCOHOLICS ANONYMOUS
Alcoholics Anonymous official website
www.aa.org

AMAZON
Source for recommended books
www.amazon.com

AMERICAN ASSOCIATION OF MARRIAGE AND FAMILY THERAPY
AAMFT official website
www.aamft.org

AMERICAN PSYCHIATRIC ASSOCIATION
American Psychiatric Association official website
www.psych.org

AMERICAN PSYCHOLOGICAL ASSOCIATION
American Psychological Association official website
www.apa.org

BOOKS4SELFHELP.COM
Good choices for self-help books
www.books4selfhelp.com

HERE-TO-LISTEN.COM
Jennifer J. Sowle, PhD, professional website
www.here-to-listen.com

MINDFULNESS RESEARCH GUIDE
Research and publication database on mindfulness
www.mindfulexperience.org

NAMI, NATIONAL ALLIANCE ON MENTAL ILLNESS
Mental health education, advocacy, and support
www.nami.org

NATIONAL ASSOCIATION OF SOCIAL WORK
NASW official site
www.socialworkers.org

NATIONAL INSTITUTE OF MENTAL HEALTH (NIMH)
Research in mental health
www.nimh.nih.gov

PSYCHOLOGY TODAY
Current articles in psychology for the general public
www.psychologytoday.com

THE INTERNATIONAL ENCYCLOPEDIA OF THE SOCIAL SCIENCES
Reference for terms and definitions
www.gale.cengage.com/iess/content.htm

Books

Bandler, Richard. Grinder, John. *The Structure of Magic, Vol. I: A Book about Language and Therapy.* (Science and Behavior Books, 1976).

Beattie, Melody. *Codependent No More: How to Stop Controlling Others and Start Caring for Yourself.* (Hazelden Foundation, 1986, 1992).

Beattie, Melody. *The Language of Letting Go: Hazelden Meditation Series.* (Hay House Inc., 2005).

Bourne, Edmund J. *The Anxiety & Phobia Workbook (Fifth Edition)* (New Harbinger Publications, 2011).

Goldstein, Elisha. *The Now Effect: How a Mindful Moment Can Change the Rest of Your Life.* (ATRIA, Simon & Schuster, 2012).

Hendrix, Harville. *Getting the Love You Want: A Guide for Couples (20th Anniversary Edition).* (Holt Paperbacks, 2008).

Lowen, Alexander. *Narcissism: Denial of the True Self.* (Touchstone, 1997).

Pipher, Mary. *Reviving Ophelia: Saving the Selves of Adolescent Girls.* (Penguin Group, 1994).

Smith, Manuel J. *When I Say No, I Feel Guilty.* (Random House, 2011).

Self-Help Groups

ADULT CHILDREN OF ALCOHOLICS (ACA)
www.adultchildren.org

ADULT SURVIVORS OF CHILD ABUSE (ASCA)
www.ascasupport.org

AL-ANON
www.al-anon.alateen.org

ALCOHOLICS ANONYMOUS (AA)
www.aa.org

CO-DEPENDENTS ANONYMOUS (CODA)
www.coda.org

SURVIVORS OF NARCISSISM ABUSE
www.narcissismfree.com

SURVIVORS OF SEXUAL ABUSE
www.rainn.org

Index

We Have
EVERYTHING®
on Anything!

The Everything® list spans a wide range of subjects, with more than 500 titles covering 25 different categories:

Business	History	Reference
Careers	Home Improvement	Religion
Children's Storybooks	Everything Kids	Self-Help
Computers	Languages	Sports & Fitness
Cooking	Music	Travel
Crafts and Hobbies	New Age	Wedding
Education/Schools	Parenting	Writing
Games and Puzzles	Personal Finance	
Health	Pets	